Red Panda

MACMILLAN McGRAW-HILL
Science

Lucy H. Daniel

Jay Hackett

Richard H. Moyer

JoAnne Vasquez

About the Cover

The red panda is also called the *lesser panda* and *red cat bear*. The red panda is about the size of a big house cat, but is neither cat nor bear! The red panda is not closely related to the giant panda either. In fact, the red panda's closest relative is the raccoon.

INQUIRY What else would you like to know about red pandas? Write your own question or questions to answer.

Macmillan McGraw-Hill

Program Authors

Dr. Lucy H. Daniel
Teacher, Consultant
Rutherford County Schools, North Carolina

Dr. Jay Hackett
Professor Emeritus of Earth Sciences
University of Northern Colorado

Dr. Richard H. Moyer
Professor of Science Education
University of Michigan-Dearborn

Dr. JoAnne Vasquez
Elementary Science Education Consultant
Mesa Public Schools, Arizona
NSTA Past President

Contributing Authors

Lucille Villegas Barrera, M.Ed.
Elementary Science Supervisor
Houston Independent School District
Houston, Texas

Mulugheta Teferi, M.A.
St. Louis Public Schools
St. Louis, Missouri

Dinah Zike, M.Ed.
Dinah Might Adventures LP
San Antonio, Texas

The features in this textbook entitled "Amazing Stories," as well as the unit openers, were developed in collaboration with the National Geographic Society's School Publishing Division.

Copyright © 2002 National Geographic Society. All rights reserved.

RFB&D ⓥ
learning through listening

Students with print disabilities may be eligible to obtain an accessible, audio version of the pupil edition of this textbook. Please call Recording for the Blind & Dyslexic at 1-800-221-4792 for complete information.

The McGraw-Hill Companies

Macmillan McGraw-Hill

Published by Macmillan/McGraw-Hill, of McGraw-Hill Education, a division of The McGraw-Hill Companies, Inc., Two Penn Plaza, New York, New York 10121.

Printed in the United States of America

ISBN 0-02-281890-1

6 7 8 9 110/043 09 08 07

Life Science

Consultants

Dr. Carol Baskin
University of Kentucky
Lexington, KY

Dr. Joe W. Crim
University of Georgia
Athens, GA

Dr. Marie DiBerardino
Allegheny University of
Health Sciences
Philadelphia, PA

Dr. R. E. Duhrkopf
Baylor University
Waco, TX

Dr. Dennis L. Nelson
Montana State University
Bozeman, MT

Dr. Fred Sack
Ohio State University
Columbus, OH

Dr. Martin VanDyke
Denver, CO

Dr. E. Peter Volpe
Mercer University
Macon, GA

Earth Science

Consultants

Dr. Clarke Alexander
Skidaway Institute of
Oceanography
Savannah, GA

Dr. Suellen Cabe
Pembroke State University
Pembroke, NC

Dr. Thomas A. Davies
Texas A & M University
College Station, TX

Dr. Ed Geary
Geological Society of America
Boulder, CO

Dr. David C. Kopaska-Merkel
Geological Survey of Alabama
Tuscaloosa, AL

Physical Science

Consultants

Dr. Bonnie Buratti
Jet Propulsion Lab
Pasadena, CA

Dr. Shawn Carlson
Society of Amateur Scientists
San Diego, CA

Dr. Karen Kwitter
Williams College
Williamstown, MA

Dr. Steven Souza
Williamstown, MA

Dr. Joseph P. Straley
University of Kentucky
Lexington, KY

Dr. Thomas Troland
University of Kentucky
Lexington, KY

Dr. Josephine Davis Wallace
University of North Carolina
Charlotte, NC

Consultant for Primary Grades

Donna Harrell Lubcker
East Texas Baptist University
Marshall, TX

Teacher Reviewers (continued)

Beth Lewis
Wilmington, North Carolina

Cindy Hatchell
Wilmington, North Carolina

Cindy Kahler
Carrboro, North Carolina

Diane Leusky
Chapel Hill, North Carolina

Heather Sutton
Wilmington, North Carolina

Crystal Stephens
Valdese, North Carolina

Meg Millard
Chapel Hill, North Carolina

Patricia Underwood
Randleman, North Carolina

E. Joy Mermin
Chapel Hill, North Carolina

Yolanda Evans
Wilmington, North Carolina

Tim Gilbride
Pennsauken, New Jersey

Helene Reifowitz
Nesconsit, New York

Tina Craig
Tulsa, Oklahoma

Deborah Harwell
Lawton, Oklahoma

Kathleen Conn
West Chester, Pennsylvania

Heath Renninger Zerbe
Tremont, Pennsylvania

Patricia Armillei
Holland, Pennsylvania

Sue Workman
Cedar City, Utah

Peg Jensen
Hartford, Wisconsin

Letter from Sally Ride

When I became an astronaut, I blasted off on a great adventure. The space shuttle rocketed off the launch pad. Only eight-and-a-half minutes later I was floating weightless in space! That trip into space was a dream come true. The dream began when I was a girl. And studying science made it possible!

When I was in third grade, I got to look through a simple telescope. I saw the planet Mars. When I learned about its huge volcanoes and deep canyons, I wanted to explore it someday.

Maybe some of you have dreams like mine. You might dream of exploring Mars, or curing cancer, or saving an endangered species. Whether you want to become a scientist or not, science will help you understand the world we live in. It will encourage you to investigate things for yourself and to ask questions. These things are important no matter what you do!

My love of science launched me into space. Science can take you places, too!

Reach for the stars!

Sally K. Ride

Be a Scientist! PAGE S1

Where Plants and Animals Live PAGE B1

UNIT C

Earth Science

Our Earth PAGE C1

UNIT D
Earth Science

Cycles on Earth and in Space PAGE D1

Activities

UNIT D

UNIT E

UNIT F

For Your Reference

Science Handbook

Health Handbook

FOLDABLES™

by Dinah Zike

Using Foldables for Data Collection

A Foldables organizer is a 3-D, interactive graphic organizer. It can be a valuable learning tool to help you organize, review, and remember information. You will find suggestions for using Foldables organizers to help you collect and record data in Quick Lab activities throughout this book.

Basic Shapes

The figures on this page illustrate the basic folds that are the building blocks for all Foldables organizers used in the Quick Labs. The basic folds have friendly names, such as "hot dog fold," so that you can easily visualize and remember what they look like. Step-by-step folding instructions for each type of Foldables organizer used in the Quick Labs are given on pages R41–R44.

Hot Dog Fold

Shutter Fold

Hamburger Fold

Valley Fold

Mountain Fold

Science Safety Tips

Here are some important safety rules that you should follow.

In the Classroom

- Read all of the directions. Make sure you understand them. When you see **BE CAREFUL!**, be sure to follow the safety rule.

- Listen to your teacher for special safety directions. If you don't understand something, ask for help.

- Wash your hands with soap and water before an activity.

- Be careful around a hot plate. Know when it is on and when it is off. Remember that the plate stays hot for a few minutes after it's turned off.

- Wear a safety apron if you work with anything messy or anything that might spill.

- Wipe up a spill right away, or ask your teacher for help.

- Tell your teacher if something breaks. If glass breaks, do not clean it up yourself.

- Keep your hair and clothes away from open flames. Tie back long hair, and roll up long sleeves.

- Wear safety goggles when your teacher tells you to wear them. Wear them when working with anything that can fly into your eyes or when working with liquids.

- Keep your hands dry around electrical equipment.

- Don't eat or drink anything during an experiment.

- Put equipment back the way your teacher tells you to.

- Dispose of things the way your teacher tells you to.

- Clean up your work area after an activity, and wash your hands with soap and water.

In the Field

- Go with a trusted adult—such as your teacher or a parent or guardian.

- Do not touch animals or plants without an adult's approval. The animal might bite. The plant might be poison ivy or another dangerous plant.

Responsibility

- Treat living things, the environment, and one another with respect.

What on Earth made this?

A dinosaur!

Science is a way of understanding the world around us. Scientists often ask questions about what they observe. They call on many skills to help them answer these questions. This process of asking and answering questions in science is called inquiry.

In this section, you will see how scientists use inquiry, reading, math, writing, and technology to learn about dinosaurs.

Inquiry Skills

These are the inquiry skills scientists use. You can use these skills, too.

Observe

Infer

Classify

Measure

Use numbers

Communicate

Predict

Interpret data

Form a hypothesis

Use variables

Experiment

Make a model

Define based on observations

Are you an observant person? You might look out the window to see if it is raining. You might even listen for rain on the windowsill. You make observations throughout your day. Observations on the world around us often raise questions.

The diagram on this page shows processes that scientists use to answer questions. Many call this the "scientific method." Scientists don't always use all of the steps. They may not use them in the same order.

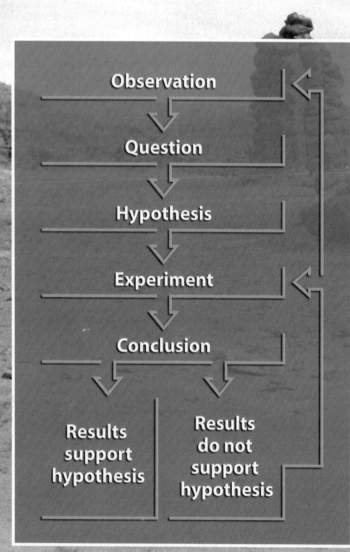

Observation

Question

Hypothesis

Experiment

Conclusion

Results support hypothesis

Results do not support hypothesis

Inquiry Skills

When you make observations, you use these skills.

Observe Use your senses to learn about an object or event.

Classify Place things that share properties together in groups.

Measure Find the size, distance, time, volume, area, mass, weight, or temperature of an object or an event.

Visual Literacy

More than half the information you get comes from pictures, or visuals. Pictures, maps, graphs, charts, and diagrams are tools. Using these tools to understand what you read and observe is called *visual literacy*.

The scientist in this photo is uncovering dinosaur footprints. What can scientists learn about dinosaurs by observing their footprints?

Do you ask "why" questions when you are curious about things? The work of scientists often starts with an unanswered question. Scientists then suggest a possible answer that can be tested with an experiment. This is known as *forming a hypothesis*. A good hypothesis must

▸ be based on what you observe.
▸ be testable by doing an experiment.
▸ be useful in predicting new findings.

Which of these dinosaurs was a meat eater and which was a plant eater? Form a hypothesis to answer this question.

S 4

Reading in Science

Before doing an experiment to answer a question, scientists often read to try to find the answer or to find out what others have learned from their experiments. You can use these reading strategies and skills to help you understand science. While you read, ask yourself these questions:

▶ **Compare and Contrast** How are two things alike? How are they different?

▶ **Main Idea and Supporting Details** What is the paragraph about? Which details add more information?

▶ **Predict** What do you think will happen next?

▶ **Cause and Effect** Why did something happen? (This is the cause.) What happened as a result? (This is the effect.)

▶ **Draw Conclusions** What do I know from the evidence?

▶ **Sequence of Events** What happened first, next, and last?

▶ **Summarize** What is this lesson or paragraph about?

Inquiry Skills

When you ask questions and form hypotheses, you use these skills.

Infer Form an idea from facts or observations.

Form a hypothesis Make a statement that can be tested to answer a question.

Define terms based on observations Put together a description that is based on observations and experiences.

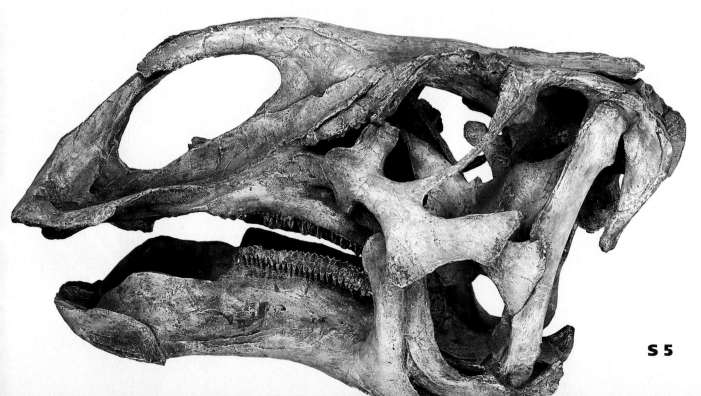

Now it's time to test your hypothesis with an experiment. In experiments you change one variable to see what happens with another variable. For example, you might make a model to find out how the type of soil affects the shape of a dinosaur's footprint. What would happen if you changed both the type of soil and the size of the dinosaur?

Experiments must be able to be repeated, too. This allows scientists to evaluate and compare each other's work. They can check their own work too! So a good experiment must:

▶ change only one variable at a time.
▶ be able to be repeated.

Technology Literacy

In an experiment, scientists use tools to collect and analyze data. They may use simple tools, such as clocks and rulers. They also use more powerful tools, such as microscopes and computers.

Information Literacy

Information literacy begins with knowing how to search for and use books, magazines, and newspapers. Today, information literacy also includes searching for information on CD-ROMs, DVDs, and the Internet.

Inquiry Skills

When you experiment, you use these skills.

Experiment Perform a test to support or disprove a hypothesis.

Use variables Identify things in an experiment that can be changed or controlled.

Predict State possible results of an event or experiment.

Make a model Make something to represent an object or event.

Whaat's one important part of a science experiment? Collecting good data! When data are collected they may then be explained, or interpreted. Collecting and interpreting data often requires working with numbers.

This scientist will measure and record the length and weight of the dinosaur fossil she is studying.

Math Literacy

Scientists often use math skills when they collect and interpret data as part of their experiments. A Math Link in each lesson of this book asks you to use several types of math skills, including:

▶ **Number Sense and Operations** This includes estimation, addition, subtraction, multiplication, and division.

▶ **Measurement** This includes using and converting standard and metric units of size, distance, time, volume, area, mass, weight, or temperature.

▶ **Data Analysis and Probability** This includes calculating the likelihood that an event will happen and making and interpreting bar graphs and line graphs.

▶ **Problem Solving** This means using skills and strategies to solve problems.

Inquiry Skills

When you collect and interpret data, you use these skills.

Use numbers Order, count, add, subtract, multiply, and divide to explain data.

Measure Find the size, distance, time, volume, area, mass, weight, or temperature of an object or an event.

Interpret data Use the information that has been gathered to answer questions or solve a problem.

You've collected and interpreted data. Now what? It is time to draw a conclusion. A conclusion states whether your data support your hypothesis. But what if your data do not support your hypothesis? Perhaps different experiments are needed. Perhaps a new question will result.

Scientists also share with others what they have found. This allows scientists around the world to stay informed. And it allows scientists to check each other's work.

Scientists also share what they have learned with the public. Have you ever been to a museum with displays of dinosaur fossils like this?

Inquiry Skills

When you draw conclusions and communicate results, you use this skill.

Communicate Share information.

Writing in Science

Writing is a tool you can use to communicate, or share information, about science. A **Writing Link** in each lesson of this book asks you to use one of these types of writing:

▶ A **Personal Narrative** tells about an event in your life.

▶ **Writing a Story** uses characters, setting, and a sequence of events.

▶ **Persuasive Writing** tries to get your readers to agree with your opinion.

▶ **Explanatory Writing** tells how to make or do something.

▶ **Writing That Compares** tells how two things are alike and different.

▶ **Expository Writing** presents facts and explains ideas.

Using Your Book

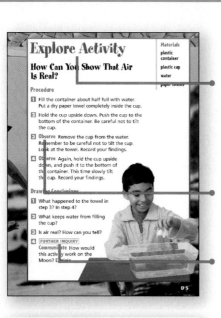

The **Explore Activity** is a hands-on way to learn about the lesson. The title is in the form of a question that you will answer in the activity.

The **inquiry skills** in the Explore Activity are the same skills that scientists use.

The last step of the activity provides an opportunity for **further inquiry**.

You can use different kinds of **Foldables™ organizers** to collect and record data in the Quick Lab.

Inquiry skills are also used in the Quick Lab.

Each Inquiry Skill Builder focuses on a specific **inquiry skill**.

Other **inquiry skills** are also reinforced in the Inquiry Skill Builder.

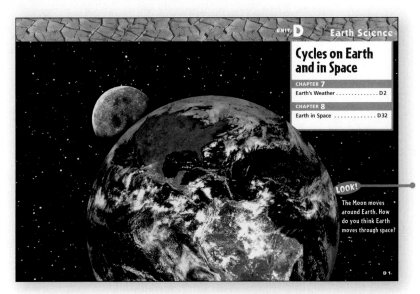

Visuals include both **photographs** and **graphics**. This question will help you get information from the photograph at the beginning of each unit of this book.

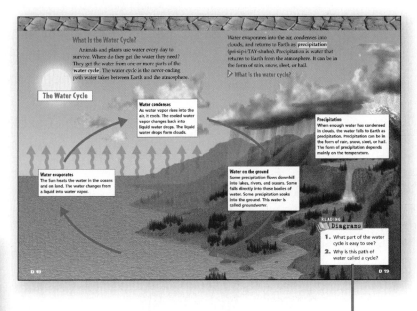

Throughout all chapters of this book you will get information by **reading graphics**. Graphics are pictures such as:
• diagrams
• charts
• maps
• graphs

Learn Through Reading

This box contains the **Main Idea** of the lesson. Keep the main idea of the lesson in mind as you read.

Before Reading Read the large red question before you read the page. Try to answer this question from what you already know.

During Reading Look for new **Vocabulary** words highlighted in yellow. Look at the pictures. They will help you understand what you are reading.

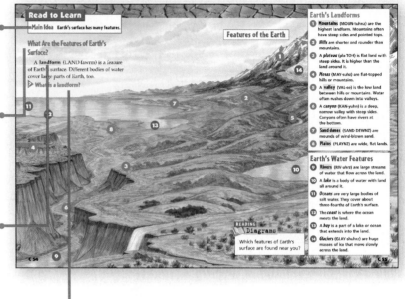

After Reading This arrow points to a question. It will help you check that you understand what you have read. Try to answer the question before you go to the next large red question.

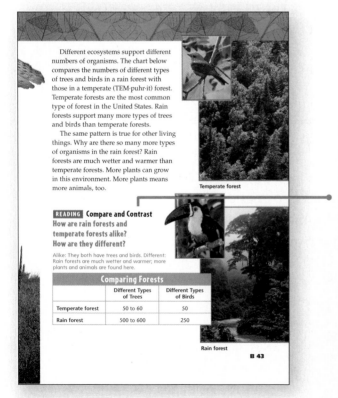

On one page in each lesson, you will find a question that practices the **Chapter Reading Skill**. In any chapter, you will find one of these skills:

- compare and contrast
- main idea and supporting details
- predict
- cause and effect
- draw conclusions
- sequence of events
- summarize

Learn Through Writing and Technology

At the end of every lesson, you can log on to **e-Journal** for tips and suggestions about how to write a research report.

Think and Write questions at the end of every lesson give you an opportunity to write about what you learned in the lesson.

A **Writing Link** at the end of every lesson allows you to express yourself through several different types of writing:
• Personal Narrative
• Writing a Story
• Persuasive Writing
• Explanatory Writing
• Writing That Compares
• Expository Writing

A **Technology Link** at the end of every lesson gives you an opportunity to log on to our Web site www.science.mmhschool.com for additional links.

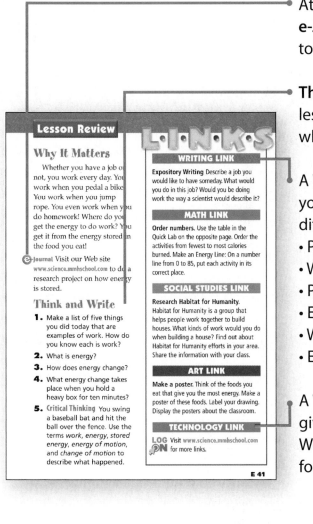

Lesson Review

Why It Matters

Whether you have a job or not, you work every day. You work when you pedal a bike. You work when you jump rope. You even work when you do homework! Where do you get the energy to do work? You get it from the energy stored in the food you eat!

e-Journal Visit our Web site www.science.mmhschool.com to do a research project on how energy is stored.

Think and Write

1. Make a list of five things you did today that are examples of work. How do you know each is work?
2. What is energy?
3. How does energy change?
4. What energy change takes place when you hold a heavy box for ten minutes?
5. Critical Thinking You swing a baseball bat and hit the ball over the fence. Use the terms *work, energy, stored energy, energy of motion,* and *change of motion* to describe what happened.

L·I·N·K·S

WRITING LINK

Expository Writing Describe a job you would like to have someday. What would you do in this job? Would you be doing work the way a scientist would describe it?

MATH LINK

Order numbers. Use the table in the Quick Lab on the opposite page. Order the activities from fewest to most calories burned. Make an Energy Line: On a number line from 0 to 85, put each activity in its correct place.

SOCIAL STUDIES LINK

Research Habitat for Humanity. Habitat for Humanity is a group that helps people work together to build houses. What kinds of work would you do when building a house? Find out about Habitat for Humanity efforts in your area. Share the information with your class.

ART LINK

Make a poster. Think of the foods you eat that give you the most energy. Make a poster of these foods. Label your drawing. Display the posters about the classroom.

TECHNOLOGY LINK

LOG ON Visit www.science.mmhschool.com for more links.

E 41

Meet a Scientist

Dr. Paul Williams
Plant Pathologist

As a third grader, Paul Williams loved to grow plants. "For me, plants were fun to play with." Williams went to college in Wisconsin. There he learned that diseases were attacking the cabbage plants. Williams wanted to help. He traveled the world collecting seeds. Dr. Williams combined many of those seeds to develop a new kind of cabbage. He named it "Fast Plant." These super-speedy plants took about five weeks—not two months—to go through a growth cycle. Fast Plants have changed the way farmers grow crops.

In 1997, astronauts took Fast Plants into space. They proved that plants grow the same way there as on Earth! Who knows? One day, Paul Williams's cabbages may be feeding people on Mars!

Fast Plants have been grown on six space missions since 1997.

TIME FOR KIDS

TOP 5 Plants and You

If you like plants, here are some careers to consider:
1. Botanist: Studies plant biology and environment.
2. Plant physiologist: Examines plant and its genes.
3. Soil conservationist: Maps, identifies, and classifies soil.
4. Horticulturist: Improves plants for crops or medicines.
5. Agronomist: Studies how plants, soil, and the environment interact.

Write About It

1. How did Paul Williams's Fast Plant help people?
2. What did astronauts prove about plants growing in space?

LOG ON Visit www.science.mmhschool.com to learn more about scientists who study plants.

Write About It questions on selected Sally Ride Science, Time for Kids, and magazine-style features give you an opportunity to write about what you learned.

A **LogOn reference** on every Sally Ride Science, Time for Kids, and magazine-style feature allows you to learn more about each topic.

Science Magazine

Star Time

Can you tell time without a clock or a calendar? Yes, you can—by using the Sun and the stars!

Thousands of years ago, that's just what people did. Farmers used the position of the stars to tell the time of year.

Stargazers noticed that stars moved together across the sky. They also observed that stars were not evenly scattered. Some groups of brighter stars reminded people of familiar things – a lion, a hunter, a bull, a scorpion. We call these groups of stars constellations. As the seasons change, the constellations move across the sky.

Look at the sky at 8 p.m. one clear winter evening. Find the constellation Orion, the hunter. Check it again after one hour. Why is Orion moving? It's not! Earth is rotating, and you're on Earth. So you're the one who's moving!

The constellation Orion, the hunter.

Orion will be in a slightly different spot each night. This is because Earth is traveling around the Sun. As Earth moves, your view of the sky changes. In late spring, Orion disappears below the horizon. During the summer you'll see other constellations, such as Leo, the lion. But you won't see Orion again until late fall. In one year, Earth will circle the Sun once. Then Orion will be back in the same place in the sky.

Even today, our units of time are linked to the motions of our planet. The time it takes for Earth to rotate once is called one day. We break that day into parts— hours, minutes, and seconds. The time it takes Earth to revolve once around the Sun is called one year. The calendar is a daily reminder that we live on a planet!

Some stars are brighter than others.

What Did I Learn?

1. What did ancient people use to predict the seasons?
   A rocks
   B stars
   C animals
   D plants

2. Why do the stars appear to move across the sky at night?
   F Earth is rotating.
   G Orion, the hunter, is chasing them.
   H The stars don't appear to move.
   J The constellations are revolving around the Sun.

LOG ON Visit www.science.mmhschool.com to learn more about astronomy.

D 42   D 43

Sally Ride Science

There are **What Did I Learn? questions** on selected Sally Ride Science, Time for Kids, and magazine-style features. Answering the questions gives you an opportunity to practice using a standardized test, multiple choice format.

Chapter 1 Review

Vocabulary

Fill each blank with the best word or words from the list.

conifers, A78
embryo, A26
energy, A18
environment, A8
flowering plants, A28
heredity, A77
organism, A6
reproduction, A7
respond, A8
root, A17

1. Living things, such as carrots and frogs, are _____.

2. Organisms use food to get _____.

3. Shivering when you are cold is one way that you _____ to the environment.

4. _____ hold plants in the ground and take in water.

5. The young plant inside the seed is called a(n) _____.

6. The passing of certain characteristics from parent to offspring is called _____.

7. When a plant bends toward sunlight it is responding to its _____.

8. One feature all living things share is _____.

Two types of plants that make seeds are:

9. _____

10. _____

Test Prep

11. Which of the following did Robert Hooke discover with a microscope?
    A cells
    B cork
    C organs
    D organisms

12. What transports water and nutrients in a plant?
    F seeds
    G leaves
    H stems
    J flowers

13. What is a very young tree called?
    A acorn
    B sapling
    C seed
    D spore

14. Conifers are trees that
    F change color in the fall
    G produce seeds in cones
    H produce seeds in flowers
    J wilt in the summer

15. Wind, insects, and animals help plants reproduce by bringing together eggs and
    A pollen
    B oxygen
    C organisms
    D water

Concepts and Skills

16. **Reading in Science** How do the different parts of a plant help it survive?

17. **Critical Thinking** On a cold day, you might see icicles that have grown from the roof of a building. Does this mean icicles are living? Explain your answer.

18. **INQUIRY SKILL Experiment** Plan a plant experiment. You need to find out if temperature or the amount of daylight is more important for a plant to grow. Describe your experiment.

19. **Product Ads** Some ads on TV try to make you hungry, so that you respond by eating the foods shown. Describe an ad like that you have seen. Did it make you respond?

20. **Scientific Methods** Predict whether a seed can germinate without sunlight. Write a plan to test your prediction.

Did You Ever Wonder?

INQUIRY SKILL Use Variables You learned that plants respond to sunlight. Investigate how plants respond to different conditions. Tell how you would test your ideas.

LOG ON Visit www.science.mmhschool.com to boost your test scores.

A 34   A 35

A two-page **review** at the end of each chapter allows you to show what you know using a variety of assessment formats:
- fill-in
- multiple choice
- short answer

Performance Assessment

RECYCLE and Reuse

Your goal is to demonstrate how a group of used objects can be reused to do something else.

What to Do

Look at a group of used items. Think of a way to use the items to do something different. For example you could reuse an old plastic bag as a waterproof liner for your book bag. You could reuse a soft drink bottle as a piggy bank. Write down your ideas. Pick one idea and try it.

Draw Conclusions

Why is recycling or reusing something better than throwing it away? Write a paragraph to answer this question.

Form a Landform

Your goal is to make a model of three different kinds of landforms.

What to Do

Write down the name of three different kinds of landforms. Tell what you know about how each landform was formed. Draw pictures of the landforms, or use modeling clay or other art materials to model them.

Draw Conclusions

How might the three landforms change over time?

C 80

Performance Assessment at the end of every unit provides an opportunity to demonstrate what you've learned through hands-on activities and projects.

UNIT A

Looking at Plants and Animals

LOOK!

Beavers cut trees and
branches to build their homes.
How do beavers cut trees?

Looking at Plants and Animals

CHAPTER

Plants

Did You Ever Wonder?

How tall can a tree grow? The record is 112 meters
(368 feet). This is the height of a coast redwood, a
tree found in Oregon and California. Redwoods
are some of the oldest and tallest trees.

INQUIRY SKILL Form a Hypothesis How fast do you
think a coast redwood grows? What does it need
to grow?

A 2

How Living Things Are Alike

Vocabulary

organism, A6
reproduction, A7
environment, A8
respond, A8
cell, A10

Get Ready

What do you see in this picture? Some objects are living. Some objects are nonliving. How can you tell a living thing from a nonliving thing?

Inquiry Skill

You infer when you form an idea based on facts or observations.

Explore Activity

What Are the Features of Living Things?

Materials

25 pea seeds

25 pieces of gravel (pea-size)

hand lens

2 plastic cups

piece of white paper

teaspoon

water

Procedure

1. **Measure** Work with a partner. Place one teaspoon of pea seeds on the white paper. Place one teaspoon of gravel next to the pea seeds.

2. **Observe** Look at the seeds and gravel with the hand lens. Compare the seeds and the gravel. Record your observations.

3. Mark a plastic cup A. Place the seeds in it. Mark the other plastic cup B. Place the gravel in it. Pour the same amount of water into each cup. Make sure the seeds and gravel are completely covered with water.

4. **Predict** What do you think will happen after two days?

5. **Observe** Look at the soaked seeds and gravel every few hours for two days. Record your observations.

Drawing Conclusions

1. What is the living thing? How do you know?

2. **Infer** What are some features of living things?

3. FURTHER INQUIRY **Infer** Are you a living thing? How do you know?

Main Idea All living things have common features.

What Are the Features of Living Things?

An **organism** (AWR·guh·niz·uhm) is a living thing. How can you tell an organism from a nonliving thing? There are certain ways to tell a living thing from a nonliving thing.

Living Things Grow and Change

A living thing grows. It starts out small. Then it gets bigger. An oak tree begins as an acorn. Then it grows to become a green *sapling* (SAP·ling). This is a very young tree.

Organisms also change as they grow. The way a living thing changes during its life is called *development* (di·VEL·uhp·muhnt). As an oak sapling grows, the branches and trunk become thicker and stronger. The oak tree also changes its shape and color as it develops.

Acorn

Large tree

Green sapling

READING Diagrams

How does an oak tree develop?

Young tree

A 6

None of these puppies is an exact copy of its parents. Each puppy has a mixture of features from both parents.

Red tulip

Living Things Reproduce

Another feature of living things is that they make more of their own kind. Plants grow from seeds. Chicks hatch from eggs. Some animals, such as puppies, are born live from their mother. All these are examples of **reproduction** (ree·pruh·DUK·shuhn). This is the way organisms make more of their own kind.

How is a puppy similar to its parents? Some new living things, or offspring, are not exact copies of their parents. Instead, they have characteristics of both parents. Most animal offspring, including you, are not exact copies of their parents.

Yellow tulip

▷ **What are two features of all living things?**

Orange tulip

The color of a tulip depends on the color of its parents.

How Do Organisms React to Change?

All organisms live in an **environment** (en·VIGH·ruhn·muhnt). An environment is made up of everything that surrounds an organism. It includes air, water, soil, and other organisms.

Living Things Respond

When the environment changes, an organism may **respond** (ri·SPAHND) to that change. To respond is to react. All living things respond to many changes.

Both plants and insects respond to light. Plants bend toward light. Insects fly toward it. The leaves on some trees respond to a change in season. In autumn they turn colors, then fall off the branches. Animals also respond to a change in season. Bears eat a lot of food as winter nears. Then they sleep or rest through the winter in a cave.

You respond to your environment in many ways, too. You may shiver if you are cold. What other ways do you respond to changes in your environment?

As it prepares to sleep through the winter, a bear eats a great deal of food—including berries.

▷ **How does a plant respond to the environment?**

Sunflowers respond by turning toward the sunlight.

The cuttlefish changes
color to communicate.

How Do Living Things Communicate?

Most living things *communicate* (kuh·MYEW·ni·kayt),
which means to share information. To communicate,
organisms send, collect, and respond to signals.

How do living things communicate?
They communicate in many ways. Fireflies
flash lights to attract mates. Some birds
sing to mark the area where they live.
When a male red-winged blackbird
sings, it is saying to other males,
"Stay out of my territory!" The
cuttlefish changes skin color and
texture. This alerts other animals
that it is looking for food.

When a red-winged
blackbird sings,
other male red-
winged blackbirds
know to keep
their distance.

To receive communications, living things use
their senses. The senses of sight, smell, hearing,
and touch can all receive information.

▷ **What senses do living
things use to communicate?**

What Are the Smaller Parts of Living Things?

Microscope

More than 300 years ago, scientist Robert Hooke looked at a thin piece of cork through a *microscope* (MIGH·kruh·skohp). A microscope is a device that uses glass lenses, similar to those in eyeglasses. The lenses allow people to see very small things. Hooke saw that the cork was made of tiny boxlike shapes that he called **cells**.

Cells are the basic building blocks of life. Since Hooke's time scientists have learned that all living things are made of cells. Your own body is made of billions of cells.

Plant and animal cells have many of the same parts. Both plant and animal cells are filled with *cytoplasm* (SIGH·tuh·plaz·uhm). Cytoplasm is a clear, jellylike material. Both types of cells also have a *cell membrane*. A cell membrane is the thin outer covering of the cell.

These cork cells are similar to the ones Hooke saw in 1665.

Plant Cell

Cell membrane

Nucleus

Cytoplasm

Cell wall

Chloroplast

READING
Diagrams

What are the parts of a plant cell?

Each cell also has a *nucleus* (NEW·klee·uhs). The nucleus is the control center of the cell.

In other ways plant cells are very different from animal cells. Plant cells are usually larger and have a boxlike shape. Animal cells come in a wide variety of shapes. A plant cell also has a *cell wall*, which is a stiff layer outside the cell membrane. Animal cells lack cell walls.

Most plant cells have green *chloroplasts* (KLAWR·uh·plasts). Chloroplasts make food. Animal cells do not have chloroplasts.

Animal Cell

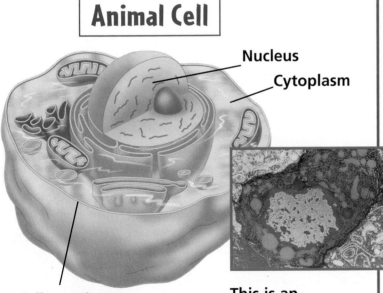

Nucleus

Cytoplasm

Cell membrane

This is an animal cell.

How Many Cells?

FOLDABLES Make a Foldables Half-Book. (See p. R41.) Label the book as shown.

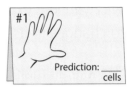

#1

Prediction: _____ cells

1. **Predict** On the front of the Foldables book, trace around your hand. Make the smallest dot you can on the hand. Write down the number of cells you think it covers.

2. **Use Numbers** Make a circle. This circle represents the ink dot on the hand. Fill the circle with beans. How many beans did you use?

3. **Interpret Data** Each bean represents a skin cell. How many skin cells are under the ink dot?

4. How did your prediction compare to this number? Record your answer on the inside of the Foldables book.

READING Draw Conclusions
Why are cells called the basic building blocks of life?

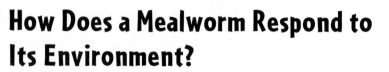

Inquiry Skill
B U I L D E R

How Does a Mealworm Respond to Its Environment?

In this activity you will experiment to find out how a mealworm responds to changes in its environment.

BE CAREFUL! Handle animals with care.
Wash your hands after handling mealworms.

Materials
mealworm

hand lens

toothpick

ruler

Procedure

1 **Observe** Look at the mealworm with the hand lens. How does it move? Very gently, touch it with a toothpick. Record your observations.

2 Plan several ways to change the mealworm's environment. Be sure the changes will not harm it. Record your plans in a chart like the one shown.

3 **Experiment** Test the statements. Record your results. Repeat the experiment. Compare these results to those recorded on the chart.

If Statement	Then Statement	Results
If something gets in the mealworm's path	then it will change its path	
If...	then...	

Drawing Conclusions

How does the mealworm respond to changes in its environment?

Lesson Review

Why It Matters

All living things are different. However, they all share the same features. All living things grow, take in food and air, get rid of waste, and reproduce.

It is important to be able to identify living things. Only living things are made of cells.

e-Journal Visit our Web site www.science.mmhschool.com to do a research project on living things.

Think and Write

1. What is an organism?

2. How is a living thing different from a nonliving thing?

3. What features do all animal and plant cells have in common?

4. INQUIRY SKILL **Experiment** How would you test the way a plant may respond to changes in its environment?

5. Critical Thinking What if your pet dog lost its sense of smell? How would this change the way it responds to its environment?

L·I·N·K·S

WRITING LINK

Explanatory Writing Suppose you are an underwater explorer. You find something that looks like the picture below. You are not sure if it is a living thing. How can you find out? Explain your discovery.

MATH LINK

Solve a problem. How small do you think a typical animal cell is? Look at the red dash. You could line up more than 300 cells along it. How many cells do you think you could line up along the blue dash?

ART LINK

Create a poster. Make a poster that shows an animal cell. Label all the parts.

TECHNOLOGY LINK

LOG ON Visit www.science.mmhschool.com for more links.

The Needs of Plants

Vocabulary

mineral, A16

root, A17

stem, A17

leaf, A18

energy, A18

oxygen, A19

Get Ready

A cactus lives in a hot, dry desert. A pine tree grows on a snowy mountain. A coconut tree thrives on a sandy beach. These three plants are very different, yet they have the same needs as all other plants. Do you know what plants need to live and grow?

Inquiry Skill

You observe when you use one or more of the senses to identify or learn about an object.

A 14

Explore Activity

What Do Plants Need?

Materials

soaked pea seeds from Lesson 1

6 half-pint cartons

4 ½ cups of soil

water

water with nutrients

metric ruler

Procedure

1 Measure Place $\frac{3}{4}$ cup of soil in each carton. Plant the seeds, and cover them with a thin layer of soil.

2 Label the cartons *Light*, *Water*, *Nutrients*, *No Light*, *No Water*, and *No Nutrients*.

3 Put the carton labeled *No Light* in a dark place. Put the remaining cartons in a sunny area. Water the cartons labeled *Light*, *No Light*, *Water,* and *No Nutrients*. Water the carton labeled *Nutrients* with water containing nutrients.

4 Measure Look at the plants. Measure and record the height of each plant twice a week.

5 Record what you see in a table like the one shown here.

Plants	Day 1	Day 3	Day 5	Day 7
Light				
Water				
Nutrients				
No light				
No water				
No nutrients				

Drawing Conclusions

1 Which plants are the healthiest after two weeks? How do you know?

2 What do seeds need to grow into healthy plants?

3 FURTHER INQUIRY **Infer** What else do you think plants need to survive? Explain your answer.

Main Idea All plants have the same basic needs.

What Are the Needs of Plants?

Like all living things, plants have certain needs. Plants need sunlight, water, and air to live. Plants also need **minerals** (MIN·uhr·uhlz). A mineral is a naturally occurring substance that is neither plant nor animal.

The parts of plants help them to get or make what they need. What parts do you see on the bean plant?

Field of bean plants

Leaves

Stem

Roots

The roots, stem, and leaves of this bean plant work together to get what the plant needs to live and grow.

All plants get water and minerals from the soil. The **root** is the plant part that grows underground. Roots help hold the plant in the ground. Roots also help take in water and minerals that the plant needs.

The **stem** is the part that supports the plant. It helps the plant stand upright. It carries minerals and water from the roots. It also carries food from the leaves to other parts of the plant.

Some plants, such as mosses, are simple plants. They don't have real roots or stems. These plants do not grow tall. Instead, they form low-growing mats in damp places to get water directly from the soil.

Other plants, such as the redwood tree, have many roots and a large stem. They can grow very tall.

The trunk of a redwood tree is its stem. Its roots are spread out underground. Why can a redwood tree grow so tall?

▷ **What are the needs of plants?**

A moss plant uses rootlike structures to get the water it needs. It grows low to the ground because it has no stem to carry water and minerals to its leaves.

Leaves

Stem

Roots

Tiny holes on the underside of a leaf take in air.

Why Does a Plant Need Leaves?

The **leaves** (singular, *leaf*) are the main food-making part of the plant. Many leaves have broad, flat surfaces that help them take in sunlight. Leaves are green because of *chlorophyll*. Chlorophyll traps the **energy** (EN·uhr·jee) in sunlight for the plant.

The leaf also helps the plant get the air it needs. Each leaf has tiny holes that take in air for the plant. The leaf uses a gas in the air called *carbon dioxide*. The plant uses the Sun's energy to combine carbon dioxide and water to make food. The stem then carries the food to the other parts of the plant.

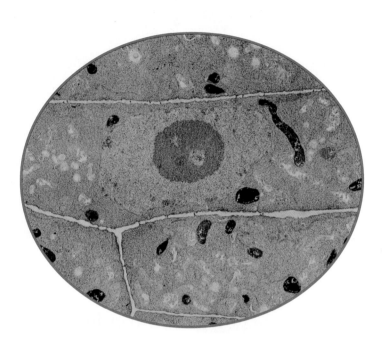

Chloroplasts, shown here as small parts inside a leaf cell, contain chlorophyll. This is where the plant makes food.

Plants use the food they make to stay alive. When we eat plants or other animals that eat plants, we use this food, too.

When leaves make food for a plant, they give off **oxygen** (AHK·suh·juhn). Oxygen is a gas that is in air and water. People and animals need oxygen to live. You inhale the oxygen made by a plant with each breath you take.

▷ **Why are leaves green?**

QUICK LAB

Water Moves in a Plant

FOLDABLES™ Make a Three-Tab Book. (See p. R43.) Label the tabs as shown.

#2	#3	#4
Predict	Observe	Infer

BE CAREFUL! Wear goggles.

1. **Measure** Put about 5 cm (2 in.) of water in a clear plastic cup. Add about ten drops of food coloring.

2. **Predict** Put a freshly cut celery stalk in the cup for two hours. What do you think will happen? Write your answer under the Predict tab.

3. **Observe** What did you observe after two hours? Write and draw your answer under the Observe tab.

4. **Infer** How does water travel through a plant? Write your answer under the Infer tab.

How Do Plants Respond to Their Environment?

Have you ever seen a plant leaning toward a sunlit window? This is one way that plants respond to their environment. A plant responds to light by growing toward it.

Some trees and shrubs drop their leaves as the days grow shorter and colder. These plants respond to the change in seasons from summer to winter.

Plants also respond to other things in the environment. For example, roots may grow toward water. The ability to respond to the environment helps a plant to live, grow, and meet its needs.

Morning glories turn toward the Sun.

READING Draw Conclusions
How do plants respond to sunlight?

The trees in this grove are responding to the cooler temperatures of autumn.

L·I·N·K·S

Why It Matters

We depend on plants for food. We eat the roots, stems, and leaves of plants. The cereals we eat are made from plants. We eat animals that eat plants. However, people need plants for more than food. We also breathe the oxygen that plant leaves make.

e-Journal Visit our Web site **www.science.mmhschool.com** to do a research project on plants.

Think and Write

1. What is oxygen?

2. What do plants need?

3. Why do most plants have roots, a stem, and leaves?

4. What if you put a plant in the middle of a room? The room has walls on three sides. On the fourth side, there is a sunny window. In which direction will the plant grow? Why?

5. **Critical Thinking** The saguaro cactus has no leaves, but its stem is green. Where do you think the cactus makes its food?

MATH LINK

Make a bar graph. Go on a plant hunt. Write down the different kinds of plants you find. Then group them into categories, such as grasses or trees. Make a graph to show how many of each category you found.

WRITING LINK

Writing That Compares Choose two plants. Measure each plant once a week for a month. Record your results in a two-column chart. Use your chart to write a paragraph that compares and contrasts the two plants.

LITERATURE LINK

Read *Save Our Park Trees* to learn about a tall, old oak tree that was alive 200 years ago. When you finish reading, think about what you would tell the people who would want to cut down this tree. Try the activities at the end of the book.

SAVE OUR PARK TREES
written by Barbara Adams
illustrated by Rick Brown

TECHNOLOGY LINK

LOG ON Visit **www.science.mmhschool.com** for more links.

STAYING ALIVE

Water, sunlight, and nutrients keep plants alive and growing. Plant leaves absorb sunlight and use it to make food. Trees grow tall and use their leaves to collect sunlight. However, some plants are equipped to live in places with very little water, sunlight, or nutrients. See how different environments affect the type of plants that live there.

The cactus lives in the desert. The plant's roots absorb and store rainfall. Some roots grow way out to absorb as much water as possible. The cactus also stores water in its thick stem. The plant's spines protect the plant and prevent it from losing water.

Cactus

Fern

Ferns grow on the ground, far from sunlight. These plants prefer the shade. They don't use as much of the Sun's light to make their food.

Venus's-flytrap

Soil doesn't supply all the nutrients a Venus's-flytrap needs. To get enough nutrients, the plant catches and eats insects!

Moss

Mosses grow close to the ground. They don't need much sunlight. Some even grow in the shade. Their leaves are like tiny magnifying glasses. They focus any available sunlight into the plant.

What Did I Learn?

1. Where could a cactus get water if it hasn't rained for a long time?

A its stem
B its leaves
C nearby streams
D from insects

2. The Venus's-flytrap gets nutrients it needs from

F leaves.
G rainwater.
H insects.
J the Sun.

LOG ON Visit www.science.mmhschool.com to learn more about plants.

The Life Cycle of a Plant

Vocabulary

life cycle, A26

embryo, A26

heredity, A27

flowering plant, A28

conifer, A28

Get Ready

Have you ever planted a seed and watched it grow into a plant? What happened to the plant as time passed? Look at the trees in the photograph. How do you think a tree changes as it grows?

Inquiry Skill

You infer when you form ideas from facts or observations.

Explore Activity

How Does a Plant's Life Begin?

Materials

5 pea seeds

hand lens

plastic cup

$\frac{1}{4}$ cup of water

paper towel

self-sealing plastic bag, pint-size

toothpick

Procedure

1 **Observe** Look at the seeds with the hand lens.

2 Place the seeds in the cup, and cover them with water. Soak the seeds overnight.

3 **Observe** Look at a seed with the hand lens.

4 Use the toothpick to separate the two halves of the seed. Use the hand lens to observe each half. Draw what you see.

5 Moisten a folded paper towel, and place it inside the plastic bag. Place the other four seeds at the bottom of the plastic bag on top of the paper towel. Seal the bag.

6 **Observe** Observe the seeds each day. Record your observations.

Drawing Conclusions

1 How did the seeds change after they were soaked? What did you find between the two halves of the seed?

2 **FURTHER INQUIRY** **Infer** Which seed part provides food for the young plant as it grows from the seed? Design and conduct an experiment to test your ideas.

Main Idea Plants grow and reproduce in many ways.

How Does a Plant's Life Begin?

A seed begins a bean plant's **life cycle** (LIGHF SIGH·kuhl). A life cycle is all of the stages in an organism's life. A plant begins life, grows, develops, reproduces, and dies.

A seed is a tiny capsule that contains a plant **embryo** (EM·bree·oh). A plant embryo is a young plant that is just beginning to grow. Each seed also contains food for the embryo. The food helps the embryo survive during the time it cannot make its own food. A tough outer case protects the embryo.

Seeds do not always *germinate* (JUR·muh·nayt) right away. A seed that germinates begins to grow. Seeds can wait for months, or even years, until the conditions for growth are right. A seed needs water, nutrients, and the right temperature to germinate and grow.

The life cycle of a plant can be short or long. A tomato plant lives for a few months.

Germination of a Bean Seed

Bean seed

Embryo

New root and stem

Adult bean plant

After the seed germinates, it grows into a young plant. This plant is called a *seedling*. A seedling looks like its parent.

New plants look like their parents because of **heredity** (huh·RED·i·tee). Heredity is the passing of characteristics from parent to offspring.

Have you ever seen purple corn? Corn kernels can be purple as well as yellow. Color is a characteristic that is passed from the parent corn plants to their offspring. The size of the ear of corn and the height of the plant are passed on, too.

What differences do you observe in these corn kernels?

▷ **What stages does a plant go through during its life cycle?**

Light or Shade?

FOLDABLES Make a Foldables Shutter. (See p. R42.) Label the tabs as shown.

1. Gather two plastic cups and the seedlings from the Explore Activity.

2. Cover the outside of one cup with black paper.

3. Wet some paper towels, and place one in each cup. Put a seedling on the paper towel.

4. Place both cups on a sunny windowsill. Place a piece of black paper over the top of the cup covered with paper. Make sure the towels are kept wet.

5. **Observe** Look at the seedlings after two days. Record what happened under the tabs of your Foldables shutter.

6. **Infer** What does this tell you about a seedling's needs? Write your answer on the back of your Foldables shutter.

With   Without

How Are Seeds Made?

Most plants, such as the pea plant, make seeds. There are two main groups of plants that reproduce by making seeds. They are **flowering plants** and **conifers** (KAHN·uh·fuhrz). Flowering plants are plants that produce seeds in flowers. Most plants in the world are flowering plants. Conifers are trees that produce seeds in cones. Pine trees and spruce trees are conifers.

Flowering Plants

Flowers have male parts and female parts. The female parts make eggs that become seeds.

The male parts make *pollen* (PAHL·uhn). Pollen is a powdery material that is needed by the eggs to make seeds.

To make seeds, pollen and eggs must come together. The wind, insects such as bees, or birds can bring pollen to eggs. Many animals like the sugary liquid in flowers. This liquid is called *nectar* (NEK·tuhr). While the animals drink nectar, pollen rubs off on their bodies. When they move to other flowers, some of the pollen is delivered to the female flower parts.

Over time flowers turn into fruits that contain seeds. A seed might grow into a new plant.

Life Cycle of a Flowering Plant

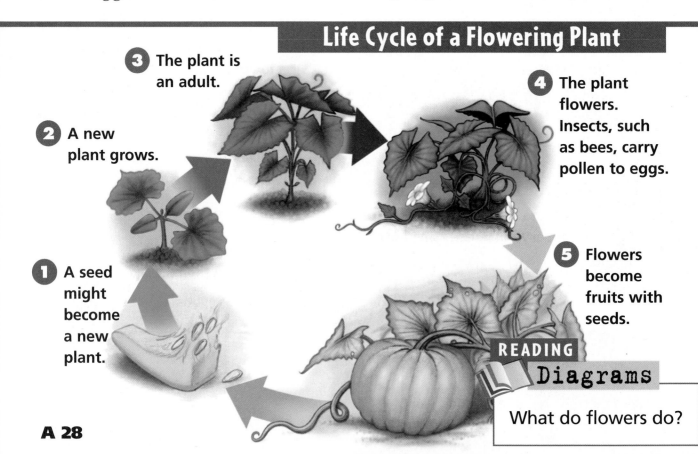

3 The plant is an adult.

2 A new plant grows.

4 The plant flowers. Insects, such as bees, carry pollen to eggs.

1 A seed might become a new plant.

5 Flowers become fruits with seeds.

READING Diagrams

What do flowers do?

Conifers

Some plants don't have flowers. They make seeds in other ways. Have you ever seen a pine cone? Pine cones come from conifers. Conifers include pine trees, spruces, and hemlocks. Their leaves look like needles or brushes.

A pine tree makes two kinds of cones. It makes small pollen cones and large seed cones. Wind blows pollen from the small cones to the large cones. When pollen attaches to the large cone, a seed is made. Seeds grow inside the large cones. When the seeds are ripe, they fall to the ground. If conditions are right, each seed can germinate and start growing. Over time, the seed may become a tree.

Female pine cone

Life Cycle of a Conifer

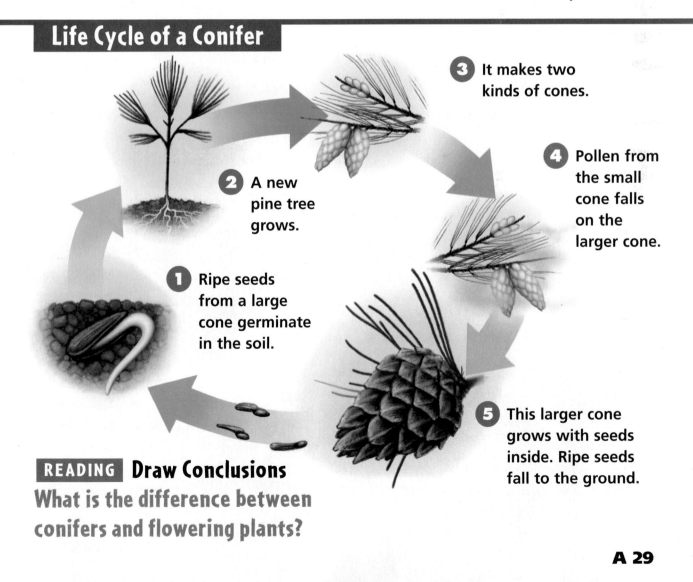

2 A new pine tree grows.

3 It makes two kinds of cones.

4 Pollen from the small cone falls on the larger cone.

1 Ripe seeds from a large cone germinate in the soil.

5 This larger cone grows with seeds inside. Ripe seeds fall to the ground.

READING Draw Conclusions
What is the difference between conifers and flowering plants?

A 29

What Other Ways Do Plants Reproduce?

Many plants can reproduce without seeds. Some can grow new plants from parts of themselves. These pieces are called *cuttings*, because a piece of the plant is cut off. If a leaf or piece of a stem from certain plants is placed in water, new roots will grow.

A *bulb* is an underground stem. One type of bulb is the onion. An onion plant can make several bulbs. Each bulb can grow into a new onion plant just like the parent plant.

Do you know what a *tuber* (TEW·buhr) is? You may have eaten a mashed one for dinner last night! A potato is a tuber. A tuber is an underground stem. New plants that grow from a tuber are just like the parent plants.

Mosses and ferns use *spores* (SPAWRZ) to reproduce. Spores are not as tough as seeds. They do not have a food supply. When a spore gets light, water, and nutrients, it can grow into a new plant.

▷ **What are two other ways plants reproduce without seeds?**

This bulb will grow into an iris plant.

New roots grow from this cutting.

This potato is a tuber. Each white spot, called an eye, can grow a new plant.

Each orange spot on this fern contains hundreds of spores.

Why It Matters

Flowering plants make almost all of the food you eat. Different foods come from different parts of plants. In any meal you might eat the flowers, fruits, seeds, leaves, stems, or roots. Flowering plants are also eaten by cows, sheep, chickens, and other animals.

e-Journal Visit our Web site **www.science.mmhschool.com** to do a research project on the stages in a plant's life cycle.

Think and Write

1. Describe the stages in a plant's life cycle.

2. What is a seed?

3. What are the ways plants can reproduce, other than with seeds?

4. Where do conifers and flowering plants produce seeds?

5. Critical Thinking How can insects be helpful in your garden?

L·I·N·K·S

WRITING LINK

Writing a Story Imagine that you are a seed that has just been formed. Write about your journey to find the right conditions for growth. What happens to you along the way? Where do you end up? Share your story with your classmates.

MATH LINK

Make a chart. Research some of your favorite vegetables to find out what plant part they come from. Make a chart that lists the different plant parts, such as seed, leaf, stem, root, and tuber. Compare how many of each you find.

ART LINK

Make a seed collage. Gather seeds of different shapes and sizes. Glue down the seeds to create a design or picture.

TECHNOLOGY LINK

 LOG ON Visit **www.science.mmhschool.com** for more links.

Spuds in Space

Ed Galindo teaches in Idaho, a state where farmers grow a lot of potatoes. Mr. Galindo and his students wondered if potatoes would grow someplace a little different—outer space!

With help from NASA, the class did an experiment. They planted potatoes in special soil provided by NASA. The soil was similar to soil found on Mars. The space shuttle *Atlantis* carried the planted potatoes into space. There the potatoes grew with very little gravity. The class grew another set of potatoes on Earth. Then they compared the two sets of potatoes. Guess what they discovered? The potatoes in space grew twice as big as those grown on Earth!

Like all good experiments, Spuds in Space suggested new questions. Why did the potatoes grow larger in space than on Earth? Will other plants grow in space as well as the potatoes did? Mr. Galindo and his students are busy trying to find the answers.

Students' experiment, Spuds in Space

Ed Galindo

Collecting data

What Did I Learn?

1. What did Mr. Galindo's students wonder about?

   A Could potatoes grow in space?
   B Could carrots grow in space?
   C How tasty are potatoes grown in space?
   D Is there gravity on the space shuttle?

2. What were the results of the experiment?

   F The potatoes didn't grow in space.
   G Only a few potatoes grew in space.
   H The potatoes grew larger in space.
   J The potatoes grew smaller in space.

LOG ON Visit **www.science.mmhschool.com** to learn more about space.

Chapter 1 Review

Vocabulary

Fill each blank with the best word or words from the list.

conifers, A28   heredity, A27

embryo, A26   organism, A6

energy, A18   reproduction, A7

environment, A8   respond, A8

flowering   root, A17
   plants, A28

1. Living things, such as carrots and frogs, are _____.

2. Organisms use food to get _____.

3. Shivering when you are cold is one way that you _____ to the environment.

4. _____ hold plants in the ground and take in water.

5. The young plant inside the seed is called a(n) _____.

6. The passing of certain characteristics from parent to offspring is called _____.

7. When a plant bends toward sunlight it is responding to its _____.

8. One feature all living things share is _____.

Two types of plants that make seeds are:

9. _____

10. _____.

Test Prep

11. Which of the following did Robert Hooke discover with a microscope?

   A cells

   B cork

   C organs

   D organisms

12. What transports water and nutrients in a plant?

   F seeds

   G leaves

   H stems

   J flowers

13. What is a very young tree called?

   A acorn

   B sapling

   C seed

   D spore

14. Conifers are trees that _____.

    F change color in the fall

    G produce seeds in cones

    H produce seeds in flowers

    J wilt in the summer

15. Wind, insects, and animals help plants reproduce by bringing together eggs and _____.

    A pollen

    B oxygen

    C organisms

    D water

Concepts and Skills

16. **Reading in Science** How do the different parts of a plant help it survive?

17. **Critical Thinking** On a cold day, you might see icicles that have grown from the roof of a building. Does this mean icicles are living? Explain your answer.

18. INQUIRY SKILL **Experiment** Plan a plant experiment. You need to find out if temperature or the amount of daylight is more important for a plant to grow. Describe your experiment.

19. **Product Ads** Some ads on TV try to make you hungry, so that you respond by eating the foods shown. Describe an ad like that you have seen. Did it make you respond?

20. **Scientific Methods** Predict whether a seed can germinate without sunlight. Write a plan to test your prediction.

Did You Ever Wonder?

INQUIRY SKILL **Use Variables** You learned that plants respond to sunlight. Investigate how plants respond to different conditions. Tell how you would test your ideas.

 LOG ON Visit **www.science.mmhschool.com** to boost your test scores.

CHAPTER

2

Animals

Did You Ever Wonder?

Have you ever seen these birds? They are puffins.
Puffins live along the cold ocean shores of Alaska and
Canada. Look at their feet and beaks.

INQUIRY SKILL Observe How do you think they find
food? What do you think they eat?

A 36

The Needs of Animals

Get Ready

It is a hot day, and you have been playing for hours. Your mouth and throat feel dry and scratchy. All you can think about is a glass of cold water. You are thirsty, and your body needs water. Is water all your body needs?

Inquiry Skill

You observe when you use one or more of the senses to learn about an object.

Explore Activity

What Do Animals Need to Live and Grow?

Procedure

BE CAREFUL! Handle animals with care. Wash your hands after handling caterpillars.

1 Place the caterpillar food in the bottom of the plastic cup.

2 Carefully put the caterpillar in the cup. Cover the cup with the lid.

3 Place the caterpillar in a cool place out of the sunlight.

4 Observe Look at the caterpillar once a day for two weeks. Record what you see.

Drawing Conclusions

1 How did your caterpillar change during the two weeks?

2 What happened to the food?

3 What do caterpillars need to live and grow?

4 FURTHER INQUIRY
Experiment How could you test to see if another living thing does the same things as the caterpillar at different times in its life?

Read to Learn

Main Idea All animals need certain things to live and grow.

What Do Animals Need to Live and Grow?

What do you need every day to live and grow? All animals have certain needs. They all need food, water, air, and a place to live. Animals live in places where their needs are met. If these needs are not met, an animal cannot survive.

Food is a very important need of animals. Food gives an animal *energy* (EN·uhr·jee). Energy is the ability to do work. An animal is like a machine. Both need energy to run. Fuel, such as gasoline, runs a machine. Food is an animal's fuel.

Animals cannot make their own food. They get the food they need from eating other living things. This means that animals are *consumers*. A consumer is an organism that cannot make its own food. It gets energy by eating other organisms.

Some animals hunt and eat other animals for their food.

A koala bear is eating a leaf.

These lion cubs meet their needs in the grassland. Other lions protect them, and they find food and water here.

Different kinds of animals find their food in different ways. Many animals eat only plants or plant parts. Plant eaters can be large or small. Many insects eat leaves, stems, or seeds. Mice and some birds eat seeds. Elephants eat stems and leaves.

Still other animals eat both plants and animals. Brown bears eat fish, seeds, and other animals.

This raccoon is eating a fish.

▷ **Why do animals need food?**

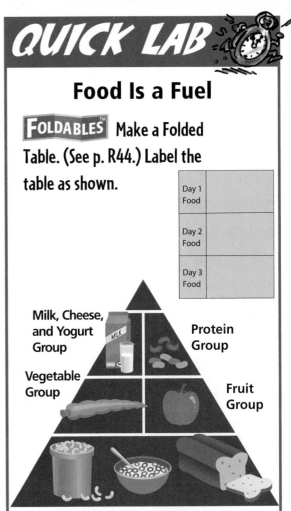

QUICK LAB

Food Is a Fuel

FOLDABLES Make a Folded Table. (See p. R44.) Label the table as shown.

Day 1 Food	
Day 2 Food	
Day 3 Food	

Milk, Cheese, and Yogurt Group

Protein Group

Vegetable Group

Fruit Group

Bread, Cereal, Rice, and Pasta Group

1. **Predict** Do you eat something from every food group most days?

2. For each of the next three days, record everything that you eat on your Foldables table.

3. **Interpret Data** Next to each item on your list, write the name of the food group it belongs to.

4. Did you eat something from every food group? Compare your results with those of your classmates.

How Do Animals Get Air and Water?

Animals need air because it contains *oxygen*. Oxygen is an important gas. You can live for a few days without food or water. However, you would die in just a few minutes without oxygen. All animals need oxygen to get the energy they need from food.

How do animals get oxygen? Many animals take in oxygen through their lungs. Lungs are body parts inside the chest. Many land animals breathe with lungs. So do some water animals, such as dolphins and whales. They swim to the surface to breathe.

Fish and some other water animals breathe with gills. Gills are body parts that take in oxygen from the water.

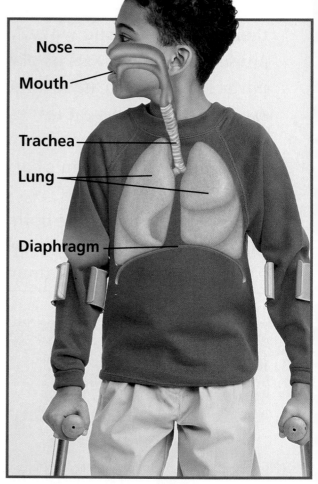

Nose
Mouth
Trachea
Lung
Diaphragm

Oxygen enters your body through your mouth and nose.

Fish take in oxygen with gills.

Why do you think all animals need water? The answer is simple. All animals are made up mostly of water. Approximately 60 percent of the human body is made up of water. This water does not stay in the body. It leaves as sweat and liquid waste. Drinking replaces lost water.

Water has several important jobs. It helps the body use food as fuel. It helps some animals stay cool, and it helps get rid of body wastes. Wastes can be poisonous if they remain in the body.

▷ **What are two ways animals get oxygen?**

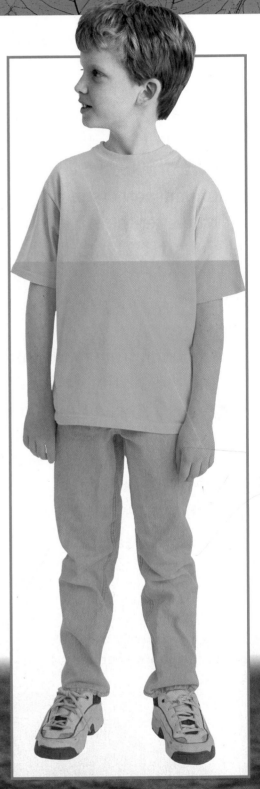

The human body is more than half water.

This whale has lungs to take in oxygen.

How Do Animals Find Shelter?

Remember that animals live in places where they can meet their needs. They live in all parts of the world. Some live on high mountains; others in deep oceans.

Wherever they live, animals find **shelters** (SHEL·tuhrz). A shelter is a place or object that protects an animal. Animals use shelters to stay safe.

Bats hang from walls inside caves during the daytime. Kangaroo rats dig holes in the ground for shelter. Beavers build their own shelters called lodges. They use trees to build their lodges at the edge of the water.

▷ **What is a shelter?**

Bats find shelter in caves during the day. They hunt for food at night.

Many deserts are hot in the day and cool at night. Kangaroo rats sleep in holes during the day and search for food at night.

This lodge helps protect the beaver from its enemies.

How Do Animals Respond to Inner Needs?

How do you know you are hungry? Does your stomach make noises? Some needs, such as needing food, are inner needs. To meet inner needs, signals inside an organism's body tell it what to do. When you are hungry, your brain gets the message: Eat!

A dolphin swimming underwater begins to run out of oxygen. Waste gas also builds up in its body. These events give the dolphin's brain a message: Go up for air!

A horse running on a hot day sweats and loses body water. The horse's brain gets a message: Drink!

What happens when you play games or run? Do you sweat and lose body water?

How do you think you would feel after playing basketball?

▶ **How does your body tell you that it is time to drink?**

After running, the horse will probably be very thirsty.

How Do Animals Respond to Changes in Their Environment?

How do you respond if you step outside and find that it is very warm? You may take off your jacket. How might you respond if it is cold? You might shiver. You might put on a hat and gloves. When you do these things, you are responding to a change in your environment.

Living things respond to changes in their environment in different ways. For example, insects are attracted to flowers in bloom. Lizards find sunny spots to warm themselves.

What happens when the weather gets colder? Some animals gather food for the winter. Geese and butterflies **migrate** (MIGH·grayt). Animals that migrate move to another place, where it is warmer. Bears and other animals find places to **hibernate** (HIGH·buhr·nayt). Animals that hibernate rest or sleep through the cold winter. These are ways animals increase their chances of survival.

Changes in the seasons, including temperature and length of day, signal some birds to migrate.

Bees are attracted to flowers in bloom.

Lizards lie in the sunlight to warm their blood.

READING **Compare and Contrast** How do lizards and bees respond to their environment?

Why It Matters

All animals have needs. People have needs, too. Think about the air you breathe, the food you eat, and the water you drink. Everything you need is found in the environment. That's why it's important to take care of the environment. Taking care of the environment now will help take care of everyone's needs in the future.

e-Journal Visit our Web site www.science.mmhschool.com to do a research project on animals.

Think and Write

1. What are the basic needs of animals?

2. Why do animals need food?

3. How do animals take in oxygen?

4. What if you were going on a trip to the North Pole? What might your needs be?

5. Critical Thinking Why would an animal leave its shelter?

L·I·N·K·S

WRITING LINK

Explanatory Writing Choose a pet you might like to have. Find out what the needs of this pet are. Write a paragraph explaining how new pet owners can take care of this animal.

MATH LINK

Solve a problem. You have been counting birds and squirrels. You see a total of 32 legs and 10 animals. How many birds do you see? How many squirrels?

ART LINK

Make a diorama. Build a shoe-box diorama for your favorite animal. Make sure to include ways your animal will find food, water, and a place to live.

TECHNOLOGY LINK

Science Newsroom CD-ROM Choose *Heads and Tail* to learn where animals live and grow.

LOG ON Visit www.science.mmhschool.com for more links.

Chasing Butterflies

Students at the Blake School in Minnesota read about monarchs. They learned that monarchs east of the Rocky Mountains fly to Mexico in the fall. Monarchs west of the Rocky Mountains fly to the coast of California. Some fly up to 4,000 kilometers (2,500 miles). They fly by day and rest at night. The trip takes up to three months.

The students went to the eastern monarchs' winter home. It's in the mountains west of Mexico City. There the kids saw millions of monarchs. The butterflies stay in Mexico until spring. Then they fly north. The females lay eggs along the way.

As temperatures drop in the fall, monarchs migrate south.

Kids Did It!

Now the Blake students want to help protect the places where monarchs rest during the winter. They are using the Internet to let people know how important these places are. Without somewhere to rest, monarchs would disappear!

 LOG ON Visit **www.science.mmhschool.com** to learn more about butterflies.

What Did I Learn?

1. Where do monarchs that live east of the Rocky Mountains fly to?

   A Mexico
   B California
   C the Blake School
   D Minnesota

2. When do the monarchs leave Mexico?

   F spring
   G summer
   H winter
   J fall

How Animals Grow

Vocabulary

metamorphosis,
A52

inherited trait,
A56

learned trait,
A56

Get Ready

How do animals change over a lifetime? Compare a dog and a caterpillar. Both change as they grow, but in very different ways. Which animal seems to grow more? Which animal seems to change more?

Inquiry Skill

You **communicate** when you share information.

Explore Activity

How Does a Caterpillar Change As It Grows?

Materials

caterpillar and container from Lesson 4

hand lens

Procedure

BE CAREFUL! Handle animals with care.

1 **Observe** Look at the caterpillar with the hand lens. Make a drawing of it.

2 **Observe** Look at the caterpillar each day for two weeks. Record your findings. Include a drawing of what the caterpillar looks like.

3 How has the caterpillar changed?

Drawing Conclusions

1 What happened to the caterpillar?

2 What does the caterpillar become when it is an adult?

3 **Classify** In what ways are the young and adult forms different?

4 FURTHER INQUIRY
Communicate Which animal seems to change more—the caterpillar or a dog? How do you know?

Main Idea Animals go through changes as they live and grow.

How Do Animals Change As They Grow?

The stages of an animal's life cycle are similar to those of a plant's life cycle. A life cycle is all of the stages in an organism's life. Animals go through these stages:

- **Birth** The animal's life begins.
- **Growth and Change** The animal gets larger. It may take on a new form.
- **Reproduction** The animal creates new animals like itself.
- **Death** The animal's life ends.

Some animals, such as people, get larger as they grow older. Unlike people, some animals go through life cycle changes called **metamorphosis** (met·uh·MAWR·fuh·sis). *Metamorphosis* means a change in body form. It causes big changes in insects such as the butterfly and smaller changes in insects such as the grasshopper.

Other animals, such as frogs and toads, also go through metamorphosis. For example, young frogs live only in water. Adult frogs live both in and out of water. Their bodies must change to live in different places.

Stage 1: Egg
A female lays an egg on a leaf.

This grasshopper goes through three stages during its life cycle.

▷ **What is metamorphosis?**

Metamorphosis of a Monarch Butterfly

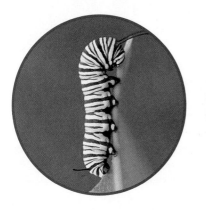

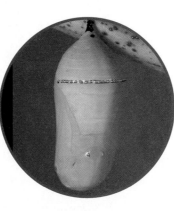

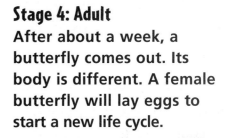

Stage 2: Caterpillar
A caterpillar hatches from the egg.

Stage 3: Pupa
(PYEW·puh) The organism forms a hard case around itself.

Stage 4: Adult
After about a week, a butterfly comes out. Its body is different. A female butterfly will lay eggs to start a new life cycle.

Metamorphosis of a Frog

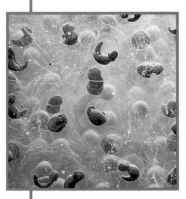

Stage 1: Egg
A female lays eggs in water.

Stage 2: Tadpole
A fishlike tadpole hatches from each egg.

Later in Stage 2: Tadpole Changing to an Adult
A tadpole grows legs, and its tail shortens. At this stage the animal is not quite a tadpole and not quite a frog.

Stage 3: Adult
A tadpole's tail finally disappears. It is a frog. A female frog lays eggs to start a new life cycle.

How Do the Life Cycles of Other Animals Compare?

Have you ever seen a kitten or puppy grow into an adult? What changes did it go through?

Almost all animals come from eggs. Some offspring, such as frogs, chickens, and turtles, hatch from eggs outside the female's body. After hatching, frogs go through metamorphosis. Chickens and turtles do not go through metamorphosis.

Other offspring, such as dogs and bears, grow and develop inside the female's body. They look a lot like the adults. As they grow and change, they do not go through metamorphosis. Use this diagram to compare the life cycles of a bear, a chicken, and a turtle.

READING Compare and Contrast
How are the life cycles of the bear, chicken, and turtle the same? How are they different?

Bear

Newborn Cub
A bear egg develops inside a female's body. A bear is born live. The baby bear feeds on its mother's milk.

Adult
Adult bears begin to reproduce at between $2\frac{1}{2}$ and 6 years of age. One to four cubs are born at a time.

Young Cub
The young bear is called a cub. Its mother watches it closely. The cub will not be ready to live on its own until it is $1\frac{1}{2}$ to 2 years old.

Eggs

Chicken eggs develop outside the female's body. Adults warm eggs by sitting on them. The warmth helps the offspring develop.

Adult

To show they are ready to reproduce, roosters have bright feathers. Most chickens live for four or five years.

Young Chick

Baby chickens, or chicks, have soft, yellow feathers. With time the young chicks grow big and strong.

Turtle

Eggs

Turtle eggs develop outside the female's body. They are usually soft and leathery. The loggerhead turtle buries about 100 eggs at a time in beach sand.

Adult

Turtles begin to reproduce when they are between 3 and 8 years old. Most turtles live for at least 50 years.

Young Turtle

The baby turtle has a special knob on its nose. This helps it break out of its shell. Once hatched, the baby is on its own. It immediately begins to walk toward the sea.

READING

Diagrams

How is a young turtle different from a bear cub or a young chick?

A 55

QUICK LAB

Name That Trait!

FOLDABLES Make a Two-Pocket Book. (See p. R42.) Label the book as shown.

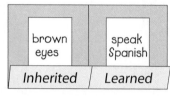

brown eyes	speak Spanish
Inherited	Learned

1. On each of two index cards, write a trait that can be inherited. On each of two other cards, write a trait that can be learned. Do not show your partner what you write.

2. Take turns holding up a card. Ask your partner to identify the trait as inherited or learned.

3. **Classify** Use the Foldables book to sort the cards into two groups.

4. **Communicate** Make more trait cards. Place them in the Foldables book. Explain if each trait is learned or inherited.

What Are Traits?

Have you ever been told, "You have your mother's eyes"? This is an example of an **inherited trait** (in·HER·it·uhd TRAYT). Inherited traits are characteristics that come from your parents.

How do you inherit traits? Both parents contribute special material to their offspring. This material determines traits such as hair and eye color.

Not all traits are inherited. Some are **learned traits**. These are things that are taught or learned by doing. You learn to ride a bicycle or speak a language.

▷ **What inherited trait and learned trait do you see here?**

Why It Matters

As you get older, you will go through many changes. Knowing the stages of the life cycle helps you better understand these changes. By studying the life cycles of animals, you can appreciate nature more.

e-Journal Visit our Web site www.science.mmhschool.com to do a research project on the life cycles of animals.

Think and Write

1. How many stages are in a butterfly's life cycle?

2. What is metamorphosis?

3. Which kinds of animals are born live? Which hatch from eggs?

4. What if you have a dog that rolls over when you tell it to? Is this an inherited trait or a learned trait? Explain.

5. **Critical Thinking** You might see many caterpillars at certain times of the year. Why do you think some people might be worried about trees then?

L·I·N·K·S

WRITING LINK

Personal Narrative You are still growing and changing. How do you think you will change by the end of the year? Write a paragraph about something you want to learn to do by then. How will you learn it?

MATH LINK

Make a line graph. Measure and record your height now. Predict how tall you might be at the end of the school year. Measure your height each month to check your prediction. Use this information to make a line graph. Describe what your graph shows.

LITERATURE LINK

Read *Sharks* to learn about a variety of different sharks. When you finish reading, list the facts you learned about sharks. Are the facts different from what you thought about sharks before you read the book? Try the activities at the end of the book.

TECHNOLOGY LINK

LOG ON Visit www.science.mmhschool.com for more links.

WHY SO MANY

EGGS?

WHAT A WAY TO GET A MEAL!

Frog eggs

A female frog can lay thousands of eggs at a time. Lots of frogs live in the same pond, so imagine all the frog eggs there could be! Will the pond soon overflow with twisting and turning tadpoles?

Probably not. Many fish eat frog eggs. Some kinds of frogs eat other frogs' eggs, too. Sudden cold weather can chill and kill the eggs. If insecticides or other chemicals get into the pond, the eggs will absorb them and die. If a pond dries up, so do the eggs!

Some eggs will survive and become tadpoles. However, fish and ducks eat tadpoles. Cold or dry weather or water pollution can kill tadpoles. Some might not find enough food. All in all, few tadpoles live to become adult frogs.

Although they lay lots of eggs, the number of frogs worldwide goes down every year. Water and air pollution are two causes. People have also filled in many ponds where frogs once laid their eggs. Without places for frogs to live, the number of frogs may continue to decrease.

Write ABOUT IT

1. Why do frogs lay large numbers of eggs?
2. Most birds lay just a few eggs. How do the eggs survive?

LOG ON Visit www.science.mmhschool.com to learn more about animal survival.

Parts of Animals

Vocabulary

tissue, A62

organ, A62

system, A62

Get Ready

What types of body parts do you have? All animals have body parts that do special jobs. What are those jobs? Look at this tree snail. How do you think its parts help it to survive?

Inquiry Skill

You predict when you state possible results of an event or experiment.

Explore Activity

What Are the Parts of an Insect?

Materials

caterpillar in a 5-inch clear-plastic petri dish

hand lens

sheet of white paper

toothpick

paper towels

Procedure

BE CAREFUL! Handle animals with care. Wash your hands after handling caterpillars.

1. Work with a partner. Cover your work area with a piece of white paper.

2. **Observe** Look at the caterpillar. What parts do you see? Draw the caterpillar.

3. **Observe** Use the hand lens to look at the caterpillar. Draw the parts you see now.

4. **Experiment** Use the toothpick to touch the caterpillar gently. How does it move when it is touched?

Drawing Conclusions

1. What are the parts of a caterpillar?

2. How does a caterpillar use its parts?

3. **FURTHER INQUIRY**
   Predict What parts do you think are inside a caterpillar? Research to check your prediction.

> **Main Idea** Different body parts help an animal to survive.

How Are Organisms Put Together?

Cells are the building blocks of all living things. Cells can be very different from one another, even inside the same organism. The cells in your heart are very different from those in your brain.

A **tissue** (TISH·ew) is made of a group of cells that are all alike. Tissues in your heart are made of muscle cells. Tissues in your brain are made of nerve cells. Heart and brain tissues look different and act in different ways.

An **organ** (AWR·guhn) is a group of tissues that work together to do a job. The heart, liver, brain, and stomach are organs. The skin is your body's largest organ.

Some organs work together in body **systems** (SIS·tuhmz). A system is a group of parts that work together. Each body system has a certain job to do.

Your body has many body systems. The digestive system gets energy from food. The nervous system lets you think and feel. It also works with the muscular system to move the body.

▷ **What is a system?**

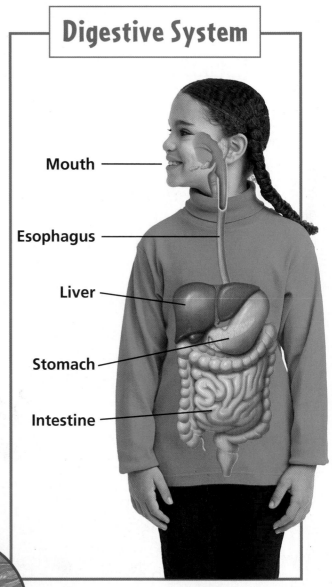

Digestive System

Mouth —

Esophagus —

Liver —

Stomach —

Intestine —

The digestive system is made up of many organs. The stomach is one of these organs. Smooth muscle tissue shown here makes up the stomach.

What Body Parts Protect and Support?

Your skin is like a wall between your body and everything around it. It keeps important materials inside. It keeps other materials outside.

Different animals have different kinds of parts that protect and support. Here are some of these parts.

Wool is the soft, curly hair of sheep. Wool keeps sheep very warm.

- Skin and scales keep water that is inside the body from escaping. They also keep outside water from moving inside. Fish are covered with scales. Humans and many other animals are covered with skin.

A lizard has tough, waterproof skin.

- Fur, feathers, and wool keep an animal warm. Many animals that live in cold places, such as polar bears, have very thick fur.
- Hard body coverings, such as shells, both protect and support. A crab's shell is very tough and hard. It protects the crab's inside parts, which are very soft.
- Bones support animals on the inside. Many animals have strong bones that help keep body parts in place.

READING **Compare and Contrast**
What are some ways outer coverings protect an animal?

A 63

What Body Parts Move or Collect Information?

Body parts that move help animals survive in many ways. Animals move to find food and eat food. They move to build homes, help their young, and escape danger. They need moving parts even to talk or sing. Put your hand on your throat and make a noise. Can you feel the moving parts?

Animals can move their legs, feet, hands, and wings. They can move their heads, backs, and tails. What other moving parts do animals have?

Animals also need to collect different kinds of information. Eyes get information from light. Ears receive sounds. The skin senses touch. The nose smells information. The tongue senses different tastes. Information about the world around them helps animals stay alive.

▶ **What are two ways your body collects information?**

Cats lick their kittens to keep them clean.

This snowshoe hare has to move quickly to survive.

How Do Animals Take In and Get Rid of Materials?

Animals need to take in air, food, and water. To do this, many animals use a nose and mouth, just like you do. Air travels from the nose and mouth to the lungs. There, oxygen from the air enters the body. The mouth is also the first part of the digestive system.

Other animals use different parts to take in materials. Earthworms have thin skin that lets air and water soak through. Fish breathe through gills. Clams and oysters do not eat with mouths. Instead, they trap small bits of food from the water.

Animals also need to get rid of wastes. When you breathe out, you get rid of a waste gas called carbon dioxide. Animals have body systems to get rid of solid and liquid wastes.

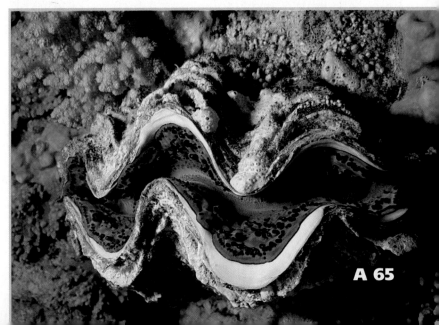

Sharks have very sharp teeth. The teeth easily tear food into pieces a shark can swallow.

▷ **What is one part animals use to take in materials?**

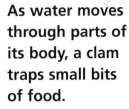

As water moves through parts of its body, a clam traps small bits of food.

Inquiry Skill
BUILDER

Comparing Animals

Classifying information helps you make sense of the world. How can classifying animals help you understand them?

Procedure

1 List ten different animals. You may wish to find pictures of the animals in magazines or other reference materials.

2 **Classify** Think of a way to divide the animals into groups. For example, one way is body covers. Give each group a name that explains what the group members have in common.

3 **Communicate** List the name of the group and its members in a table like the one shown below.

4 Think of another way to group the same animals. Repeat steps 2 and 3 two more times.

Drawing Conclusions

1 **Interpret Data** Is there only one way to classify animals? Explain your answer.

2 **Communicate** How did you decide how to group the animals?

Way of Classifying	Groups	Animals in Groups
First way of classifying: body covers	hair	bear, moose, walrus, squirrel
	scales	fish, snake
	feathers	robin
	hard shell	ant, clam, snail
Second way of classifying:		

L·I·N·K·S

Why It Matters

Next time you look at an animal, think about its different body parts. Each part has a job. Your own body is also made of parts that perform jobs. Right now you are using some parts to gather information. Which parts are you using?

℮-Journal Visit our Web site **www.science.mmhschool.com** to do a research project on the parts of animals.

Think and Write

1. Compare cells, tissues, and organs.

2. Describe three different body coverings of animals.

3. Why is it important to have different parts?

4. **INQUIRY SKILL** **Classify** How might you classify the following body parts: ears, skin, brain, hands, mouth?

5. **Critical Thinking** Explorers find something that they think is an animal. The object has no way for materials to enter its body. Could it be an animal? Explain.

WRITING LINK

Expository Writing How do your moving parts help you survive? Make a chart. In one column, list your moving parts. In the second column, tell how each helps you survive. Use the information in your chart to write a paragraph.

MATH LINK

Solve a problem. A one-year-old alligator weighs about 4 pounds. A two-year-old alligator can weigh between 9 and 12 pounds. What is the most weight an alligator can gain between year one and year two?

LITERATURE LINK

Read *Claws and Wings and Other Neat Things* to learn about animals and their special body parts. Try the activities at the end of the book.

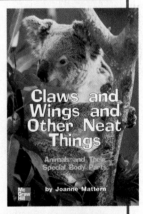

Claws and Wings and Other Neat Things

Animals and Their Special Body Parts

by Joanne Mattern

TECHNOLOGY LINK

Science Newsroom CD-ROM Choose *Hide and Seek* to learn about the outer coverings of different animals.

LOG ON Visit **www.science.mmhschool.com** for more links.

Kinds of Animals

Get Ready

What's your favorite animal? Is it a dog, a cat, or a bird? Imagine that someone had never seen animals before. How would you describe them?

Inquiry Skill

You **communicate** when you **share information**.

Scales

Gills

What Are Fish?

A **fish** is an animal that lives its
whole life in water. Many fish have long,
narrow bodies. Some fish are almost flat! A fish's body
is shaped to move easily through water. Scales and a
slimy coating also help fish move through water.

Like people, fish need oxygen to live. Fish use
gills to get oxygen from water. The water comes
through the fish's mouth, then moves through the
gills behind the fish's head. The gills take in oxygen,
and the water passes out.

A fish is cold-blooded. This means that its body
temperature changes with the surrounding
temperature. When the water gets cold, the fish's
temperature drops. When the water warms up, the
fish's temperature rises.

▷ **How do fish get oxygen?**

What Are Amphibians and Reptiles?

An **amphibian** (am·FIB·ee·uhn) is a cold-blooded animal that spends part of its life in water and part on land. A frog is an amphibian. So is a salamander.

Frogs lay eggs in water. When an egg hatches, a tadpole appears. A tadpole has a tail and gills, like a fish. When it gets older, it grows legs and lungs. Its tail disappears. It becomes an adult frog that can live on land.

A **reptile** (REP·tuhl) is an animal that lives on land and has a waterproof skin. Lizards, turtles, and snakes are reptiles. They are cold-blooded animals. They need the Sun to warm their bodies.

What kind of animal is this salamander?

READING **Compare and Contrast** How are amphibians and reptiles alike? How are they different?

A snake has tough skin that keeps water inside. What kind of animal is a snake?

What Are Birds?

A **bird** is an animal that has a beak, feathers, two wings, and two legs. Birds are the only animals that have feathers. Feathers keep birds' bodies smooth so that they can fly or swim easily.

A bird's front limbs are wings. Most birds use their wings to fly. Strong muscles attach the wings to the chest. Birds need strong muscles to lift off the ground and fly in the air.

Birds lay eggs that have shells. Most birds sit on their eggs to keep them warm. After the young hatch, one or both parents may care for them. Soon the young are ready to live on their own.

Most birds hatch their eggs in nests that they build.

Name That Animal!

FOLDABLES™ Make a Folded Chart. (See p. R44.) Label the chart as shown.

Animal	Number of Guesses

1. Write the name of a different animal on each of five index cards.

2. Trade your cards with another team.

3. One player picks a card. The other player asks yes or no questions about the animal. For example, does the animal have fur? Does it fly?

4. Continue playing until the animal is guessed. Count how many guesses were needed. Record the number on your chart.

An ostrich is too heavy to fly, but it can run very fast.

▶ **What do all birds have in common?**

A 73

A young dolphin and its mother

What Are Mammals?

What do a gorilla, a whale, and a cat have in common? They are all **mammals** (MAM·uhlz). A mammal is an animal with hair or fur. A mammal feeds its young with milk.

Mammals may have thick fur, thin fur, or just a few hairs. Bears and rabbits are covered with thick coats of fur. Dolphins and elephants have just a few hairs.

Female mammals make milk. They feed the milk to their young after the young are born. Most mammals are born live, rather than hatching from eggs.

Mammals are warm-blooded. Their bodies stay at the same temperature, even when it's very cold or very hot around them. Those that live in cold places have thick fur or layers of fat to keep them warm. Others live in hot places. They sweat or pant to cool themselves.

▷ **What do all mammals have in common?**

A kangaroo is a pouched mammal. The young kangaroo remains in the pouch until it is strong enough to leave it.

Why It Matters

You share the world with many animals. Each animal can be classified. A wolf is a mammal, and a robin is a bird. Both are examples of vertebrates. Worms are invertebrates. So are snails and spiders. Next time you see an animal, think about how it is classified.

e-Journal Visit our Web site www.science.mmhschool.com to do a research project on animals.

Think and Write

1. What are two large groups of animals?

2. What features do all birds have in common? Do all birds fly?

3. What are two characteristics of mammals?

4. Choose an animal in your neighborhood or school. What kind of animal is it? How would you describe it?

5. Critical Thinking To which group do humans belong—fish, amphibian, reptile, bird, or mammal? Why?

MATH LINK

Solve a problem. The ostrich is the world's largest living bird. It is about 108 inches tall. Measure how tall you are in inches. How much taller than you is the ostrich?

WRITING LINK

Persuasive Writing Suppose you have to choose a national symbol for the United States. Some people want the bald eagle. Benjamin Franklin wants the turkey. What animal would you pick? Write a letter. Tell why the animal you chose should be our national symbol. Use reasons to persuade.

LANGUAGE ARTS LINK

Use a dictionary. The word *amphibian* comes from two Greek words meaning "having a life of two kinds." Why is this a good name for frogs, toads, and other amphibians? Now use a dictionary to find the word *reptile*. Why is this a good name for snakes, alligators, and lizards?

TECHNOLOGY LINK

LOG ON Visit www.science.mmhschool.com for more links.

Chapter 2 Review

Vocabulary

Fill each blank with the best word from the list.

amphibians, A72   **mammal,** A74

bird, A73   **migrate,** A46

fish, A71   **organ,** A62

hibernate, A46   **reptiles,** A72

inherited trait,   **shelter,** A44
   A56

1. Having straight black hair is an example of a(n) _____.

2. A place that keeps an animal safe is called a(n) _____.

3. An animal that has feathers, two wings, and two legs is a(n) _____.

4. A(n) _____ is a group of tissues that work together to do a job.

5. An animal with body hair or fur that feeds its young with milk is a(n) _____.

Two ways animals respond to their environment is to **6.** and **7.** .

Three groups of cold-blooded animals are:

8. _____

9. _____

10. _____.

Test Prep

11. You need food because it _____.

   A contains oxygen

   B contains water

   C uses carbon dioxide

   D gives you energy

12. A crab's shell is a body part that _____.

   F gets information

   G protects and supports

   H moves

   J takes in materials

13. Which statement is true about your skin?

   A It senses information.

   B It keeps water inside the body from escaping.

   C It keeps harmful materials out.

   D All of the above.

14. Fish use _____ to get oxygen from water.

   F scales

   G gills

   H lungs

   J organs

15. The best definition of a cold-blooded animal is an animal _____.

    A whose body temperature changes

    B that grows thick fur to keep it warm

    C that migrates south

    D that hibernates during the winter

Concepts and Skills

16. **Reading in Science** Describe the life cycle of each animal shown above. Compare and contrast these animals.

17. **Critical Thinking** A mother sea turtle may have a hundred babies at once. A mother elephant gives birth to one baby at a time. How does each mother care for her baby?

18. INQUIRY SKILL **Classify** Many animals move by using their legs, fins, or wings. Think of two animals for each type of movement. Make a table. Write the names of animals in the table.

19. **Decision Making** Juanita's pet cat is about to have kittens. Juanita cannot keep all the kittens in her home. She is trying to find people who will give good homes to the kittens after they are born. What would you tell Juanita?

20. **Scientific Methods** What are some movements an insect makes to help it survive? Write down a plan that describes how you could find out.

Did You Ever Wonder?

INQUIRY SKILL **Experiment** You have seen how animals grow and change. Choose an animal to investigate. Find out how the animal grows, and compare its growth to yours.

LOG ON Visit www.science.mmhschool.com to boost your test scores.

Dr. Paul Williams

Plant Pathologist

As a third grader, Paul Williams loved to grow plants. "For me, plants were fun to play with."

Williams went to college in Wisconsin. There he learned that diseases were attacking the cabbage plants. Williams wanted to help. He traveled the world collecting seeds. Dr. Williams combined many of those seeds to develop a new kind of cabbage. He named it "Fast Plant." These super-speedy plants took about five weeks—not two months—to go through a growth cycle. Fast Plants have changed the way farmers grow crops.

In 1997, astronauts took Fast Plants into space. They proved that plants grow the same way there as on Earth! Who knows? One day, Paul Williams's cabbages may be feeding people on Mars!

Fast Plants have been grown on six space missions since 1997.

TOP 5 Plants and You

If you like plants, here are some careers to consider:

1. Botanist: Studies plant biology and a plant's environment.
2. Plant physiologist: Examines a plant and its genes.
3. Soil conservationist: Maps, identifies, and classifies soil.
4. Horticulturist: Improves plants for crops or medicines.
5. Agronomist: Studies how plants, soil, and the environment interact.

Write About It

1. How did Paul Williams's Fast Plant help people?
2. What did astronauts prove about plants growing in space?

Photo courtesy of University of Wisconsin-Madison

LOG ON Visit www.science.mmhschool.com to learn more about scientists who study plants.

Plenty of Plants

Your goal is to make a poster that shows different ways plants reproduce.

What to Do

Observe the plants on this page. Make a poster that shows different ways that plants reproduce. Draw a picture of each plant. Write a sentence that tells how the plant reproduces.

Draw Conclusions

What do all forms of plant reproduction have in common?

Make an Animal Book

Your goal is to make a book that tells about animal parts.

What to Do

Use four sheets of paper. Cut out four pictures of animals from magazines. Glue each picture to a sheet of paper. Below the picture, tell about the body parts that help the animal survive. Make a cover for your book.

Draw Conclusions

What body parts do all of the animals shown in your book share?

My Animal Book

Life Science

UNIT B

Where Plants and Animals Live

LOOK!

The red-eyed tree frog can climb trees. What body parts help it climb?

Where Plants and Animals Live

Relationships Among Living Things

Did You Ever Wonder?

What kinds of plants and animals live in the Chesapeake Bay? Recently people have been helping to protect this environment. As a result the numbers of plants and animals that live here are increasing.

INQUIRY SKILL Communicate What can you do to help the living things in your environment?

Ecosystems

Get Ready

Do you think a caribou could survive in a desert? Caribou live in the cold Arctic tundra. Their thick fur keeps them warm. Their strong hooves help them walk over the ground. Look at the picture of the caribou. What are their surroundings like? Why do you think they live where they do?

Inquiry Skill

You observe when you use one or more of the senses to learn about an object or event.

Explore Activity

What Can You Find in an Ecosystem?

Materials

meter tape

ball of yarn

4 clothespins

hand lens

Procedure

1. **Measure** Mark off an area of ground that is 1 meter square. Stick a clothespin into the ground at each corner. Wrap yarn around the tops of the clothespins.

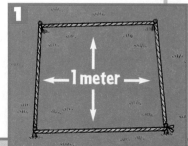

2. **Observe** Use your hand lens to look at the living and nonliving things in this area.

3. Use a chart to record what you see. Label each object *living* or *nonliving*.

4. Share your findings with a classmate. Compare the environments each of you observed.

Drawing Conclusions

1. How many different kinds of nonliving things are in your environment? What did you have the most of?

2. Choose one living thing you observed. What are the characteristics of this organism?

3. FURTHER INQUIRY **Infer** What are the characteristics of another living thing that might live here? How do you know?

Read to Learn

Main Idea Ecosystems are made up of living and nonliving things.

What Makes Up an Ecosystem?

Plants and animals live with one another. They also depend on one another to stay alive. They depend on nonliving things, too, like rocks, soil, water, and air. Together, all the living and nonliving things in a place make up an **ecosystem** (EK·oh·sis·tuhm). Ecosystems can be large or small. Earth can be thought of as one large ecosystem. An ecosystem can also be as small as the space under a rock.

All the living things in an ecosystem make up a **community** (kuh·MYEW·ni·tee). The community on the grasslands includes zebras, giraffes, and other animals, along with trees and grasses.

A population of zebras live on the grassland.

Each community is made up of many different **populations** (pahp·yuh·LAY·shuhnz). A population is all the members of a single type of organism. All the giraffes on a grassland make up the giraffe population. All the zebras make up the zebra population.

Different populations make up a community.

A tree is one part of a forest ecosystem. It is also home to birds, insects, and squirrels. For these animals the tree is a **habitat** (HAB·i·tat). A habitat is a living thing's home. Living things get food, water, and shelter from their habitat.

The different parts of an ecosystem affect one another. Insects live in the tree's bark. Birds build nests from twigs. The tree grows in soil and takes in water and air.

Some parts of an ecosystem are so small you cannot see them! Tiny organisms live in the soil. They break down materials such as leaves and add them to the soil.

READING **Summarize**
What are some of the living and nonliving things in an ecosystem?

1 Leaves fall from the tree during autumn.

2 Small organisms in the soil break down the leaves.

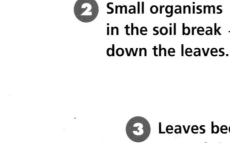

3 Leaves become part of the soil.

4 The tree grows in the soil.

What Habitats Are Found in a Pond?

A frog needs food, water, and shelter. It gets all of these things at a pond. The pond is the frog's habitat.

Some plants and animals live only in parts of the pond. A sunfish stays in the water. Raccoons live along the banks. Lily pads float on the water's surface. The pond provides many different habitats.

A pond is an ecosystem. A pond is also a *wetland*. Wetlands are a mix of land and water ecosystems. Marshes and swamps are also wetlands. Wetlands are important because they provide homes for many different types of plants and animals.

▷ **How can a pond provide different habitats?**

Habitats

① The Banks
Plants like ferns and mosses live along the pond's banks. Animals include insects, mice, snakes, raccoons, and birds.

② The Water's Edge
Plants on the water's edge live partly underwater. Animals include salamanders, snails, and water bugs.

③ Shallow Water
Floating plants live in the shallow water. Frogs sit on lily pads, and turtles lie on rocks to bask in the sunlight.

④ Deep Water
Floating plants live here, too. Fish live in the deep water.

READING Diagrams

1. What are two habitats shown in the diagram?

2. Choose three of the living things that live in a pond. Make a chart that shows each organism's habitat.

A Pond Ecosystem

Populations

5 Great Blue Heron
The heron flies from place to place. It comes to the pond for its favorite foods.

6 Dragonfly
Young dragonflies live in the water. They breathe through gills. Adult dragonflies live out of the water.

7 Bladderwort
The bladderwort is a floating plant. Its stems and leaves have air sacs. When a small organism touches an air sac, it is sucked inside and eaten!

8 Algae
Algae are tiny organisms. A pond may contain billions of algae.

Inquiry Skill
BUILDER

What Makes Up a Forest Community?

You have learned that a community is all the living things in an ecosystem. Different ecosystems have different communities. For example, the pond community includes bladderworts, frogs, algae, and dragonflies. What makes up a forest community? Look at the picture on this page. Use your observations to define a forest community.

Procedure

1. **Observe** Make a list of all the things you see in the picture of the forest.

2. **Classify** Which of the things on your list are living? Which are nonliving?

Drawing Conclusions

Define Terms Using your list, explain what a forest community is.

Why It Matters

People can help habitats. Many people are carefully watching habitats. They look for changes. When they find a problem, they try to solve it. For example, a plant disease may have killed many plants in an area. Scientists may find ways to help plants produce seeds and grow back.

e-Journal Visit our Web site www.science.mmhschool.com to do a research project on ecosystems.

Think and Write

1. What is an ecosystem?

2. What are some members of a pond community?

3. How is a community different from a population?

4. INQUIRY SKILL **Define Terms** Think about the habitat of a pet dog. List some of the characteristics of the habitat. Use your list to write your own definition of *habitat*.

5. **Critical Thinking** How would a pond ecosystem change if the water in the pond dried up?

MATH LINK

Solve a problem. An ecosystem has frogs, dragonflies, great blue herons, and floating plants. How many animals are in the community? How many populations are there? Use the graph below.

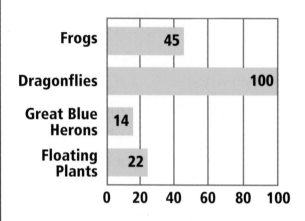

Frogs	45
Dragonflies	100
Great Blue Herons	14
Floating Plants	22

0 20 40 60 80 100

WRITING LINK

Explanatory Writing Make a list of different insects that live in your neighborhood. Tell how insects help or use other living things.

SOCIAL STUDIES LINK

Make a map. Make an outline map of your state. Draw the major bodies of water. Include mountains, rivers, and any other important features. Label your map.

TECHNOLOGY LINK

LOG ON Visit www.science.mmhschool.com for more links.

You Depend on Plants and Animals!

What would your life be like without plants and animals? It would be different. You depend on plants and animals in many ways.

Do you ever wear cotton clothes? Cotton is a plant fiber. Are you sitting on a wooden chair or holding a wooden pencil? Wood comes from trees. The trunks and branches of trees are wood. Do you like eating fruits and vegetables? If so, you like to eat plants.

You even use plants while you breathe! Every time you breathe in, you take in a gas called oxygen that comes from plants.

How do you depend on animals? Animals provide meat and other foods. Milk, ice cream, cheese, and eggs all come from animals.

How Cloth Is Made

1. Cotton is stripped or picked from the plants.
2. Cotton fibers are separated from cotton seeds.
3. Dirt is removed from the fibers.

4. The fibers are spun into yarn.
5. The yarn is woven into cloth.

6. The cloth is cut and sewn to make clothing.

Do you own a wool sweater or mittens? Wool is usually made from a sheep's soft, curly fleece.

Leather is made from animal skins. Shoes, gloves, and wallets are often made of leather.

Some people depend on animals to help them get around. Some animals can be trained to be great helpers—and pals.

Cows provide people with milk.

What Did I Learn?

1. Which of the following is not provided by trees?

   A wooden chair
   B pencil
   C wool
   D paper

2. What step comes after cotton fibers are separated from cotton seeds?

   F The fibers are spun into yarn.
   G The yarn is woven into cloth.
   H The cloth is cut and sewn into clothing.
   J Dirt is removed from the fibers.

 LOG ON Visit www.science.mmhschool.com to learn more about plants and animals.

Food Chains and Food Webs

Get Ready

Would you eat grass for lunch? No, you would not. For a donkey, however, grass makes a fine meal. Cows, horses, sheep, and buffalo eat grass, too! Other animals, like eagles and lions, never eat grass. Different animals eat different things. What kinds of foods do you eat?

Inquiry Skill

You **classify** when you group similar things together.

B 14

Explore Activity

Where Does Food Come From?

Procedure

1 Observe Look at the picture of the pizza. What types of foods do you see? Make a list.

2 Classify Next to each thing on your list, record whether the food comes from a plant or an animal. Write *P* for plant and *A* for animal.

3 Look at your list of foods that come from animals. From which animal does each food come? What food does that animal eat?

Drawing Conclusions

1 If there were no plants, which foods would be left to make pizza? (Hint: Think about what animals eat to survive.)

2 Infer Do all foods come from plants? Explain your answer.

3 Write down a food that you like to eat. List all of the ingredients in this food.

4 FURTHER INQUIRY **Classify** Make a chart that shows where each ingredient in your favorite food comes from.

Main Idea Animals depend on plants for their food.

The plant is a producer.

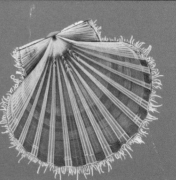

What Makes Up a Food Chain?

What is food? Food is material that organisms use to get energy. All food comes from organisms called **producers** (pruh·DEW·suhrz). Producers make food from water, air, and energy from sunlight. Green plants and some one-celled organisms are producers.

The insect is a consumer.

Desert Food Chain

Plant makes food   Insect eats plant   Vole eats insect

Ocean Food Chain

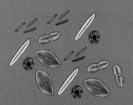 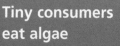

Algae make food   Tiny consumers eat algae   Shellfish eats tiny consumers

Animals are **consumers** (kuhn·SEW·muhrz). Consumers are organisms that eat producers or other consumers.

Together, producers and consumers make up a **food chain**. A food chain is a series of organisms that depend on one another for food. Food chains start with producers. Consumers eat those producers. Other consumers eat the first consumers.

▷ **What is an example of a producer? A consumer?**

READING
Diagrams

1. What are the first and last organisms in the desert food chain? In the ocean food chain?

2. How are the two food chains different? How are they alike?

Snake eats vole

Hawk eats snake

Small fish eat shellfish

Large fish eats small fish

Killer whale eats large fish

B 17

How Are Materials Recycled?

What do you think happens to a leaf that falls from a tree? Over time organisms break the leaf apart and return it to the soil. These kinds of organisms are called **decomposers** (dee·kuhm·POH·zuhrz). A decomposer breaks down dead plant and animal material. It recycles chemicals so that they can be used again.

Producers, consumers, and decomposers work together to recycle materials through an ecosystem. Producers use the recycled material to make new food. Consumers eat the food. When producers and consumers die, decomposers recycle the dead material. The cycle goes on and on.

This cycle helps reduce garbage. Without decomposers Earth would be covered with dead plant and animal material. When decomposers eat plant and animal material, they make compost. Compost is a mix of decaying leaves, vegetables, and other living matter.

Decomposers are breaking down leaves. The leaves will become part of the soil.

Decomposers include fungi. You can see fungi growing on this tree.

On a cold morning, you might see a compost pile steaming. That is because this process gives off heat. Compost piles heat up for the same reason that you heat up when you exercise. Like your muscles, the decomposers are working hard and are using lots of fuel. When they use lots of fuel, heat is produced.

READING **Summarize**

What is the job of a decomposer?

How does composting help recycle plant and animal material?

QUICK LAB

Decomposers

FOLDABLES Make a Folded Table. (See p. R 44.) Lable the table as shown.

BE CAREFUL! Don't open the sealed bag.

Day 1	
Day 2	
Day 3	
Day 4	
Day 5	
Day 6	
Day 7	

1. Put some apple pieces in a plastic bag. Seal the bag.

2. **Observe** Leave the apples in the bag for one week. Observe the apples every day. Record your observations in the table.

3. What happened to the pieces of apple? Record your findings on the back of the table.

4. What does this activity tell you about decomposers? Write your answer on the back of the table.

5. **Infer** What would happen if there were no decomposers? Write your answer on the back of the table.

What Is a Food Web?

An owl and a hawk are not in the same food chain. They are still connected, however. Both eat many of the same things, like mice and snakes.

In the desert owls and hawks are parts of the same **food web**. A food web is made up of several food chains that are connected.

Look at the single desert food chain on page B16. Now compare it with the food web shown below. Notice how the food chains connect to one another. Try to find the chain with grass, jackrabbit, and coyote.

Herbivore
An animal that eats only plants is called a *herbivore*. Jackrabbits and prairie dogs are herbivores.

Carnivore
An animal that eats only other animals is called a *carnivore*. Hawks, snakes, owls, and coyotes are carnivores.

Different consumers eat different kinds of food. Some consumers eat only plants. Some eat only animals. Still others eat both plants and animals. Each group has a special name. This name ends with the letters *vore*. *Vore* means "eater."

▶ **What groups of animals are part of a food web?**

READING
Diagrams

1. What are three different food chains in the food web?

2. If the jackrabbits left the desert, how would the food web change?

Omnivore
An animal that eats both plants and animals is called an *omnivore*. Javelinas, small piglike animals, are omnivores. They eat insects, cacti, and other desert plants.

What Is an Energy Pyramid?

You can group organisms by their positions in food webs. Each group forms its own level on an **energy pyramid** (EN·uhr·jee PIR·uh·mid). An energy pyramid is a diagram that shows how energy moves through an ecosystem.

Each level in an energy pyramid has more members than the level above it. There are more producers than plant eaters. There are more plant eaters than meat eaters. For every bald eagle, there might be hundreds of insects and thousands of plants.

> ▷ **Are there more producers or consumers in an ecosystem?**

READING

Diagrams

How do the levels compare in an energy pyramid?

Energy Pyramid

Animals that are not hunted by other animals

Animals that eat other animals

Animals that eat plants

Plants

L·I·N·K·S

Why It Matters

You are a consumer. You are part of a food web. You probably depend on many different producers as well as other consumers for food. You also depend on decomposers to recycle plant and animal materials in your ecosystem.

e-Journal Visit our Web site www.science.mmhschool.com to do a research project on food chains.

Think and Write

1. Where does food come from?

2. What is a producer? A consumer? A decomposer?

3. How are food webs different from food chains?

4. How can composting be used to recycle discarded plant and animal material? Explain your answer.

5. **Critical Thinking** What would happen if an ecosystem had more consumers than producers? Could this ecosystem last? Why?

WRITING LINK

Writing a Story Create a picture book. Write a story about the food web. Include yourself as a character. Remember to have a beginning, a middle, and an end to the story. Include a diagram of the food web in your story.

MATH LINK

Solve a problem. Eli is collecting fresh vegetables for a pizza. He picks 14 tomatoes, 6 peppers, and 3 onions. How many more tomatoes than peppers did Eli pick? Explain how you found your answer.

SOCIAL STUDIES LINK

Use a map. Petrified Forest National Park is located in Arizona. Use a map to find out where in the state it is located. Research and list the plants and animals that live there. Find out how this ecosystem has been affected by humans.

TECHNOLOGY LINKS

Science Newsroom CD-ROM Choose *Chains of Life* and *Down to Earth* to learn more about food chains and food webs.

LOG ON Visit www.science.mmhschool.com for more links.

Roles for Plants and Animals

Get Ready

What do these fish need to survive? What do these plants need to survive? Do you think they might need each other? What would you do to take care of the living things in an aquarium?

Inquiry Skill

You make a model when you make something that represents objects or events.

Explore Activity

How Do Living Things Meet Their Needs?

Materials

gravel

guppy or goldfish

small water plants

2-L plastic drink bottle

bottom of another drink bottle with holes

fish food

Procedure

BE CAREFUL! Handle animals carefully. Measure materials carefully.

1. **Make a Model** Put a 3-cm layer of gravel into the plastic drink bottle. Fill the bottle with water as shown. Anchor the plants in the gravel.

2. Cover the bottle with the bottom of another bottle. Do not place it in direct sunlight.

3. After two days, gently place the fish in the bottle. Add a few flakes of fish food.

4. **Observe** Look at your ecosystem every day for two weeks. Feed the fish twice each week. Record your observations.

Drawing Conclusions

1. What did the fish need to survive? What did the plants need to survive?

2. What might happen if the plant was not part of the ecosystem?

3. **FURTHER INQUIRY** **Experiment** How do frogs meet their needs? Predict what kind of ecosystem you would need to build to find out. How do you know?

Main Idea Living things depend on one another in many ways.

How Do Living Things Use Air?

What do you need from the air around you? You can't see it, but you take it in with every breath. It's a gas called oxygen. All animals need oxygen. Animals that live in water get their oxygen from the water.

Plants need gases from the air, too. They need carbon dioxide to make food. They also need oxygen to use food. During the day plants make their own food. At night they get oxygen from the air, just like animals.

Where do these gases come from? They come from plants and animals! Plants make oxygen, a gas that animals need. Animals give off carbon dioxide, a gas that plants need.

Trees give off oxygen.

Plants give off oxygen.

Fish take in oxygen.

Trees take in carbon dioxide.

Plants take in carbon dioxide.

Fish give off carbon dioxide.

Animals and plants take part in the **carbon dioxide and oxygen cycles** (KAHR·buhn digh·AHK·sighd AND AHK·suh·juhn SIGH·kuhlz). The carbon dioxide and oxygen cycles are the trading of these two gases. The gases move from one population to another in both water and land ecosystems. If gases were used up instead of exchanged, living things would die.

Where does the world's supply of oxygen come from? Plants in large forests make a lot of oxygen. Trees are the world's largest organisms that make oxygen. However, the most important source of oxygen lives in the oceans. Tiny one-celled organisms called algae make more oxygen than all the land plants in the world.

▷ **How are you part of the carbon dioxide and oxygen cycles?**

People take in oxygen.

People give off carbon dioxide.

What Do Populations Depend on?

Visit a forest, and you may see animals eating. Mice and rabbits eat grasses and shrubs. Beetles eat leaves. Owls and hawks swoop down from the sky to catch mice. Populations depend on the resources in the community.

Owls, coyotes, wolves, and many other animals are hunters. Animals that hunt for food are called **predators** (PRED·uh·tuhrz). The animals that predators eat are called **prey** (PRAY).

Predators have body parts that allow them to hunt and catch prey. Some are able to run very fast. Many have a keen sense of smell or sight.

This gecko will have a tasty treat.

A heron catches a fish.

A lion cub begins to hunt at the age of six months.

Do prey depend on predators? You might not think so. However, predators help control the populations of many animals. If predators disappeared, the numbers of their prey would rise quickly. After the prey ate all the food that was available, many of them would die.

Not all meat eaters kill what they eat. Have you ever seen a crow pick at a dead animal? Crows are **scavengers** (SKAV·uhn·juhrz). Scavengers eat dead animals. Crayfish, crabs, vultures, and many other animals are scavengers.

▷ **Why do prey need predators?**

Vultures

A hyena is a scavenger. Why are scavengers important?

This snake is eating an egg.

The oxpecker and the buffalo help each other.

Cows help cattle egrets find food.

How Can Populations Affect Each Other?

To many fish, sea anemones are very dangerous. Their tentacles contain a strong poison. However, the clownfish can swim near an anemone without being harmed! Its body is coated with special slime that protects it.

The clownfish and anemone help each other. When a clownfish feels threatened, it swims to the anemone's tentacles for safety. The anemone feeds on scraps that fall out of the clownfish's mouth.

The buffalo and oxpecker also help each other. An oxpecker pecks insects out of the skin of a buffalo. It also calls out loudly when it sees danger. This warns the buffalo.

How do the sea anemone and clownfish help each other?

Sometimes one population helps another without being helped in return. Cows help cattle egrets in this way. Egrets follow cows wherever the cows go. The cows are so big that they stir up insects and other small animals. The egrets eat these insects and animals. The cows help the egrets find food but receive no help in return. They are not harmed, either.

Sometimes one population does harm another. Look at the tapeworm. It is a **parasite** (PAR·uh·sight). A parasite is an organism that lives on or inside another organism. The organism a parasite lives with is called the **host** (HOHST).

A tapeworm attaches itself inside the host. The host can be a human or another animal. The tapeworm takes in food that the host has digested. Parasites like tapeworms can make their host sick. Sometimes they kill their host.

Fleas are parasites on dogs. They live on a dog's skin and take in its blood. Fleas harm dogs but rarely kill them.

A tapeworm is a parasite.

▷ **What is a parasite?**

Fleas are parasites. They live on cats and dogs.

QUICK LAB

Traveling Seeds

FOLDABLES™ Make a Folded Chart. (See p. R44.) Label the chart as shown.

Prediction	Results

1. **Predict** What will happen when you toss seeds onto a piece of fake fur? Record your prediction on the chart.

2. **Experiment** Test your prediction. Have your partner hold up the fur. Toss different seeds at it. Record the results on the chart.

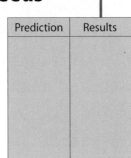

3. Which seeds stuck to the fur? Were your predictions correct? Write your answer on the back of your Foldables chart.

How Do Animals Help Plants Reproduce?

An oak tree makes seeds called acorns. Acorns might grow into new oak trees if they land in the right place. Most acorns fall right under the tree. Is this a good place for acorns to grow? No, it is not. There is not enough light.

How can acorns be moved? Animals help! Squirrels find the acorns. They bury them in the ground to store them for winter. They eat many of the acorns, but a few acorns are forgotten. They stay buried in the ground, far from the tree. They might grow into new trees.

READING **Summarize**
How do squirrels help oak trees reproduce?

Why It Matters

Some organisms can be both helpful and harmful. Bacteria are just such an organism. They are one-celled living things. They are helpful because they are decomposers. Decomposers break down dead plant and animal matter. Decomposers help recycle Earth's materials.

e-Journal Visit our Web site **www.science.mmhschool.com** to do a research project on prey and predators.

Think and Write

1. What are the carbon dioxide and oxygen cycles?

2. What are predators and prey?

3. Give an example of two organisms that help each other survive.

4. How do squirrels help oak trees reproduce?

5. **Critical Thinking** Most parasites harm their host but do not kill it. Why does a parasite need a living host?

L·I·N·K·S

MATH LINK

Make a graph. A shark can smell its prey 400 meters (440 yards) away. It can hear sounds about 910 meters (1,000 yards) away. Make a bar graph to show this information.

WRITING LINK

Expository Writing Write a list of questions you would ask if you could interview a predator. Research the animal to find the answers. With a partner, record the interview. Play the recording for the class.

LITERATURE LINK

Read *Kit Foxes* to learn how two kit foxes find a den and raise a family. When you finish reading, think about an animal that might live in your neighborhood. Try the activities at the end of the book.

Kit Foxes

Written by Jennifer Jacobson • Illustrated by Pat Traub

TECHNOLOGY LINK

LOG ON Visit **www.science.mmhschool.com** for more links.

LONG LIVE THE RAIN FORESTS

Where can you find a monkey small enough to fit it your hand? Where can you find a frog that can soar like a bird? Or find a flower the size of a chair? These treasures live in the world's tropical rain forests. Rain forests are wet, warm lands that are home to many living things.

Millions of kinds of plants and animals live in rain forests. The plants help us because they make oxygen, an important gas in the air. Rain forest plants also provide many of the world's medicines.

Sadly, large chunks of rain forest are destroyed every minute. The forests are being destroyed for many reasons. Loggers cut down trees and sell the lumber. Farmers clear land for cattle and crops. Miners dig up the land to take the minerals below. More than half of the world's rain forests are gone already.

Banana tree

A tropical butterfly

This Blue Morpho butterfly is one of millions of insects that live in the rain forest.

People around the world now understand why rain forests are important. People are working hard to save them. You can help, too. Learn more about rain forests. Tell your friends and the adults you know what you find out.

Write ABOUT IT

1. Why do people destroy rain forests?
2. Do you think rain forests are worth saving? Why or why not?

LOG ON   Visit www.science.mmhschool.com to learn more about rain forests.

Chapter 3 Review

Vocabulary

Fill each blank with the best word from the list.

community, B6   **parasite,** B31
consumer, B17   **predator,** B28
decomposer, B18   **prey,** B28
habitat, B7   **producer,** B16
host, B31   **scavenger,** B29

1. The place where an animal lives and grows is its _____.

2. All the living things in an ecosystem make up a(n) _____.

3. Bacteria are a kind of _____ because they break down dead plant and animal material.

4. A crow is a(n) _____ because it eats dead animals.

5. A _____	hunts for	6. _____.
7. A _____	lives on or in a(n)	8. _____.
9. A _____	eats foods made by a(n)	10. _____.

Test Prep

11. Plants and animals exchange carbon dioxide and _____.

   A food
   B oxygen
   C water
   D molds

12. All the following are consumers in a pond EXCEPT _____.

   F algae
   G herons
   H frogs
   J dragonflies

13. Animals can help plants by _____.

   A making food
   B finding water
   C spreading seeds
   D providing energy

14. Bacteria are helpful because they _____.

   F produce food
   G spoil food
   H are parasites
   J recycle materials

15. A parasite depends on a

_____.

A scavenger

B producer

C host

D decomposer

Concepts and Skills

16. Reading in Science Use this diagram to explain a food chain. Write a short paragraph that explains your answer.

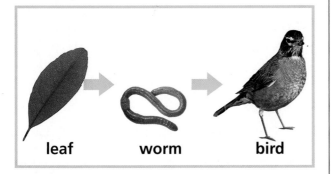

leaf   worm   bird

17. Product Ads Some insects are pests. Some ads claim their products are strong enough to kill many insects. Write down ways these products might affect a food chain.

18. Decision Making The sign says, "Do not feed the ducks." You brought some bread to the pond. Would you feed the ducks? Write a paragraph explaining your decision.

19. Critical Thinking A pack of coyotes moves to a new ecosystem. They eat many rabbits. What can happen to the ecosystem? Explain your answer in writing.

20. INQUIRY SKILL **Define Terms Based on Observations** Using your observations, write a definition of an aquarium ecosystem. Describe the parts of the ecosystem and how they work together.

Did You Ever Wonder?

INQUIRY SKILL **Communicate** A habitat is an organism's home. It provides food and shelter, as well as protection. How might people help to conserve the places where organisms live?

LOG ON Visit **www.science.mmhschool.com** to boost your test scores.

CHAPTER 4

Ecosystems in Balance

Did You Ever Wonder?

What fish lives in both oceans and rivers? The answer is the salmon. Salmon are born in rivers, then move to oceans. At the end of their lives, they swim up the same river in which they were born. The journey is dangerous!

INQUIRY SKILL Infer Why do you think salmon return to the river?

Competition Among Living Things

Get Ready

Who gets the bug? All of the young birds want it. Plants and animals compete for their basic needs. One of these needs is space. Does the amount of space available affect the way plants grow?

Inquiry Skill

You **infer** when you form an idea from facts or observations.

B 40

Explore Activity

How Much Room Do Plants Need?

Materials

soil

bean seeds

4 milk cartons

measuring cup

water

masking tape

marker

Procedure

1. Cut the tops from the milk cartons. Use the masking tape and the marker to label the cartons A to D. Use the measuring cup to fill each carton with the same amount of soil.

2. **Use Variables** Plant 3 bean seeds in carton A. Plant 6 bean seeds in carton B. Plant 12 bean seeds in carton C and 24 bean seeds in carton D.

3. **Predict** What do you think each carton will look like in 14 days? Record your predictions.

4. **Experiment** Place the cartons in a well-lighted area. Water the plants every two days. Use the same amount of water for each carton. Record any changes you observe in the plants.

Drawing Conclusions

1. How do the plants in carton D compare with the plants in the other cartons?

2. What are the plants competing for?

3. Repeat this activity. Compare your results. What happened?

4. FURTHER INQUIRY **Infer** How do plants in your neighborhood compete for what they need to grow?

Main Idea Plants and animals compete for the things they need.

How Much Room Do Organisms Need?

Competition (kahm·pi·TISH·uhn) for space affects how plants grow. Competition occurs when organisms with similar needs work against one another to get what they need to live. Organisms share and compete for space, water, food, and oxygen.

Desert plants compete for water. A cactus soaks up all of the moisture in a single area. No other plants can grow in this area.

Rabbits compete for food. If there are too many rabbits, all of the grass will be eaten. Some of the rabbits won't survive.

Predators also compete. Predators are animals that hunt for food. Predators compete for prey. *Prey* try to escape from predators. Predators compete with each other. Hawks, owls, and snakes all compete to catch mice for food.

The owl is a predator. The mouse is its prey.

These cacti are competing for water. How does that explain why they grow so far apart?

Different ecosystems support different numbers of organisms. The chart below compares the numbers of different types of trees and birds in a rain forest with those in a temperate (TEM·puhr·it) forest. Temperate forests are the most common type of forest in the United States. Rain forests support many more types of trees and birds than temperate forests.

The same pattern is true for other living things. Why are there so many more types of organisms in the rain forest? Rain forests are much wetter and warmer than temperate forests. More plants can grow in this environment. More plants means more animals, too.

Temperate forest

READING **Compare and Contrast**
How are rain forests and temperate forests alike? How are they different?

Comparing Forests

	Different Types of Trees	Different Types of Birds
Temperate forest	50 to 60	50
Rain forest	500 to 600	250

Rain forest

Musical Chairs

FOLDABLES™ Make a Three-Tab Book. (See p. R42.) Make a Venn diagram on your Foldables book as shown.

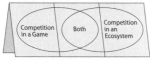

Competition in a Game | Both | Competition in an Ecosystem

1. Play a game of musical chairs.

2. **Experiment** Change the number of chairs you play with. How does this affect the game? Record your observations.

3. What do the players compete for in musical chairs?

4. **Communicate** How is the competition in the game like competition in a real ecosystem? Use the Venn diagram to record your answer.

Can Competition Be Avoided?

Competition is a struggle for survival. In order to survive, some organisms find ways to avoid competing. Many types of organisms share the same ecosystem. Each type of organism has its own **niche** (NICH). A niche is the job or role an organism has in an ecosystem. An organism's niche includes what an organism does, what it eats, and how it interacts with other organisms.

The forests of New Guinea are home to Victoria crowned pigeons.

For example, there are many types of pigeons in the forests of New Guinea. Each type has a different niche. This helps the pigeons avoid competition.

The Victoria crowned pigeon has a niche that includes eating fruits, berries, and large seeds. The pigeon nests in trees and searches for food on the ground of the forest.

▷ **How do pigeons in the forests of New Guinea avoid competition?**

Why It Matters

As a living thing, you have a niche in your ecosystem. Your niche includes the roles you have at home and at school. How is your niche different from the niches of other people and animals in the ecosystem?

e-Journal Visit our Web site www.science.mmhschool.com to do a research project on competition among living things.

Think and Write

1. What is competition?

2. What things do organisms compete for?

3. What is a niche?

4. Why do some ecosystems have more types of organisms than others?

5. **Critical Thinking** A gazelle and a zebra both live in the same habitat and eat plants. How do they avoid competition?

MATH LINK

Solve a problem. Look at the chart on p. B43. What is the difference between the numbers of different types of trees in the temperate forest and the rain forest? Which forest has more types of trees?

WRITING LINK

Expository Writing Observe an animal every day for one week. How is it fit for its environment? How does it compete with other living things for resources? Use your observations to write a report about the animal's niche in the ecosystem.

LITERATURE LINK

Read *The Wolves' Winter* to learn how a pair of young wolves search for a new home. When you finish reading, think about how an animal in your neighborhood might search for food. Try the activities at the end of the book.

The Wolves' Winter
by
Alice Pernick
illustrated by
Diane Blasius

TECHNOLOGY LINK

LOG ON Visit www.science.mmhschool.com for more links.

Buzzing Bees and Flower Seeds

We all know that bees buzz from flower to flower. They are collecting nectar to turn into honey. But did you know that bees are also doing another important job? Bees are helping flowers to make new flowering plants.

Flowers attract bees so that bees will land on them and get covered with pollen.

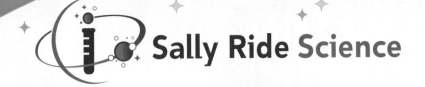

When a bee lands on a flower and sips its nectar, the bee's hairy legs and body get covered with sticky flower pollen.

This sticky pollen is good for flowers. Flowers depend on bees to drop pollen on other flowers. That is called pollination, and it is how flowers reproduce.

Many flowers have both male and female parts. Pollen contains a flower's male cells. Once pollen lands on a new flower, it makes its way inside the flower to the female cells. There the male and female cells combine, and a seed is made. This seed can grow into a new flowering plant.

The more times a bee pollinates a flower, the more seeds the flower can make. That's good for the flower. It's also good for the bee. More flowers means more nectar. More nectar means more honey. More honey means more food for the bee—and enough honey for people, too!

Some flowers use brightly colored petals to lure bees. Others give off a sweet aroma that bees like. Bees take pollen from one flower to another.

Write About It

1. Bees and flowers both benefit from pollination. How?

2. What would happen to some flowers if bees suddenly disappeared?

LOG ON Visit www.science.mmhschool.com to learn more about bees.

Adaptations for Survival

Get Ready

Could a goose perch on a tree branch? What kind of feet would be best for perching? Parts of animals are like tools. Each part has a job to do. The job of goose feet is to paddle through water. Although all birds have beaks, not all beaks are the same. How does a bird's beak help it stay alive?

Inquiry Skill

You **experiment** when you perform a test to support or disprove a hypothesis.

Explore Activity

How Does the Shape of a Bird's Beak Affect What It Eats?

Procedure: Design Your Own

1 Predict How does the shape of a bird's beak affect what it eats? Record your prediction.

2 Make a Model Look at the materials given to you. How will you use them? Record your plan.

3 Create a chart like the one here to record your data.

4 Follow your plan. Be sure to record all your observations.

Bird Beak Observations		
Type of Beak	Type of Food	Observations

Materials

chopsticks

spoon

clothespin

drinking straw

rubber worm

peanut in shell

rice

water in paper cup

Drawing Conclusions

1 Share your chart with your classmates. How are your results similar? How are they different? Why is it important to compare your results with those of your classmates?

2 Explain why different tools are better suited to different jobs.

3 Infer How does the shape of a bird's beak help it to eat the foods it needs? How do you know?

4 FURTHER INQUIRY **Experiment** Are different teeth better for eating different foods? How would you test your ideas?

B 49

Main Idea Living things have adaptations that help them survive.

What Is an Adaptation?

Tools work in different ways. Some tools are good for picking up small things. Other tools are better for picking up large things. Parts of organisms also work like tools. A bird uses its beak as a tool for eating. Different beak shapes are suited to different kinds of food.

The honeycreeper is a kind of bird. There are different types of honeycreepers. Each type has a beak that is shaped differently. Each beak shape is an **adaptation** (ad·uhp·TAY·shuhn). An adaptation is a special characteristic that helps an organism survive. How do different kinds of beaks help honeycreepers survive?

Honeycreeper beaks are just one example of adaptation. There are many others. In fact, most organisms have a variety of adaptations. Each adaptation helps the organism survive.

How is the wool of a lamb an adaptation? It keeps the lamb warm. A warm coat helps the lamb survive cold winter days. A giraffe's long neck is an adaptation, too. It helps the giraffe find food in high places. Finding food that others can't reach increases the giraffe's chances of survival.

Honeycreepers

Each type of honeycreeper has one of these three basic beak shapes.

A long, curved beak is good for eating nectar from flowers.

A beak that is short, thick, and strong is just right for eating seeds and nuts.

A straight beak is good for eating insects.

The bright coloring of a flower is an adaptation.

A frog has a long, sticky tongue and powerful legs. Both of these adaptations help the frog catch insects for food. The bright coloring of a flower is an adaptation. It attracts insects that help the flower reproduce. By reproducing, this type of plant survives.

The European Grass Snake can pretend it is dead. How does this adaptation help it survive?

READING **Compare and Contrast**

How are the different types of beaks on honeycreepers alike? How are they different?

A frog's sticky tongue and powerful legs are adaptations.

How Can Adaptations Protect Living Things?

Not all adaptations are important for getting food or reproducing. Many adaptations help protect an organism from harm.

For example, many animals have body colors or shapes that match their surroundings. Look at the animals on this page. When these animals stay still, a predator may not see them. These are examples of **camouflage** (KAM·uh·flahzh). Camouflage is an adaptation that allows an organism to blend in with its environment. It increases an animal's chance for survival. A white rabbit blends in with the snow, while brown rabbits match their forest habitat. In some cases body coloring can also hide a predator from its prey. The stripes of a tiger allow it to be unseen as it stands in tall grass.

Can you point out the pipefish among the plants? This fish holds its body straight up and down.

This Indian leaf butterfly is protected by camouflage. With its wings folded up, it looks like a dead leaf. Can you point out the butterfly?

Some animals are protected because they look like other animals. Looking like another organism is called **mimicry** (MIM·i·kree). Sometimes a gentle animal may look like a predator. For example, a snake and a snake mimic caterpillar look very much alike. One animal is a dangerous predator. The other is a harmless plant eater. Animals that eat caterpillars may avoid this one because it looks like a snake.

The wings of the grey butterfly have spots that look like eyes. These eyespots look like the eyes of a powerful hunter, the owl. A small bird looking for a meal would probably fly on by the butterfly.

The snake mimic caterpillar avoids being eaten by looking like a real snake.

▷ **How can color protect some living things?**

If you saw this butterfly among the leaves of a tree, what would you think you were looking at?

What Do Animals Do to Defend Themselves?

Animals have many ways of defending themselves against danger. Some animals have a keen sense of smell or hearing. These senses warn them of a nearby predator. Using these senses, the animals can hide or escape.

Some animals defend themselves by fighting with strong claws, sharp teeth, and powerful jaws. Others have special ways of chasing away a predator. These defenses are all important adaptations.

Some defenses are learned by animals. Other defenses are done by instinct. Instinct is a way of acting that an animal is born with. It does not need to be learned. The pictures here show instinct.

The porcupine fish inflates itself into a prickly ball when it senses a predator.

When a pill bug needs to defend itself, it curls up.

▷ **How do animals defend themselves?**

When the frill-necked lizard of Australia is attacked, it raises the stiff skin around its neck. It hisses and lashes its tail. It scares off even large snakes.

How Do Animals in Different Environments Adapt?

Organisms have adaptations that help them survive in their environment. Deserts are hot, dry places. There is little rain. Water is often deep underground. Wolves that live in a hot desert have thin coats. Cacti that live in a desert have thick stems to store water.

The tundra is a cold, dry place. Here the soil is frozen several inches down. Only very small trees are able to survive in this environment. Wolves that live in the tundra have thick fur.

▷ **How are wolves that live in the cold forest different from those that live in the hot desert?**

Adaptations in Different Environments			
	Trees	**Bears**	**Birds**
Arctic tundra	Only very small trees grow in the tundra.	A polar bear has thick white fur.	A snowy owl has white. feathers
Desert	A mesquite tree has deep roots.	No bears live in the desert.	A roadrunner has brown feathers.

READING Charts

How are the colors of the animals alike? How are they different?

B 55

Design an Animal

You know that camouflage is one way animals keep safe. In this activity you will observe an area of your classroom. When you observe something, you use one or more of your senses to learn about the objects. You will use your observations of your classroom to help you design an animal that could hide in that environment.

Procedure

BE CAREFUL! Be careful when using scissors.

1. **Observe** Select an area to observe. This area is the environment for the organism that you will design. What do you notice about the area? What colors do you see? What textures do you feel? Record your observations.

2. Create a plan with a classmate. Make a list of features that would help an organism hide in this environment.

3. Use the materials given to you to create a plant or an animal that will blend into its surroundings. Put your plant or animal into its environment.

Drawing Conclusions

1. Describe the characteristics of the organism that you made. Explain why you included each one.

2. **Infer** Some animals can change the color of their body covering. Why might they do this?

Materials

construction paper

crayons

cotton balls

yarn

scissors

tape

L·I·N·K·S

Why It Matters

People also have special adaptations that suit their environment. Your hands are a special adaptation. For example, your hands let you paint a picture, throw a ball, or play the piano. What other adaptations do you have?

e-Journal Visit our Web site www.science.mmhschool.com to do a research project on adaptations.

Think and Write

1. What is an adaptation?

2. What is camouflage? Give an example of camouflage.

3. Describe some adaptations that protect organisms.

4. INQUIRY SKILL **Observe** Look at the picture of the frog on page B51. What adaptations help it survive?

5. **Critical Thinking** Compare reptiles that live in the desert with those that live in the rain forest. In what ways would you expect them to be different? How might they be the same?

MATH LINK

Solve a problem. What if there are 15 honeycreeper families that live in a forest? If each family has five young birds, how many honeycreepers would live in this forest?

WRITING LINK

Writing That Compares Describe your favorite animal. Where does it live? What adaptations does it have to help it survive? Compare the adaptations with those of another animal, such as a horned toad or a chameleon. Write how the animals are alike and how they are different.

ART LINK

Create a poster. Design an ecosystem that shows several types of organisms using the adaptations that allow them to survive (such as camouflage or mimicry). Share your poster with your classmates.

TECHNOLOGY LINK

LOG ON Visit www.science.mmhschool.com for more links.

Changing Ecosystems

Get Ready

For many years Mount St. Helens was a sleeping volcano. Bears and elk roamed its forests. Fish swam in its streams. Wildflowers bloomed on its slopes. Then on May 18, 1980, Mount St. Helens erupted. This changed local habitats forever. How did these changes affect wildlife in the area?

Inquiry Skill

You predict when you state possible results of an event or an experiment.

Explore Activity

What Happens When Ecosystems Change?

Materials

3 predator cards:
  red hawk
  blue owl
  green snake

12 prey cards:
  4 red
  4 blue
  4 green

Procedure

1. Make the 3 predator cards and 12 prey cards listed in the Materials. Give each player one predator card. Stack the prey cards in the center of the table.

2. Take turns drawing a prey card. Keep only the prey cards that match the color of your predator card. Return all others. Play until one predator gets all four matching prey cards.

3. **Experiment** Add a card that says "fire" to the prey cards. Play the game again. Any predator who draws the fire card must leave the game. Return the fire card to the deck. Continue to play until a predator gets all four prey cards or all players are out.

Drawing Conclusions

1. What happened each time you played the game?

2. The fire card represented an ecosystem change. What effect did it have?

3. **Infer** What may happen when an ecosystem changes?

4. **FURTHER INQUIRY** **Predict** What might happen if you changed the number of prey cards? Try it.

Main Idea Changes in ecosystems affect the plants and animals that live there.

What Happens When Ecosystems Change?

Ecosystems can change. The change can be large or small. When a large change occurs, the organisms that live in that ecosystem are affected. Some have trouble surviving.

The eruption of Mount St. Helens in Washington State caused huge changes. A wind of hot steam and rock blasted the area. The wind lifted trees right out of the ground. Organisms that made their homes on or near trees were affected. The forest was buried in ash. When it rained, the ash turned muddy. Then the ash hardened into a tough crust that killed the plants underneath it. Other organisms near the ground had their habitats destroyed.

Animals that roamed the forest now had no homes. Some moved far from Mount St. Helens in search of new homes. Others could not find new habitats and died.

Melting snow and storms led to flooding along the Missouri River.

Spirit Lake below Mount St. Helens before the eruption

Spirit Lake after the eruption

Over time some organisms found new habitats. The fireweed plant began to grow right through the cracks in the crust. As one organism moved back in, others followed. After a few years, a new ecosystem began to form on the crust of ash. It is different from the ecosystem that was there before.

A volcanic eruption is one event that can change an ecosystem. A flood or drought can change an ecosystem, too. Floods are caused by heavy rains or snow. Rivers rise up over their banks and cover dry land. This drowns plants and changes habitats. A drought is the opposite of a flood. During a drought it doesn't rain for weeks or months. Rivers and lakes dry up. Plants and animals are affected. Other natural disasters, such as fires, earthquakes, and storms, can also change an ecosystem.

People change the ecosystem, too. People cut down trees and use the wood to build homes. They can make a wetland for a new supply of clean water.

> **What are three things that can cause changes in habitats?**

How do the conditions of Spirit Lake today determine how well these plants grow?

How Do Ecosystems Come Back?

After a big change, ecosystems usually come back. A fire can destroy almost all the habitats in a forest. How does a forest return? There are several stages the forest must go through.

READING

Charts

1. What happens to a forest right after it is destroyed?

2. Why do animals return after the grasses and insects instead of before them?

How a Forest Comes Back After a Fire

Stage 1 Habitat destruction
Bulbs and seeds may survive underground. They begin to grow in the ash.

Stage 2 Grasses
Over time grasses cover the bare ground. The grasses add nutrients to the soil. They also provide a home for insects. The insects attract larger animals.

Stage 3 Larger plants
Small trees begin to grow. The trees block the sunlight. Without light the grasses begin to die.

Stage 4 Forest
Small trees are replaced by larger trees. The forest is the final stage.

Organisms respond to change in one of three ways. Some organisms respond to a change in their habitat by adjusting. The fireweed on Mount St. Helens was covered by crust. It adjusted to its new habitat by growing through the crust.

This box turtle survived a forest fire.

Some organisms **perish** (PER·ish). Organisms that perish do not survive. A mouse may survive a fire. Where will it find food after the fire? If it cannot meet its needs, it may not survive. Some organisms **relocate** (ree·LOH·kayt). An organism that relocates finds a new home. Trees were destroyed on Mount St. Helens. Birds that lived in the trees could fly to new trees.

▷ **What are two ways organisms can respond to change?**

Many animals are driven away as their habitats become towns. This moose is feeding near a house.

Are Living Things Dying Out?

Natural disasters such as fires and floods can destroy habitats. People can harm habitats, too. When people replace plains or forests with new towns, organisms may lose their homes or become overcrowded. Pollution can harm organisms, too. Some animals are hunted by people.

All these things are threats to plants and animals. In many cases organisms become **endangered** (en·DAYN·juhrd). An organism is called endangered when there are very few of its kind left.

The few remaining California condors are being watched carefully so that their young can grow safely.

The loggerhead turtle lives in the Atlantic Ocean. Its habitats are being destroyed and polluted.

The rosy periwinkle of Madagascar produces a chemical proven effective in treating some forms of cancer.

People are finding ways to protect many endangered organisms. Some endangered animals live in national parks, where they are watched by rangers. Laws are being passed to stop the hunting of endangered animals.

▶ **When does an animal become endangered?**

QUICK LAB

Crowd Control

FOLDABLES™ Make a Two-Tab Book. (See p. R41.) Label the book as shown.

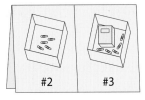

#2   #3

1. Toss 20 paper clips in a small box. Remove any two that touch each other.

2. Gather the paper clips that are left in the box. Toss them again and remove any two that touch. Repeat until there are no clips left. Count how many tosses you made. Record your answer on the first tab of your Foldables book.

3. Repeat steps 1 and 2. This time, put a book in the box so there is less room for the clips to move in. Record the number of tosses you made on the second tab.

4. **Infer** When organisms are crowded together, how do their chances of survival change? Write your answer on the inside of the Foldables book.

The Bengal tiger lives in southern Asia. Hunters have killed almost all of this kind of tiger.

Have Living Things Died Out?

The answer is "Yes." For example, all the dinosaurs that lived millions of years ago became **extinct** (ek·STINGKT). *Extinct* means that there are no more of that type of organism alive. Extinct animals include dinosaurs. Scientists are not sure what caused these animals to die out. However, we do know why many other organisms became extinct. Changes in habitats, pollution, and hunting have killed off many living things.

Many organisms are becoming extinct even today, as rain forests are cleared. In the last 500 years, 500 kinds of organisms have become extinct in what is now the United States. Endangered organisms that you read about may become extinct if we do not protect them.

READING **Compare and Contrast** What are some of the different ways organisms can become extinct?

The saber-toothed cat was similar to today's tiger. It became extinct thousands of years ago, when its prey became extinct.

Dodo birds once covered the island of Mauritius near Africa. They were hunted by people until they became extinct in 1680.

Why It Matters

Why should you care about endangered organisms? When an organism becomes extinct, it is gone forever. This changes the food web it belonged to. It also may affect products we get from the organism.

e-Journal Visit our Web site www.science.mmhschool.com to do a research project on endangered organisms.

Think and Write

1. What causes ecosystems to change?

2. How might a forest recover after a fire or flood?

3. How do organisms respond when their habitats change?

4. What happened when there were no laws to control hunting?

5. **Critical Thinking** A forest is cut down to build a parking lot. Why is this habitat change more serious than a forest fire?

L·I·N·K·S

MATH LINK

Make a graph. Look out a window for ten minutes. Record the number of animals you see. Repeat your observations each day at the same time at the same window for one week. Draw a bar graph to show how the number of animals changes each day. Use writing to explain your graph.

WRITING LINK

Persuasive Writing Describe an endangered organism that you want to save. Write an article about the organism for a newspaper. Tell why it is important to save this endangered organism.

LITERATURE LINK

Read *Rescue at First Encounter Beach* to learn how a pod of pilot whales becomes beached. When you finish reading, write a list of the ways the rescuers helped the whales. Try the activities at the end of the book.

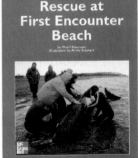

Rescue at First Encounter Beach
by Pearl Nauman
Illustrated by Anna Stewart

TECHNOLOGY LINK

LOG ON Visit www.science.mmhschool.com for more links.

Chapter 4 Review

Vocabulary

Fill each blank with the best word from the list.

adaptation, B50   **mimicry,** B53
camouflage, B52   **niche,** B44
competition, B42   **perish,** B63
endangered, B64   **relocate,** B63
extinct, B66

1. Organisms that all want the same thing are in _____.

2. The job or role an organism has in an ecosystem is its _____.

3. A characteristic that helps an organism survive in its environment is a(n) _____.

4. The white fur of the polar bear is an example of _____.

5. An adaptation in which one organism imitates or looks like another is called _____.

6. An organism that is _____ is gone forever.

When an ecosystem changes, living things may
       7. or **8.** .

When living things do not survive, that type of organism may become
       9. or **10.** .

Test Prep

11. Predators often compete for the same _____.

  A adaptation
  B prey
  C habitat
  D ecosystem

12. All the following are adaptations EXCEPT _____.

  F camouflage
  G mimicry
  H the shape of a bird's beak
  J the prey in a habitat

13. A snowy owl most likely lives in the _____.

  A tundra
  B desert
  C rain forest
  D temperate forest

14. An ecosystem can be changed by _____.

  F floods
  G droughts
  H fires
  J all of the above

15. Which of the following animals is now extinct?

   A dodo bird

   B pigeon

   C blue whale

   D elephant

Concepts and Skills

16. Reading in Science Look at the pictures below. Compare and contrast the two pictures of Spirit Lake.

Before   **After**

17. Critical Thinking One group of rabbits lives on an island without predators. A second group of rabbits lives on a different island with predators. Which group is more likely to be faster runners? Explain.

18. Safety You are exploring changes in a habitat in a nearby park. Write down some rules you might follow to be sure your study is safe.

19. Scientific Methods What animals (not pets) in your neighborhood use camouflage? Plan to make a survey of animals in your neighborhood to find out. Tell what characteristics allow each animal to blend in with its surroundings.

20. INQUIRY SKILL **Observe** Draw a picture of your favorite animal. What adaptations does your animal have? What purpose does each adaptation serve?

Did You Ever Wonder?

INQUIRY SKILL **Form a Hypothesis** You have seen that many animals have unusual behaviors that help them to survive. Think of a question such as, why does a spider not get caught in its own web? How can you find the answer?

 LOG ON Visit **www.science.mmhschool.com** to boost your test scores.

Dr. Francisco Dallmeier

WILDLIFE CONSERVATIONIST

Dr. Dallmeier and a giant sea turtle

In the rain forest of Gabon, in Africa, elephants, leopards, and reptiles prowl the land. Francisco Dallmeier and a team of scientists wanted to identify every type of plant and animal in the area. Gabon is a rain forest near the Congo River. "For the future of Gabon, it's important to know what we have there."

The team tracked down and recorded 159 types of reptiles and amphibians. They found 70 kinds of fish, 140 types of trees, and dozens of mammal species. Dallmeier also discovered several plant and animal species that had never been seen before.

Dallmeier's work has helped people understand the importance of the Gabon rain forest. He says, "We need to protect these plant and animal species. They are valuable to the natural balance of the area and our Earth."

LOG ON

Visit www.science.mmhschool.com to learn more about rain forests.

TIME FOR KIDS®

TOP 5 Rain Forest Facts

1. About 2,000 trees per minute are cut down in the rain forests.
2. Rain forests are home to millions of plant and animal species.
3. On one day in 1987, a total of 7,603 fires were burning in the Amazon rain forest.
4. Four square miles of rain forest can contain as many as 1,500 species of flowering plants.
5. Most of the plants useful in cancer treatment are found only in the rain forests.

Write About It

1. What did Dr. Dallmeier find in the Gabon rain forest?
2. Why does Dr. Dallmeier want to help protect plants and animals in the Gabon rain forest?

Composting Recycles

Your goal is to find out if a compost pile will heat up.

Materials
2 2L clear plastic drink bottles marker scissors clear 1-inch tape 1 cup of soil	grass clippings, leaves, plant peelings, newspaper strips thermometer water

What to Do

1. Have an adult help you make the compost container. Use the diagram.

2. Fill the container with grass clippings, leaves, newspaper strips, plant peelings, or a combination of these materials. Add the soil and mix it with the other materials. Moisten the substances in the container. Cover the container with the top of the first bottle (A).

3. Observe the container each day. Record what you observe on a chart.

4. With an adult, open the top and place the thermometer in the container twice each week.

5. Record the temperature on a chart.

Draw Conclusions

Did the compost pile heat up? Write a paragraph about your findings. Explain how composting can be used to recycle discarded plant and animal material.

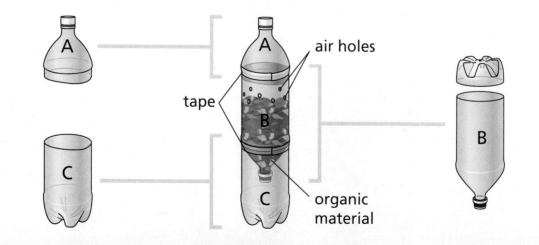

UNIT C Our Earth

Our Earth

LOOK!

The walls of the Grand Canyon show many layers of rock. How do you think the Grand Canyon formed?

CHAPTER

5

Earth's Resources

Did You Ever Wonder?

How do caves form? Most caves form in limestone.
Limestone is a type of rock. Rainwater creates tiny
holes within limestone. Over time, water dissolves, or
breaks up, the limestone. The holes grow into caves.

INQUIRY SKILL Form a Hypothesis What types of rocks
form caves?

Minerals and Rocks

Vocabulary

mineral, C6

igneous rock, C8

sedimentary rock, C8

metamorphic rock, C9

Get Ready

What is Earth like today? What was it like long ago when dinosaurs roamed the land? The clues are found in rocks. Every rock has a different story to tell.

Inquiry Skill

You classify when you place things that share properties together in groups.

Explore Activity

Materials

several
different rocks

hand lens

How Are Rocks Alike and Different?

Procedure

1. Touch each rock. Describe how each rock feels.

2. **Observe** Carefully look at each rock. Write about any lines or patterns you see.

3. **Observe** Look at each rock through the hand lens. Write or draw any new things you see.

Drawing Conclusions

1. Did any rocks feel the same? Did any rocks have similar lines or patterns?

2. Describe how the rocks are alike. Describe how they are different.

3. **Infer** Do you think the rocks are made of one material or many materials? Explain.

4. **FURTHER INQUIRY** **Classify** How might you classify the rocks into two or more groups? What physical properties of the rocks will be helpful? Try it to test your idea.

Main Idea Rocks are made of minerals.

What Are Minerals?

There are hundreds of different kinds of rocks. Rocks have many different properties. Some are light in color, and others are dark. Some are rough, and others are smooth. There are rocks that are heavy and rocks that are light. Some rocks are easily broken. Other rocks are difficult to break.

All rocks are made from types of materials called **minerals** (MIN·uhr·uhlz). A mineral is a substance found in nature that is not a plant or an animal. Minerals are the building blocks of rocks. There are more than 3,000 minerals.

Some rocks are made of many different minerals. Granite (GRAN·it) is an example of this type of rock. Other rocks are made up mostly of one type of mineral. Limestone is this type of rock.

Granite

Limestone

How do granite and limestone compare?

Not all rocks are hard. Chalk is made of a rock that is so soft you can write with it.

Hematite

Galena

A mineral's streak may not be the same as its color. Compare the streaks of hematite and galena.

There are many clues that help us tell one mineral from another. They have different colors. They can be shiny or dull. You can compare their *texture* (TEKS·chuhr). Texture is how something feels.

Another way to identify minerals is to scratch them. Hard minerals are more difficult to scratch. Many minerals leave marks behind when you rub them on something. The mark is called a streak.

▶ **How can you compare minerals?**

QUICK LAB

Mineral Scratch Test

FOLDABLES™ Make a Folded Table. (See p. R44.) Label the table as shown.

Mineral	Prediction	Observation	Order of Hardness

1. Your teacher will give you three minerals. Draw each mineral in the table.

2. **Predict** Which mineral will be the easiest to scratch? Which will be the most difficult?

3. **Observe** Test your predictions. Scratch each mineral with your fingernail, a penny, and a paper clip. Record your observations in the table.

4. **Interpret Data** Number the minerals you tested in order of hardness, from hardest to softest.

How Are Rocks Formed?

Earth's rocks form in one of three ways. Each way gives a rock its properties.

An **igneous** (IG·nee·uhs) **rock** is a "fire-made" rock. Igneous rocks form when melted rock cools and hardens. Inside Earth, melted rock cools slowly and forms rocks such as granite. Melted rock that flows to the surface cools quickly and forms rocks such as basalt (buh·SAWLT).

A **sedimentary** (sed·uh·MEN·tuh·ree) **rock** forms when sand, mud, and pebbles at the bottom of rivers, lakes, and oceans pile up. Over time these bits press together. They cement into solid rocks. Sandstone, shale, and siltstone are all examples of this kind of rock.

When a volcano erupts, melted rock material rushes out. After it bursts onto Earth's surface, the melted rock cools and hardens. This forms igneous rocks.

The third kind of rock is called a **metamorphic** (met·uh·MAWR·fik) **rock** . *Metamorphic* means "a change in form." A metamorphic rock is a rock that has changed form through squeezing and heating. Marble and gneiss (NIGHS) are examples of this kind of rock.

All over Earth you find examples of newly formed rocks. You can find rocks breaking apart, too. Wind and water can break large rocks into tiny pieces. Plants and animals can, too. Rocks break apart and re-form again and again.

▶ **How is a metamorphic rock formed?**

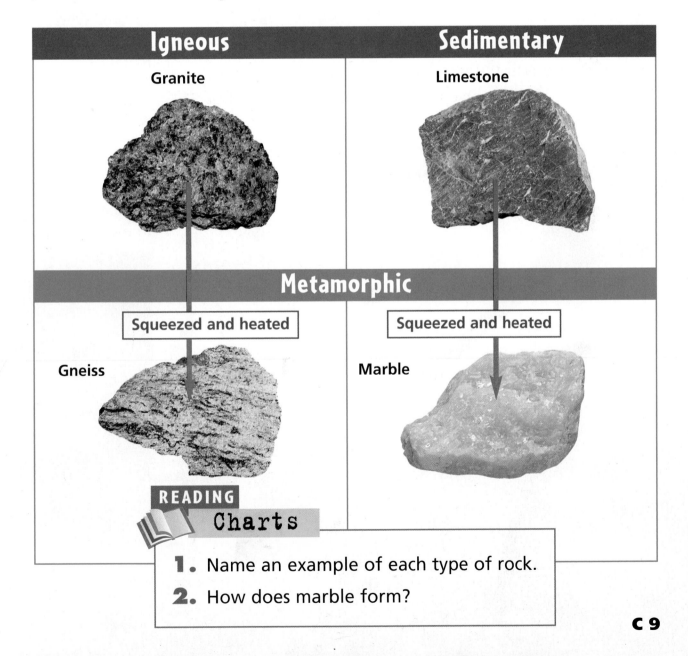

Igneous
Granite

Sedimentary
Limestone

Metamorphic

Squeezed and heated

Squeezed and heated

Gneiss

Marble

READING
Charts

1. Name an example of each type of rock.

2. How does marble form?

How Do We Use Rocks and Minerals?

Look around you. Everywhere you will see the many uses of rocks. Rocks are used to make roads, walls, and buildings. Crushed limestone is used to make cement. Clay and sand are used to make bricks.

Would you guess that glass comes from rock? Glass is made from sand, which is tiny rock pieces. Sand and other ingredients are mixed together at high temperatures. When the material cools, it becomes glass. Soil is also made of small pieces of rock. Without soil we would have no food.

You use minerals, too. People cannot live without salt, a mineral in food. Pencils contain a mineral called graphite. Metals, like iron, gold, and silver, are very useful minerals.

The outsides of these pans are covered with copper, a shiny metal.

Marble is used to make statues.

READING **Sequence of Events**
How is glass made?

These glassblowers are shaping the hot glass.

C 10

L·I·N·K·S

Why It Matters

When you walk up a mountain, you are walking over rocks. When you walk in a valley, you are walking over rocks. Rocks and minerals are not alive. However, all living things—including you—use them every day.

e-Journal Visit our Web site www.science.mmhschool.com to do a research project on rocks.

Think and Write

1. What are minerals?

2. Describe how rocks are naturally broken down into smaller pieces.

3. What are the three main groups of rocks? Give an example of each.

4. List three ways that you use rocks or minerals.

5. **Critical Thinking** People need salt to stay alive, but they do not need gold or silver. However, silver or gold costs more money than salt. Why do you think this is so?

WRITING LINK

Writing a Poem Write a poem about igneous, sedimentary, or metamorphic rocks. Tell how the rocks are formed. Describe how they look. Use rhyming words at the end of lines. You could title your poem "Poetry Rocks!"

MATH LINK

Use place value. James is building a house. The table shows the cost of different building materials. Arrange the materials from least expensive to most expensive.

Materials	Total Cost
Boulders	$185
Marble	$380
Cement	$225
Bricks	$280
Gravel	$45

LITERATURE LINK

Read *Acoma: The Sky City* to learn about an old Native American village in New Mexico. When you finish reading, think about designing your own clay pots. Try the activities at the end of the book.

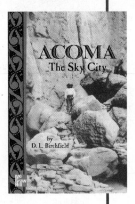

TECHNOLOGY LINK

LOG ON Visit www.science.mmhschool.com for more links.

Kinds of Soils

Vocabulary

soil, C14

humus, C14

Get Ready

Could these plants grow without soil? Plants need soil whether they grow in a garden, on the prairie, or in the forest. Many living things make their home in the soil. What do you think soil is like?

Inquiry Skill

You **observe** when you use one or more of your senses to learn about an object.

Explore Activity

What Is in Soil?

Materials

small amount of soil

piece of white paper

hand lens

Procedure

1. Spread the soil on the piece of paper.

2. **Observe** Look at the soil closely. What do you see? Are there different colors? Are there pieces of different sizes?

3. **Observe** Touch the soil. How does it feel? Smell the soil. How does it smell? Record your observations. Be sure to wash your hands after you touch the soil.

4. Use a hand lens to look at the soil. What can you see now? Record your observations.

Drawing Conclusions

1. Describe the soil. Tell how it looks, smells, and feels.

2. **Infer** What different materials make up the soil?

3. **FURTHER INQUIRY** **Form a Hypothesis** Form a hypothesis that explains how soil forms. Test your hypothesis. What did you find out?

Main Idea Soil is made of living and nonliving things.

What Makes Up Soil?

Soil is made of many different materials. They include small rocks, sand, minerals, and clay. Other materials in soil come from living things and form **humus** (HYEW·muhs). Humus is a material that was once living or was formed by a living thing. Humus adds nutrients to the soil.

Soil has spaces for air and water. These spaces are often made by plant roots and insects.

There are usually two layers of soil. The top layer is called topsoil. It is made of very small, dark particles. Topsoil has a lot of humus and minerals. It also can hold a lot of water.

Below the topsoil is a layer called subsoil. Subsoil is made of bigger, lighter colored particles. Subsoil lacks humus. Subsoil does hold water and some minerals. Below subsoil is *bedrock*. Bedrock is solid rock.

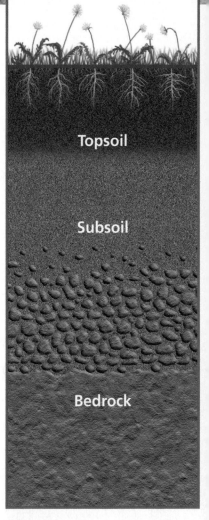

Topsoil

Subsoil

Bedrock

Topsoil forms at Earth's surface. Large rocks break into very small pieces and mix with humus.

Rich soil on this Pennsylvania farm supports the growth of many different crops.

There are many kinds of soils. Each kind is made of different types of rocks and minerals. Some soils hold more water than other soils. Some soils have more humus, too.

Different soils are found in different parts of the world. In some places the soil has a lot of clay. In other places the soil is very sandy. A few lucky places have *loam* (LOHM). Loam is a kind of soil with clay and sand. Plants grow well in loam.

Soil layers can be thick or thin. Plants grow better in thick soil than in thin soil. Windy, dry weather can make soil thinner. Mountains have thin soil because gravity pulls soil downhill.

Soil takes a long time to form. Farmers take good care of their soil. They want to use it year after year. Good soil helps many different types of plants to grow.

READING **Sequence of Events** **How does soil become thinner?**

This soil is sandy.

Loam contains clay and sand.

This soil contains red clay.

Inquiry Skill
BUILDER

How Much Water Can Soil Hold?

In this activity you will measure and compare the amounts of water held by two different soils.

Procedure

1. **Measure** Fill the measuring cup with 250 mL of potting soil. Put the soil into the cup with holes in the bottom. Pack the soil firmly. Fill the measuring cup with 100 mL of water.

2. **Experiment** Hold the cup of potting soil over an empty cup without holes. Have a partner slowly pour the water into the soil. Let the water run through the soil for two minutes.

3. **Measure** Pour the water you collected into the measuring cup. Record the volume in a chart.

4. **Experiment** Repeat Steps 1–3 using sandy soil. Record the volume.

Drawing Conclusions

1. **Infer** Which soil held more water? How do you know?

2. Which kind of soil would be better for a garden? Which would be better for a soccer field?

3. **Interpret Data** Repeat this activity and record the data in a chart. Compare your results. Compare your findings with a classmate's. What did you find out? Summarize your results.

Materials

4 paper cups, 2 with holes in the bottom

measuring cup

water

potting soil

sandy soil

watch or clock

calculator (optional)

Why It Matters

Soil is the basis for life. Good soil contains the water and minerals plants need to make food. We depend on plants for the food we eat. That's why it is important to take good care of soil. Poor soil can be improved by adding humus. Humus helps soil absorb and retain water. This helps more plants to grow.

e-Journal Visit our Web site www.science.mmhschool.com to do a research project on soil.

Think and Write

1. What materials make up soil?

2. How are soil layers different?

3. Describe three different types of soil.

4. **INQUIRY SKILL** **Measure** Every time you water a plant, water drips from the pot to the floor. How can you find out how much water the plant is losing?

5. **Critical Thinking** How does soil help plants grow? Why is this important to people?

L·I·N·K·S

WRITING LINK

Expository Writing What is life like in the soil? Earthworms, plants, and insects such as ants and some beetles all live in the soil. Write about a living thing that lives in the soil.

MATH LINK

Solve a problem. Ted poured 16.5 ounces of water into a pot of soil. He collected 9.8 ounces of water from a hole in the bottom of the pot. How much water remained in the soil?

TECHNOLOGY LINK

Science Newsroom CD-ROM Choose *Let's Grow Over This Again* to learn how crop rotation can affect the amount of nutrients in the soil.

LOG ON Visit www.science.mmhschool.com for more links.

The Farmers' Friend

Next time you eat a peanut, think of George Washington Carver. He's the man who made the peanut famous!

Carver was born into slavery. He was born in Missouri in the early 1860s. Even at a young age he liked to learn about plants. People called him "the plant doctor."

At about age 11, Carver went away to get an education. He got a job and lived with families who took him in. By 1896 he had earned two college degrees. Then he got a job at the Tuskegee Institute in Alabama. He was a teacher and head of research. His goal was to help poor Southern farmers.

George Washington Carver was always interested in plants.

Most Southern farmers grew only cotton. The plant took nitrogen (NIGH·truh·juhn) out of the soil. Carver suggested that farmers plant cotton one year. Then the next year they should plant a different crop. He wanted the farmers to use peanuts, soybeans, and sweet potatoes. Why? These plants put nitrogen back into the soil!

Carver made more than 300 products from peanuts alone! These included cheese, flour, ink, and milk substitutes. He also made more than 100 products from sweet potatoes. Some of these are flour, rubber, and glue.

Soon many companies bought the new crops. They made the new products. More and more Southern farmers rotated their crops with cotton. In time their cotton grew better, too.

George Washington Carver received many honors. He was most proud of helping the farmers. They began to earn more money. Best of all, their farmland could support generations of farmers in the future.

What Did I Learn?

1. Carver wanted farmers to grow peanuts and sweet potatoes because they

   A put nitrogen back into the soil.

   B provide people with lots of vitamins.

   C are cheaper to grow.

   D grow faster than cotton.

2. Which of the following is not a product developed by Carver?

   F flour

   G wax

   H glue

   J ink

 LOG ON Visit www.science.mmhschool.com to learn more about George Washington Carver.

Fossils and Fuels

Get Ready

The objects captured in this piece of amber were once alive. Now they are fossils. Fossils tell us the story of life on Earth billions of years ago. How do you think fossils might have formed?

Inquiry Skill

You **experiment** when you perform a test to support or disprove a hypothesis.

Explore Activity

How Are Fossils Formed?

Materials

large plastic spoon

clear glue

2 carrot slices

paper towel

Procedure

1. Squeeze a small amount of glue into the spoon. Let the glue set for a few hours.

2. Place one slice of carrot on top of the glue. Slowly add more glue until the carrot slice is completely covered. Place the spoon on a paper towel. Put the other slice of carrot next to the spoon.

3. Compare the glue and carrot to fossil insects in amber.

4. **Observe** Compare the carrot slices. Describe their color and appearance.

Drawing Conclusions

1. How did the glue change the carrot slice?

2. **Predict** Over time, will the carrot slice in the glue change more than the other carrot slice? Why?

3. FURTHER INQUIRY **Experiment** With a team member, design and conduct an experiment to test your prediction.

Main Idea Fossils teach us about Earth's past.

How Are Fossils Formed?

A **fossil** (FAHS·uhl) is the imprint or remains of something that lived long ago. People have found fossils that are more than three billion years old!

First, plants and animals die. The materials around them can preserve, or save, their shapes and body parts. Shells, teeth, bones, skin, and even footprints can become fossils.

Most fossils are found in sedimentary rocks. Remember, these rocks form when silt, sand, mud, and other materials pile up and get cemented together. Sometimes these materials cover the remains of living things. This happens gently and quickly. The remains may become fossils, as rocks form around them.

Fossils are also found in **amber** (AM·buhr). Amber is hardened tree sap. Tree sap is a sticky liquid that can harden like glue. When an insect gets stuck in tree sap, it may become a fossil in amber.

This woman is looking for fossil bones preserved in rocks.

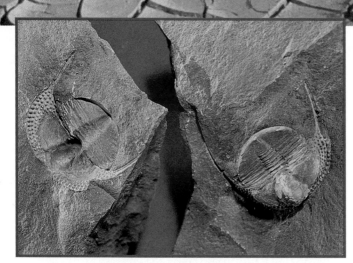

One of these fossils is a cast. The other fossil is a mold. Can you tell which fossil is the cast and which fossil is the mold? The fossil on the left is the mold, and the fossil on the right is the cast.

Shallow prints or marks in solid rock are called *imprints*. Living things made the imprints. They pressed on the materials that later turned into rock.

Shells often leave fossils called *molds*. A mold is an empty space in rock where something once was. Shell molds form after shells are buried in sand or mud. As water seeps in, it breaks down the shells. Shell-shaped spaces are left.

A *cast* is a fossil made inside a mold. A cast can form when minerals seep into a mold. As the minerals harden, they form a copy of the mold's shape.

READING Sequence of Events
What is one way that fossils can form?

Imprint Clues

FOLDABLES™ Make a Trifold Book. (See p. R42.) Label the book as shown.

(See p. R42.)

Object #1	Object #2	Object #3

1. Gather three small objects. Form some modeling clay into a thick, flat layer.

2. **Make a Model** Press an object into the clay. It should make an imprint. Carefully remove the object.

3. Repeat step 2 with two other objects.

4. **Infer** Exchange imprint models with a classmate. Try to figure out which objects were used. Record your answers in the Trifold Book.

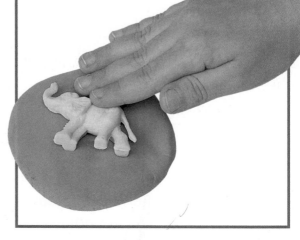

What Do Fossils Tell Us About the Past?

Fossils help us learn about what Earth was like long ago. They tell us about the plants and animals of the past.

Look at the fossil bone shown at right. The bone is very different from the bones of animals alive today. It came from a dinosaur that lived millions of years ago. Everything we know about dinosaurs comes from studying their fossils.

This man is standing next to the fossil leg of a supersaurus. Scientists estimate that supersaurus may have stood 16.5 meters (54 feet) tall! Very little is known about this dinosaur because very few fossil bones have been discovered. The diagram shows which bones have been found.

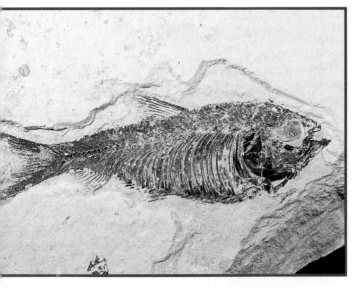

Fish fossils have been found under dry land and even inside mountains.

Triceratops is the best known horned dinosaur. It lived during the Cretaceous period.

Woolly mammoth

Elephant

Compare the woolly mammoth and elephant. How are they alike? How are they different?

Fossils can also tell how Earth has changed. Fish fossils have been found under dry land. How must Earth have changed for this to happen?

Fossils tell us how life on Earth has changed. Many types of animals that lived in the past, such as dinosaurs, are not alive today.

Look at the picture of another animal from the past, the woolly mammoth. Does it remind you of an animal you see today? The woolly mammoth is an ancient relative of the elephant.

Earth's plants have also changed. Ferns are some of Earth's oldest plants. Plants that make flowers came later.

▷ **How has life on Earth changed over time?**

What Are Fossil Fuels?

Cars, trucks, and airplanes need **fuel** (FYEW·uhl) in order to run. A fuel is a material that is burned for its energy.

Oil products, such as gasoline, are fuels. Coal and natural gas are, too. These fuels are examples of fossil fuels. Fossil fuels formed from the remains of plants and animals from long ago.

This is a lump of coal.

▷ **Where do fossil fuels come from?**

How Coal Forms

1 Millions of years ago, swamps covered large parts of Earth's land. When swamp plants died, they sank to the bottom.

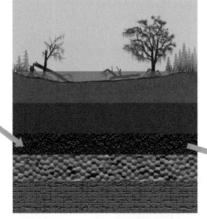

2 Layers of decayed plants formed a soft material called peat. Over time the peat was buried under layers of mud and sand.

3 The mud and sand turned to rock. Slowly the peat changed into coal.

READING Diagrams

Describe how swamp plants changed to coal.

Why It Matters

Fossils tell a story. The story is about Earth's history. It is a very long story that includes many changes. There can be changes in land and water. There can be changes in the weather. There can also be changes in living things. If you learn about the changes of the past, you can predict changes in the future.

e-Journal Visit our Web site www.science.mmhschool.com to do a research project on fossils and fuels.

Think and Write

1. What is a fossil?

2. Describe three types of fossils.

3. How do we know about dinosaurs?

4. What are fossil fuels? Give an example.

5. **Critical Thinking** We know a lot about dinosaurs. Why can we only hypothesize about what colors they were?

LINKS

MATH LINK

Make a bar graph. The table shows the lengths of different dinosaurs. Make a bar graph that shows these lengths. You may choose to research more about these dinosaurs.

Dinosaur	Length
Apatosaurus	23 meters
Allosaurus	12 meters
Triceratops	8 meters
Troodon	2 meters
Ultrasaurus	30 meters

WRITING LINK

Personal Narrative Suppose that you are a woolly mammoth. Write a letter to an elephant in the future. Include questions a woolly mammoth might ask an elephant.

SOCIAL STUDIES LINK

Write a report. Research alternative or replacement heat sources. These include geothermal, nuclear, and solar energy.

TECHNOLOGY LINK

 LOG ON Visit www.science.mmhschool.com for more links.

Water in Sea, Land, and Sky

Get Ready

How much of Earth's surface do you think water covers? Some people say that Earth has the wrong name. Maybe we should call the planet "Water"! What do you think?

Inquiry Skill

You predict when you state possible results of an experiment.

Explore Activity

Where Do Lakes Form?

Materials

clear-plastic box

modeling clay

water

Procedure:

1 **Make a Model** Place the clay in the clear-plastic box. Mold it into different landforms. Make mountains, hills, and valleys. Clay should cover most of the bottom of the box.

2 **Predict** You have modeled land without water. If you added water, where would lakes form?

3 **Observe** Gently pour water into the plastic box. Stop when you see one or more small lakes forming. Draw a diagram of the land with water. Add more water to the model.

Drawing Conclusions

1 Where did lakes form in your model?

2 Compare your model with real land and water. How are they alike? How are they different?

3 **Infer** Could lakes ever form where there are mountains? Explain.

4 FURTHER INQUIRY **Predict** Rain has been falling for many days, and Lake Elmo is rising. What do you need to know to predict where the water will go? Compare your ideas with your classmates'.

Main Idea Earth's water moves from place to place.

How Much of Earth's Surface Is Water?

Water covers nearly three-fourths of Earth's surface. A little more than one-fourth of the surface is land.

Oceans hold almost all of Earth's water. Ocean water is very salty. A few lakes have salt water, too. The Great Salt Lake in Utah is one example.

Ponds, streams, rivers, and most lakes hold fresh water. Fresh water is water without much salt. People need fresh water to live. Many plants and animals need fresh water, too.

Much of Earth's fresh water is trapped in ice. Large sheets of ice are found at the North Pole and the South Pole.

From space Earth looks blue because of all the water. This picture shows the Pacific Ocean.

If All of Earth's Water Fit into 100 Cups

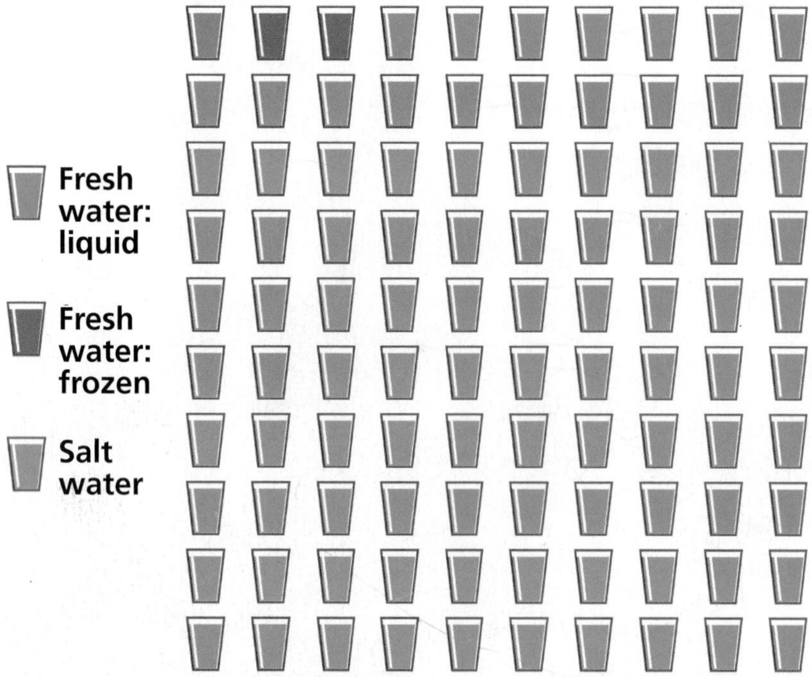

Fresh water: liquid

Fresh water: frozen

Salt water

READING Diagrams

How many cups represent Earth's fresh water?

Every day people use fresh water from lakes, rivers, and other sources. Why don't these sources dry up? The **water cycle** (WAW·tuhr SIGH·kuhl) fills them up again and again. The water cycle is the movement of water from place to place and from one form to another form.

The Sun powers the water cycle. When it heats liquid water, the water **evaporates** (i·VAP·uh·rayts). To evaporate means to change from a liquid to a gas.

Water in its gas form is called water vapor. The water vapor rises through the air. When it cools, it **condenses** (kuhn·DENS·uhz) into water droplets and ice crystals. These droplets and crystals form clouds. To condense means to change from a gas to a liquid. When water droplets and ice crystals become heavy enough, they fall to Earth's surface. This water can be in the form of rain, snow, sleet, or hail.

READING **Sequence of Events**
What are the steps in the water cycle?

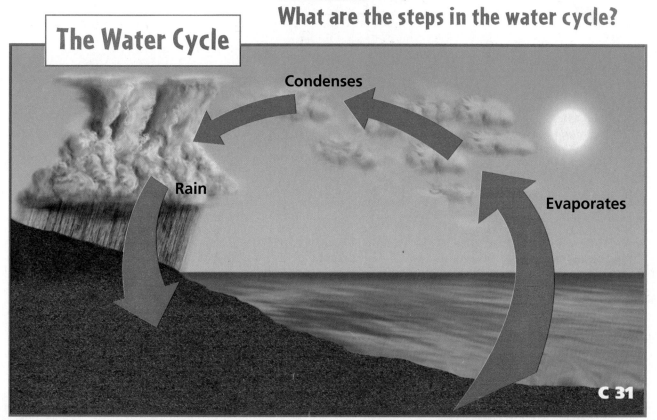

The Water Cycle

Condenses

Rain

Evaporates

How Can People in Dry Places Get Water?

When it rains, getting water is easy. In places with little rain, however, getting water can be more difficult.

In some places people build dams across rivers. A dam is a large wall that holds back a river. The water in the river gathers in a kind of lake, called a *reservoir* (REZ·uhr·vwahr). The reservoir stores water for people to use.

In other places people build pipes or ditches for water to travel through. These pipes or ditches are called *aqueducts* (AK·wuh·dukts). Aqueducts can carry water to places where it is needed.

An aqueduct brings fresh water to people.

▷ **What do dams and aqueducts do?**

The Lake Owyhee Dam in Oregon holds back a river. This creates a reservoir.

Can We Get Water from the Ground?

The next time it rains, watch what happens to the water. Some flows into streams, lakes, and rivers. However, much of it soaks into the ground.

The soil and rocks underneath the ground hold water. Water held in rocks and soil below the surface is called **groundwater**. Groundwater is stored in the cracks and spaces of underground rocks and soil.

We get groundwater by digging wells, which are deep holes. Groundwater fills the holes. We can raise the water out of the well when we need it.

▷ **How can we get groundwater?**

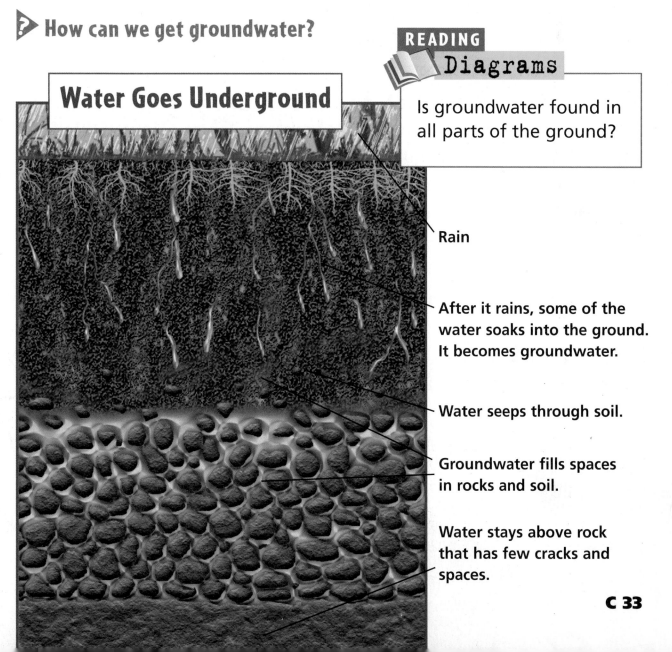

READING

Diagrams

Is groundwater found in all parts of the ground?

Water Goes Underground

Rain

After it rains, some of the water soaks into the ground. It becomes groundwater.

Water seeps through soil.

Groundwater fills spaces in rocks and soil.

Water stays above rock that has few cracks and spaces.

QUICK LAB

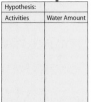

Wasting Water

FOLDABLES™ Make a Folded Chart. (See p. R44.) Label the chart as shown.

Hypothesis:	
Activities	Water Amount
Total=	liters

1. **Form a Hypothesis** How much water do you think you use in a day? Record your prediction on the chart.

2. Write on the chart each activity in which you use water.

3. Use the chart below to see how much water each activity uses.

4. **Use Numbers** Add the number of liters of water used for each activity. Calculate the amount of water used in a day.

5. Compare your results with the prediction. How can you use less water? Write your answer on the back of the chart.

How Much Water Do You Use?

Activity	Normal Use
Showering	95 liters
Bathing	150 liters
Brushing teeth	18 liters
Washing hands	8 liters
Dishwasher	60 liters
Washing clothes	220 liters

Why Should We Conserve Water?

The water cycle helps to replace the water supply. We take water from lakes, streams, and rivers. Could we ever run out of fresh water? We might if we are not careful.

People everywhere should **conserve** (kuhn·SURV) water. To conserve means to use something wisely, not wastefully. By using water wisely, we can save it for when we really need it.

Here are some ways to conserve water. Can you think of other ways?

- Turn off water faucets when you are not using them.
- Fix leaky faucets.
- Water lawns and plants only when they need water.
- Run the washing machine only with a full load of clothes.
- Take short showers instead of long showers or baths.

▷ **How can you conserve water?**

Lesson Review

Why It Matters

Think of all the ways people use water. We drink water, cook with water, bathe in water, and swim in water. We need clean, fresh water for all of these things.

People use a lot of water every day. It is important to use water wisely. How can you conserve water?

ⓔ-Journal Visit our Web site www.science.mmhschool.com to do a research project on water conservation.

Think and Write

1. Where is most of Earth's water? What kind of water is it?

2. People take water from ponds and lakes. Why don't ponds and lakes dry up?

3. Why do people build dams and aqueducts?

4. What is groundwater?

5. **Critical Thinking** Why is it important to conserve water? List some ways you can conserve water.

L·I·N·K·S

MATH LINK

Compare numbers. The chart shows how much five families spend on water in a year. What is the difference between the highest cost and the lowest cost?

Family	Water Cost
Altman	$240
Lee	$187
Colon	$154
Rodriguez	$266
Mathews	$209

WRITING LINK

Writing a Poem Write a poem about water using five lines. The letters that begin all the lines should spell *WATER* when joined together. Your poem does not need to rhyme.

ART LINK

Make a diorama. Show the water cycle or part of the water cycle. Use a shoe box, cotton or foam balls, construction paper, or other materials you like. Do not use water.

TECHNOLOGY LINK

Science Newsroom CD-ROM Choose *Waste Not Want Not* to learn different ways people can conserve water.

LOG ON Visit www.science.mmhschool.com for more links.

Saving Our Resources

Vocabulary

natural
resource, C38
renewable
resource, C40
nonrenewable
resource, C41
pollution, C42

Get Ready

Why do miners dig deep into Earth? They
are looking for useful materials, such as
metals, coal, or diamonds. Useful materials
are called resources. Mining changes the
land. People have been trying to repair the
land. How do you think mining can
change Earth?

Inquiry Skill
You infer when you form an
idea from facts or observations.

Explore Activity

How Does Mining Affect the Land?

Materials

chocolate chip cookie

4 toothpicks

paper towel

Procedure

1 Observe Place the cookie on the paper towel. Draw the cookie, and label its parts. The chips represent resources. The cookie represents the land.

2 Model Use toothpicks to remove the chocolate chips. Try not to damage the cookie. Mine all the resources from the land.

3 Observe Draw the cookie again.

Drawing Conclusions

1 How did mining change the cookie?

2 If you needed more resources than you found in the land, how could you get them?

3 Infer What are some problems people face when they mine resources from Earth?

4 FURTHER INQUIRY **Infer** How can damage to mining areas be repaired? How do you know? Test your ideas on your cookie and report your results.

Main Idea Earth's resources should be used wisely.

What Is a Natural Resource?

A **natural resource** (NACH·uhr·uhl REE·sawrs) is material on Earth that is necessary or useful to people. You use natural resources every day. They keep you alive or make your life better.

Some natural resources come from the air. You take in oxygen, a gas in the air, when you breathe.

Other natural resources come from Earth's surface. Soil is an important resource. Plants grow in soil. All animals need plants for food. Plants and animals are also natural resources. We use them for food, clothing, and many other things.

These oil wells pump oil from deep underground. Oil is found in only a few places on Earth. Oil is refined into gasoline.

Why are plants and animals important natural resources?

Water is one of the most important resources.

Still other natural resources come from below the surface. Fuels such as coal and oil are examples. Minerals such as iron, salt, and copper are, too. Sometimes people dig very deep into the ground to get these resources.

Water is a natural resource that is found above, on, and below Earth's surface. Water is a gas in the air. It falls to the surface as rain or snow. Some of it soaks into the ground, becoming groundwater.

▷ **What natural resources are being shown in these pictures?**

Treated properly, the soil will support crops year after year.

What Is a Renewable Resource?

A **renewable resource** (ri·NEW·uh·buhl REE·sawrs) is a resource that can be replaced or used over and over again. Soil and water are both renewable resources.

Farmers grow crops in soil year after year. Sometimes strong winds blow away soil. Water can wash away soil, too. While soil can be used over and over again, it takes a long time for new soil to form. It is difficult to replace lost or damaged soil. Farmers need to know how to care for soil.

Plants, animals, and water are also renewable resources. New plants are grown. New animals are raised to replace those that we use. Water moves from one part of Earth to another in the water cycle.

▶ **What are three renewable resources?**

Like other plants, trees are a renewable resource. New trees can be planted to replace the ones we use.

What Is a Nonrenewable Resource?

A **nonrenewable resource** (nahn·ri·NEW·uh·buhl REE·sawrs) is a resource that cannot be reused or replaced easily. Once a nonrenewable resource is used up, we cannot get more of it.

Nonrenewable resources include minerals, such as gems and metals. People value gems for their beauty and strength. Metals are very useful. Iron and copper are metals.

Gems are beautiful minerals.

Fossil fuels are also nonrenewable resources. Coal, oil, and natural gas are examples. Fossil fuels take millions of years to form. They also can be hard to find.

Once we find fossil fuels, we often do not keep them for long. We burn them for energy. Then they are gone forever!

▷ **What are two examples of nonrenewable resources?**

Most cars and trucks burn gasoline. Gasoline is made from fossil fuels. Will we always be able to get more gasoline?

What Is Pollution?

As we use Earth's water, air, and land, we add materials to them. When you wash your hands, you rinse soap and dirt into the water. Later, the water is cleaned. Soap and dirt are removed from the water. Sometimes Earth's resources are not cleaned. The result can be a problem called **pollution** (puh·LEW·shuhn). Pollution occurs when harmful materials get into water, air, or land. When resources are polluted, they may be unsafe to use.

Some pollution happens naturally. The water in a lake can become polluted when too much sand or soil settles in it. The lake may become a poor home for fish and plants. Volcanoes and forest fires pollute the air with dust, gas, and ashes.

Humans cause pollution, too. People add things such as soap and *fertilizers* (FUR·tuh·ligh·zuhrz) to water. Fertilizers help plants grow, but they can soak into the ground and pollute water supplies.

Smog is a kind of air pollution. It is a mixture of fog and smoke.

Forest fires cause air and land pollution. Forest fires can occur naturally, or they can be started by humans.

Air pollution is a problem in many cities. Cars, airplanes, and factories may add harmful gases and other materials to the air. Rain may bring these materials to Earth. The polluted rainwater may damage trees and buildings, and pollute water supplies.

Land pollution can be a problem, too. As Earth's population grows, people produce more trash. Trash takes up valuable space.

All living things use Earth's resources. Cleaning up pollution is always a good thing to do.

READING **Sequence of Events**
What is one way the water supply can become polluted?

In the past many people dumped their trash into rivers. Now it is against the law.

QUICK LAB

Cleaning Water

FOLDABLES™ Make a Two-Tab Book. (See p. R41.) Label the book as shown.

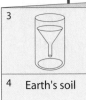

BE CAREFUL! Wear goggles.

1. **Model** Place a funnel inside the bottom half of a plastic bottle. Put a layer of gravel in the funnel, and cover it with a layer of sand.

2. Mix a cup of water with a little soil and some crushed leaves. Slowly pour the mixture into the funnel.

3. **Observe** Draw the mixture on the top tab. Describe how the mixture changed as it went through the funnel. Write your answer under the top tab.

4. How does Earth clean water? Make a diagram on the bottom tab. Write your answer under the tab.

One Person's Trash in a Year

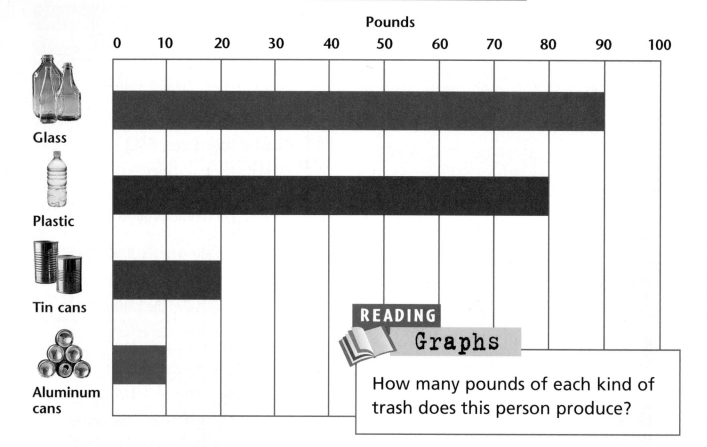

Pounds

| | 0 | 10 | 20 | 30 | 40 | 50 | 60 | 70 | 80 | 90 | 100 |

Glass

Plastic

Tin cans

Aluminum cans

READING

Graphs

How many pounds of each kind of trash does this person produce?

How Can You Conserve Resources?

If we all conserve Earth's resources, we can keep using them in the future. One way to conserve resources is to reduce our use of them. To *reduce* is to use less of something. Try to reduce your use of paper. Use all the pages in a notebook before buying a new one.

Another way to conserve resources is to reuse them. To *reuse* is to use something again and again. You might reuse grocery bags or glass jars.

A third way to conserve is to recycle. To *recycle* is to treat something so that it can be used again. Glass, paper, plastic, and metals can all be recycled.

▷ **What are three ways to conserve resources?**

Recycling lets you use something again. Do you recycle?

Why It Matters

Scientists have learned that certain materials can be recycled. For example, old plastic soft drink bottles can be made into weatherproof picnic benches. Scientists have also learned that some materials, such as gasoline, cannot be used again.

By studying the materials we use, we can learn to conserve our natural resources.

e-Journal Visit our Web site www.science.mmhschool.com to do a research project on conservation.

Think and Write

1. Give three examples of a natural resource. Discuss how each resource is used.

2. Why is water a renewable resource?

3. Why are fossil fuels a nonrenewable resource?

4. Discuss three ways to conserve resources.

5. **Critical Thinking** You bought a present for your friend's birthday. How could you wrap the present in a way that conserves paper?

L·I·N·K·S

LITERATURE LINK

Read *The Old Swimming Hole,* a story about how Nick discovers that a swimming hole has become a garbage dump. Think about something you can do to stop pollution. Try the activities at the end of the book.

WRITING LINK

Explanatory Writing What can you do to show respect for the environment? Think of a project you could do with your family or class to conserve, or save, resources. For example, you could make recycling posters to put up in your neighborhood. Write a paragraph to explain your project.

MATH LINK

Solve a problem. For five days in a row, Eli bundled 9 bags of cans and Erin bundled 3 bags. How many bags had they bundled after the fifth day?

TECHNOLOGY LINK

 LOG ON Visit www.science.mmhschool.com for more links.

CARS OF THE FUTURE

An electric car
travels down a road.

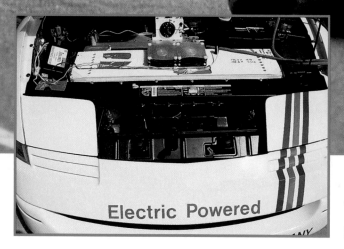

Electric Powered

This electric battery
powers the car.

Most cars today run on gasoline—a mixture of fossil fuels. However, fossil fuels may run out someday. Burning fossil fuel pollutes the air, too.

Are there other ways to power a car? Yes, there are. Cars can run on electricity! Electric cars receive power from batteries. Instead of filling a tank with gasoline, the driver recharges the batteries. Some electric cars use a little gasoline, too. The gasoline helps the batteries last longer.

Scientists have been studying electric cars for a long time. They are looking for ways to improve the cars and to build them more cheaply. By the time you learn to drive, you may be driving an electric car!

A rechargeable battery powers this car.

Today's vehicles rely on gasoline.

LOG ON Visit **www.science.mmhschool.com** to learn more about cars.

 ABOUT IT

1. What are the benefits of electric cars?
2. Do you think you will be driving an electric car someday? Why or why not?

Chapter 5 Review

Vocabulary

Fill each blank with the best word from the list.

condense, C31
conserve, C34
evaporate, C31
fossil, C22
fuel, C26
mineral, C6

natural resource, C38
nonrenewable resource, C41
pollution, C42
soil, C14

1. A substance found in nature that is not a plant or an animal is a(n) _____.

2. _____ is a mixture of tiny rocks, minerals, and decayed materials from plants and animals.

3. The imprint or remains of something that lived long ago is a(n) _____.

4. Something that is burned for its energy is called a(n) _____.

5. A material from Earth that is useful or necessary is a(n) _____.

6. Coal is a(n) _____ because it cannot be reused or replaced in a useful amount of time.

7. Smoke from a fire can cause air _____.

8. To use something wisely, not wastefully is to _____.

Two parts of the water cycle are when water:

9. _____

10. _____

Test Prep

11. The building blocks of rocks are _____.

   A minerals

   B quartz

   C living things

   D soil

12. Which of the following is true about fossils?

   F They tell us about plants of the past.

   G They tell us about animals of the past.

   H They tell us how Earth has changed.

   J All of the above.

13. Most of Earth's water is found in _____.

   A lakes

   B rivers

   C glaciers

   D oceans

14. Natural gas and oil are _____.

    F renewable resources

    G minerals

    H nonrenewable resources

    J formed by glaciers

15. Treating old materials to make them into new products is _____.

    A recycling

    B pollution

    C weathering

    D reusing

Concepts and Skills

16. **Reading in Science** Look at the chart on page C9. Describe the three main ways that rocks form.

17. **Critical Thinking** What if you are going to plant some seeds? Why might you add humus to the soil?

18. INQUIRY SKILL **Measure** Look at the graduated cylinder. How many milliliters of water are in it?

19. **Product Ads** The labels of some laundry soaps tell you that the soaps break down into harmless materials. Why is this good for something that will be put into water?

20. **Scientific Methods** Your kitchen has a leaky faucet. How can you find out how much water is wasted each day?

Did You Ever Wonder?

INQUIRY SKILL **Experiment** Evaluate what you learned about rocks. Plan a test to see which rocks could most easily form caves.

LOG ON Visit **www.science.mmhschool.com** to boost your test scores.

CHAPTER

6

Forces Shape the Land

Did You Ever Wonder?

What forces shaped these rocks? Wind and rain
shaped them over thousands of years. If you could
visit this park a thousand years in the future, what
changes might you see?

INQUIRY SKILL Predict How does Earth's surface
change over time?

Landforms

Vocabulary

landform, C54
mountain, C55
valley, C55
sand dune, C55
plain, C55
river, C55

Get Ready

What is Earth's surface like where you live? Are there mountains or hills? Is the land very flat? Maybe you live where there are lots of lakes or rivers. Maybe you live near a desert.

Earth's surface has many different features. How do you think these features are alike? How are they different?

Inquiry Skill

You **classify** when you place things that share properties together in groups.

Explore Activity

How Do the Features of Earth's Surface Compare?

Procedure

1 **Observe** How are the pictures alike? How are they different? Discuss these questions with a partner.

2 **Classify** Sort the pictures into two groups. Describe how you sorted them.

3 **Classify** Repeat step 2. This time try to sort the pictures into three groups.

Drawing Conclusions

1 What categories did you sort the pictures into?

2 **Infer** For each picture, list some living things that could live in the place shown.

3 FURTHER INQUIRY **Predict** For each picture, predict how the land might change during a year. How might it change after many years?

What Are the Features of Earth's Surface?

A **landform** (LAND·fawrm) is a feature of Earth's surface. Different bodies of water cover large parts of Earth, too.

▷ **What is a landform?**

Features of the Earth

Earth's Landforms

1 **Mountains** (MOUN·tuhnz) are the highest landform. Mountains often have steep sides and pointed tops.

2 **Hills** are shorter and rounder than mountains.

3 A **plateau** (pla·TOH) is flat land with steep sides. It is higher than the land around it.

4 **Mesas** (MAY·suhz) are flat-topped hills or mountains.

5 A **valley** (VAL·ee) is the low land between hills or mountains. Water often rushes down into valleys.

6 A **canyon** (KAN·yuhn) is a deep, narrow valley with steep sides. Canyons often have rivers at the bottom.

7 **Sand dunes** (SAND DEWNZ) are mounds of wind-blown sand.

8 **Plains** (PLAYNZ) are wide, flat lands.

Earth's Water Features

9 **Rivers** (RIV·uhrz) are large streams of water that flow across the land.

10 A **lake** is a body of water with land all around it.

11 **Oceans** are very large bodies of salt water. They cover about three-fourths of Earth's surface.

12 The **coast** is where the ocean meets the land.

13 A **bay** is a part of a lake or ocean that extends into the land.

14 **Glaciers** (GLAY·shuhrz) are huge masses of ice that move slowly across the land.

READING Diagrams

Which features of Earth's surface are found near you?

What Is Earth's Surface Like in the United States?

All of the features you just read about can be found in the United States. The map and pictures show some of these features.

READING **Cause and Effect**
Why is much of the food in the United States grown on the Great Plains?

Lakes
All states have small lakes. The Great Lakes are among Earth's largest lakes.

Coast
Nearly half of the United States borders an ocean.

Mountains
The Rocky Mountains run north to south, and they cover much of the west.

Plains
Ranging between North Dakota and Texas are the Great Plains. Farmers on the Great Plains raise much of the food we eat.

Rivers
Many rivers flow into the Mississippi River. This river empties into the Gulf of Mexico.

Lesson Review

Why It Matters

Wherever you live, the land affects you. The land on the Great Plains is good for growing grains like corn and wheat. Coasts and lakes are good places to go fishing. If you live on a mountain, you need to be good at climbing! Many places in the United States are very special.

e-Journal Visit our Web site **www.science.mmhschool.com** to do a research project on landforms.

Think and Write

1. What is a landform? Give an example.

2. Describe three different ways that water covers Earth's surface.

3. Why are the Great Plains important?

4. How is a mesa different from a plateau?

5. **Critical Thinking** Why do crops grow better on plains and in valleys than on mountains?

L·I·N·K·S

WRITING LINK

Writing a Story There are many ways to explain how the Grand Canyon was formed. Ancient people used stories to explain how it happened. Write a "how story" myth to explain how the Grand Canyon was formed. Draw pictures to help tell your story.

MATH LINK

Compare numbers. Use the table below. Arrange these states in order of shortest coastline to longest.

State	Coastline (in miles)
Alabama	53
Alaska	5,580
California	840
Delaware	28
Florida	1,350

SOCIAL STUDIES LINK

Write a letter. Explain to another person what the land is like where you live. Discuss how the land affects your life.

TECHNOLOGY LINK

 LOG ON Visit **www.science.mmhschool.com** for more links.

LESSON 7

Slow Changes on Land

Vocabulary

weathering, C60
erosion, C62
glacier, C62

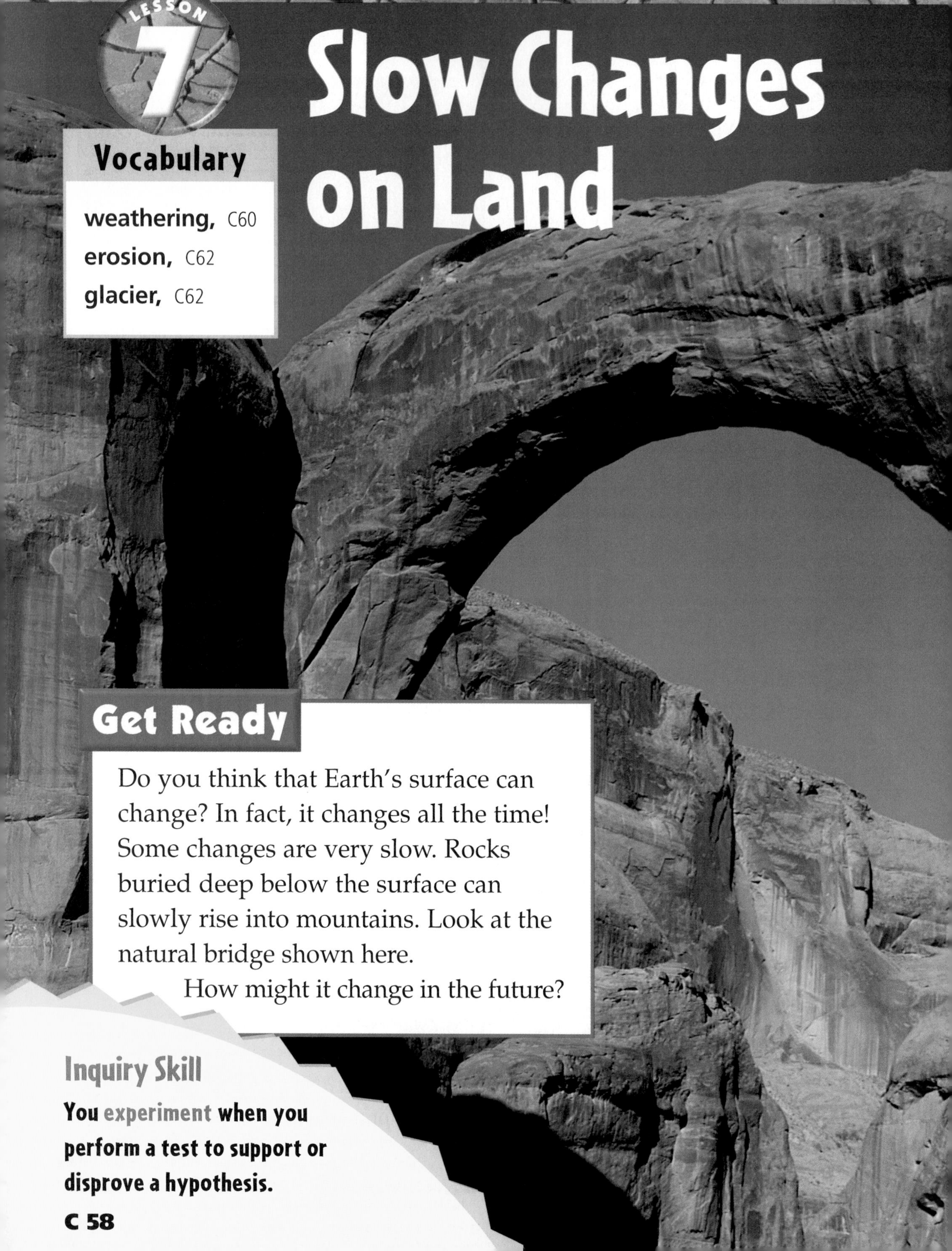

Get Ready

Do you think that Earth's surface can change? In fact, it changes all the time! Some changes are very slow. Rocks buried deep below the surface can slowly rise into mountains. Look at the natural bridge shown here.

How might it change in the future?

Inquiry Skill

You experiment when you perform a test to support or disprove a hypothesis.

Explore Activity

How Do Rocks Change?

Materials

3 pieces of chalk, different colors

sandpaper

Procedure

1. **Observe** Look at the pieces of chalk and the sandpaper. Write down what they look and feel like.

2. **Predict** What do you think will happen when you draw with the chalk on the sandpaper? Record your prediction.

3. **Experiment** Use the chalk to write or draw on the sandpaper.

4. **Observe** Look at how the chalk and the sandpaper changed each other. Record your observations.

Drawing Conclusions

1. What happened to the sandpaper and the chalk?

2. Which material changed more? Tell why you think this happened.

3. **Infer** What might happen when strong winds blow sand over rocks? How would the rocks change?

4. FURTHER INQUIRY
   Experiment What changes might you see in the chalk if you leave it outside for a week or more? Why? Try it to test your ideas.

Main Idea Weathering and erosion change Earth's surface.

How Do Rocks Change?

Even the hardest rocks can break apart. **Weathering** (WETH·uhr·ing) is the process that crumbles, cracks, and breaks rocks. Weathering usually happens slowly and can be hard to see. It may take many years to break a rock.

Weathering can happen in many ways. Rushing water weathers rocks on beaches and river bottoms. Strong winds sometimes blow sand against rocks. Growing plant roots weather rocks, too. This helps change rocks into soil.

Changing temperatures also can weather rocks. Did you know that water takes up more space when it freezes? When water freezes inside a rock, the rock may crack.

Some *chemicals* (KEM·i·kuhlz) weather rocks. Chemicals make up the air, the water, and everything around you. Some can change the minerals in rocks. The rocks may crumble or break.

▷ **What is weathering?**

How are the rocks in these two pictures changing? What is causing this change?

How a Cave Forms

Water runs through cracks in limestone.

Chemicals in the water soften the limestone. Water washes away the weathered rock. A small opening forms.

The process continues. A cave forms.

READING

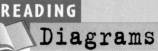
Diagrams

1. Could a cave form without water? Why or why not?

2. Do you think a cave could form in a month? In a year?

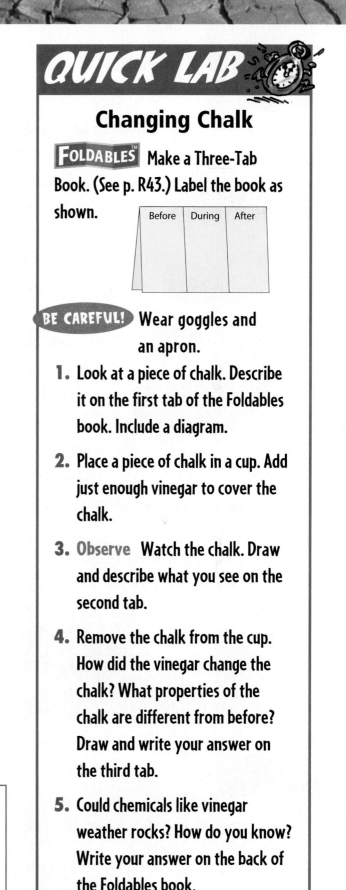

QUICK LAB

Changing Chalk

FOLDABLES™ Make a Three-Tab Book. (See p. R43.) Label the book as shown.

Before	During	After

BE CAREFUL! Wear goggles and an apron.

1. Look at a piece of chalk. Describe it on the first tab of the Foldables book. Include a diagram.

2. Place a piece of chalk in a cup. Add just enough vinegar to cover the chalk.

3. **Observe** Watch the chalk. Draw and describe what you see on the second tab.

4. Remove the chalk from the cup. How did the vinegar change the chalk? What properties of the chalk are different from before? Draw and write your answer on the third tab.

5. Could chemicals like vinegar weather rocks? How do you know? Write your answer on the back of the Foldables book.

What Happens to Weathered Rocks?

Weathered rocks and other weathered materials don't stay in one place. They are moved around in a process called **erosion** (i·ROH·zhuhn). Erosion occurs when weathered materials are carried away. Like weathering, erosion is often a slow process.

Erosion happens all around you. Rivers and streams carry weathered rocks over long distances. Gravity can pull rocks down mountains and hills. Strong winds blow soil and sand.

A **glacier** (GLAY·shuhr) can cause erosion, too. A glacier is a huge mass of moving ice. Gravity may move a glacier from high land to low land. A glacier may also spread over flat land. Wherever it goes, it moves rocks and other things in its path.

Gravity, helped by wind or animals, may move these rocks down the mountain.

▷ **When does erosion occur?**

Glaciers form when more snow falls than melts away. When glaciers become large enough, they creep downhill.

How Do People Change Earth's Surface?

How is the land changing?

People change Earth's surface every day. Some changes are very small, like digging a hole in your backyard. Other changes are larger.

In some places, people want more land. To make room, sometimes forests are cut down. In the past, wetlands sometimes were drained. Wetlands are ponds and swamps. Today most wetlands are protected by environmental laws.

Roads change Earth, too. Builders may dig into hills or mountains so that a road can cross. When it rains, roads and parking lots do not let water soak through. The water rushes away instead.

We need to change Earth's surface for many reasons. By changing it wisely, we can keep Earth a wonderful place to live.

Builders need to dig rocks out of mountains to make room for roads.

READING **Cause and Effect**
How do people cause changes in Earth's surface?

Inquiry Skill
BUILDER

SKILL Form a Hypothesis

Which Materials Settle First?

What happens to materials that are carried away by erosion? In this activity you will model an experiment that finds the answer. The first step in the experiment is to form a hypothesis. A hypothesis is an answer to a question that can be tested.

Materials

large plastic jar with a lid

measuring cup

pebbles

sand

soil

water

Procedure

1 **Observe** Look at the pebbles, soil, and sand. Describe each of these materials. How do they compare with one another?

2 **Form a Hypothesis** When pebbles, sand, and soil are mixed together with water, how do they settle? Which material forms the bottom layer? Which forms the top? Form a hypothesis that answers these questions.

3 **Experiment** Pour one cup of each material into the jar. Fill the jar almost to the top with water. Seal the jar tightly with a lid. Shake the jar.

4 **Observe** Let the jar sit for several hours. Observe the contents of the jar. Record your observations.

Drawing Conclusions

1 Compare the results of the experiment with your hypothesis. Did the results support your hypothesis?

2 Which material settled first? Which materials settled second and last? How do you know?

3 **Interpret Data** Repeat this activity. Compare these results with the results from the first time. What happened when you repeated the activity? Compare your findings with a classmate's. What did you find out? Summarize your findings.

Why It Matters

Earth's surface is changing. Weathering and erosion usually are slow changes. Cutting forests can speed up these changes. In many places people are planting forests. They are also letting water fill low areas, making wetlands. By taking care of Earth, we can keep it a good home.

e-Journal Visit our Web site www.science.mmhschool.com to do a research project on erosion.

Think and Write

1. List three things that cause weathering.

2. List three things that cause erosion.

3. Describe two slow processes that change Earth's surface.

4. **INQUIRY SKILL** **Form a Hypothesis** Would clay or sand be more easily washed away by rain?

5. **Critical Thinking** Ted built a sidewalk from rocks. He lives where the winters are cold. How might the sidewalk change over time?

L·I·N·K·S

SOCIAL STUDIES LINK

Use a map. Glaciers are found in only some places in the United States. Use maps to find three glaciers. Research what they are like.

MATH LINK

Compare sand, pebbles, and rocks. Gather three cups that are exactly the same. Fill one cup with rocks. Fill the second cup with pebbles. Fill the third cup with sand. Next, add water to each cup until the water reaches the top.

Predict which cup holds the least water. Explain your prediction. To find the answer, hold the rocks or sand back as you pour the water into a measuring cup.

WRITING LINK

Writing That Compares Thousands of years ago, caves were important to  humans. What might it be like if you lived in a cave? Describe your daily activities. Compare them to your activities today.

TECHNOLOGY LINK

LOG ON Visit www.science.mmhschool.com for more links.

ERASING EROSION

Soil is very important, especially on farms. Crops need rich soil to help them grow. Wind and rain can wash away, or erode, farm soil. Farmers try to slow erosion and protect their farmland.

During the 1930s the Great Plains were very dry. Most plants in Kansas died. Dust storms carried away loose soil. Now farmers plant trees and terrace hillsides to keep the soil in place.

Terrace (TER·is) farming protects the soil. "Shelves" are cut into the sides of a hill. The flat shelves hold rainwater better than a steep hillside!

People fight erosion. They reseed the prairies and terrace the farmland in hilly fields.

Contour (KAHN·tewr) farming protects the soil, too. Crops are planted around hills in rows. Each row soaks up rainwater as it runs down the hill.

Rows of trees can be planted between crop fields. The trees help break the force of the wind. Gentle winds don't carry away as much soil as strong winds.

Cover crops can help save soil. These crops are not for harvesting. They are planted in empty fields. Their roots hold the soil in place during storms.

LOG ON Visit www.science.mmhschool.com to learn more about erosion.

What Did I Learn?

1. What is one way of controlling erosion?

   A terrace farming
   B planting cover crops in empty fields
   C planting rows of trees to slow the wind
   D all of the above

2. Contour farming and terrace farming both

   F carry away rich soil.
   G follow the shape of the land.
   H rely on trees to block the wind.
   J speed up erosion.

Fast Changes on Land

Get Ready

What do you think has happened to the land under this house? Sometimes land can change in just a few hours. How do you think Earth's land changes in a gentle rain? How do you think it changes in heavy rain?

Inquiry Skill

You make a model when you make something to represent an object or an event.

Explore Activity

How Do Gentle and Heavy Rains Change Earth's Land?

Materials

2 trays

soil and sand mixture

water

spray bottle

cup

Procedure: Design Your Own

1. **Make a Model** Pour equal amounts of the mixture into two trays. At one end of each tray, pat the mixture to model a hill. Make both hills alike. Draw a picture of the two lands you modeled.

2. **Form a Hypothesis** Do gentle or heavy rains change Earth's land more? Work with a classmate. Decide on a plan to test your hypothesis, using available materials.

3. **Experiment** Carry out your plan. Draw the two lands as they look at the end of the experiment.

Drawing Conclusions

1. How do the two lands you modeled compare?

2. Which kind of rainfall causes more erosion?

3. FURTHER INQUIRY **Observe** You experimented on model landforms. How do you think your results compare with changes in the real world? Observe changes in the land after gentle and heavy rains. Compare these examples of erosion to changes in this activity.

Main Idea Storms, earthquakes, volcanoes, and other events change Earth's surface quickly.

Hurricane damage from Hurricane Andrew

How Can Land Change Quickly?

Violent weather, such as hurricanes, tornadoes, and floods, can change Earth's surface quickly.

A **hurricane** (HUR·i·kayn) is a violent storm with strong winds and heavy rains. Hurricanes are the largest and most powerful of all storms. They form over the oceans, where they can become many, many miles wide. Their winds move in a circle pattern at speeds of 125 kilometers (approximately 78 miles) per hour or more!

Most hurricanes die out before they reach land. Those that move over the land act like giant bulldozers. Rain, wind, and giant waves damage or destroy most things in their path. Houses, bridges, roads, and cars may be swept away. Trees are uprooted, and lives can be lost. Coastlines can be changed and soil eroded quickly—often in a few minutes or hours.

A **tornado** (tawr·NAY·doh) is a small, powerful windstorm over land. It looks like a giant funnel. Winds swirl very fast in a tornado, sometimes 240 kilometers (approximately 150 miles) per hour or faster. Tornadoes may travel for many miles, damaging houses, other buildings, and anything else in their path.

A **flood** is a huge flow of water over land that is usually dry. Heavy rains can cause floods, as can melting snow or breaking dams. Rivers that normally hold back water overflow their banks. Floods can carry away rocks and soil, and destroy plants, houses, and buildings.

READING Cause and Effect

How do hurricanes, tornadoes, and floods change the land?

Most tornadoes form in wide, flat places.

QUICK LAB

Weather Adds Up

FOLDABLES™ Make a Folded Table. (See p. R44.) Label the table as shown.

Weather	New York, U.S.A	Cairo, Egypt	My City
Average Winter Temperature	0°	15°C	
Average Yearly Rainfall	107 cm	0-10 cm	

1. **Interpret Data** Look at the table below. Record the data on your Foldables table. What is the difference in winter temperatures between the two cities? Which city has more rainfall?

2. On your Foldables table, add weather information about the place where you live. How does the weather in each city compare with the weather where you live?

3. **Infer** A stone monument was moved to New York City from Egypt. The surface of the monument changed very quickly in New York. Why do you think this happened? Write your answer on the back of your table.

Weather in New York City and Cairo

	New York, USA	Cairo, Egypt
Average winter temperature	0°C	15°C
Average yearly rainfall	107 cm	0 to 10 cm

How Do Earthquakes and Volcanoes Change the Land?

Another event that changes Earth's surface quickly is an **earthquake** (URTH·kwayk). An earthquake is a sudden movement in the rocks that make up Earth's crust.

Earthquakes begin far below the surface. Forces within Earth build up, then break Earth's rocks suddenly. The breaking rocks shake the ground above them.

Some earthquakes are so weak that they can hardly be felt. Others are very strong. Strong earthquakes crack roads and cause buildings to fall. When earthquakes strike cities, they can cause great damage. Power lines and water pipes can break. Fires can start and be hard to put out.

Earthquakes may cause landslides, too. The earthquake loosens the rocks on the side of a mountain or hill. The land tumbles down, burying or sweeping aside things in its path. Landslides can also come from melting snow or heavy rains.

This damage to a road in Oakland, California, was caused during the 1989 earthquake.

This house was damaged in a landslide.

Other kinds of sudden changes come from **volcanoes** (vahl·KAY·nohz). A volcano is an opening in Earth's surface. The word *volcano* is also the name of the mountain that builds up around this opening.

Sometimes melted rock, gases, and pieces of rock and dust are forced out of a volcano. This event is called an eruption. Some volcanoes may stay quiet for hundreds of years, then erupt suddenly. Other volcanoes erupted in the past but will never erupt again.

The ash, gases, and melted rock from volcanoes can cause a lot of damage. Melted rock that flows onto the ground is called *lava*. Lava can cover everything in its path and start fires.

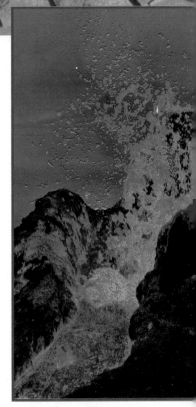

Lava is melted rock that is very, very hot.

▷ **What are earthquakes and volcanoes?**

How a Volcano Forms

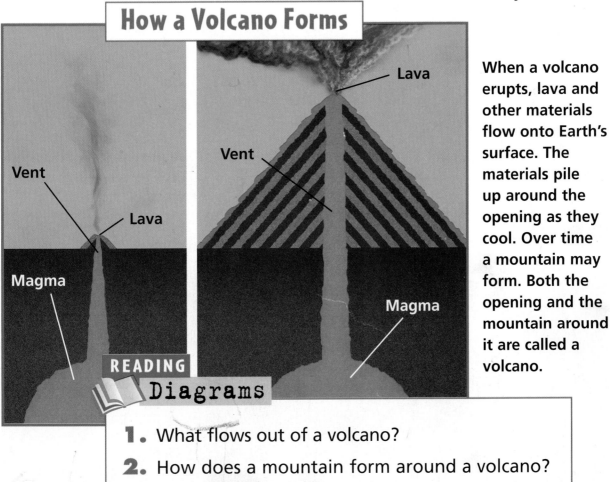

Vent

Lava

Magma

Vent

Lava

Magma

When a volcano erupts, lava and other materials flow onto Earth's surface. The materials pile up around the opening as they cool. Over time a mountain may form. Both the opening and the mountain around it are called a volcano.

READING

Diagrams

1. What flows out of a volcano?

2. How does a mountain form around a volcano?

How Can Erosion Work Quickly?

Remember that erosion is the carrying away of soil, sand, and other weathered materials. Usually erosion changes the land slowly. Sometimes, however, erosion causes fast changes.

The photo shows piles of sand called *dunes*. At beaches and other sandy places, winds blow sand into sand dunes. These dunes do not stay the same for long. As the wind changes, they become smaller or larger, or shift position.

Wind can also blow loose soil. Usually plants hold soil in place. In the 1930s, however, dry weather in the Great Plains killed many crops. The soil became very dry and turned to dust. When strong winds came, they blew thick, black clouds of dust across the plains. People called the plains the Dust Bowl.

Today farmers know better ways to plant crops and to care for soil. No one wants to see huge dust storms again!

▷ **What is the Dust Bowl?**

These sand dunes are at the beach.

The dust storms of the 1930s forced many farmers from their homes.

Why It Matters

Volcanoes, earthquakes, tornadoes, and hurricanes can quickly change Earth's landforms. They can also cause a great deal of damage.

e-Journal Visit our Web site www.science.mmhschool.com to do a research project on earthquakes and volcanoes.

Think and Write

1. Describe three events that cause sudden changes in the land.

2. Describe how earthquakes change the Earth.

3. How can a mountain build around a volcano?

4. What caused the dust storms of the 1930s?

5. **Critical Thinking** Of the storms and events discussed in this lesson, which could strike where you live? Which could not strike? Explain your answer.

L·I·N·K·S

WRITING LINK

Persuasive Writing Have you lived through a bad storm? If not, ask a friend or adult who has. Then write a public service announcement that tells how to prepare for a storm. Tell how the storm changes people, plants, animals, or the land.

LITERATURE LINK

Read *The Hurricane Hero* to learn about Joe Duckworth. He was the first person to fly an airplane right into the center of a hurricane. Try the activities at the end of the book.

The Hurricane Hero

Written by Robin Bloksberg
Illustrated by Linda Graves

MATH LINK

Make a bar graph. The Richter scale rates earthquakes according to their magnitude, or size. Use research materials or the Internet to find the magnitude of five major earthquakes. Use this information to make a bar graph.

TECHNOLOGY LINK

LOG ON Visit www.science.mmhschool.com for more links.

Vocabulary

Fill each blank with the best word from the list.

earthquake, C72   **plain,** C55
glacier, C62   **river,** C55
hurricane, C70   **valley,** C55
landform, C54   **volcano,** C73
mountain, C55   **weathering,** C60

1. A violent storm with wind and heavy rain is a(n) _____.

2. Any feature on Earth's surface is called a(n) _____.

3. A huge mass of ice and snow that moves is a(n) _____.

4. An opening in Earth's crust through which melted rock and other materials are forced out is a(n) _____.

5. Any process that causes rocks to crack, crumble, and break is _____.

6. A sudden movement in the rocks that make up Earth's crust is called a(n) _____.

Write the name of the landform on the line where it belongs.

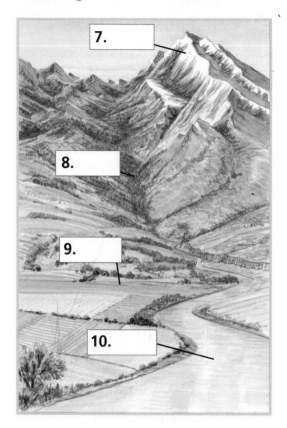

7.

8.

9.

10.

Test Prep

11. How are hills different from mountains and plateaus?

A Hills are smaller than mountains and plateaus.

B Hills are taller than mountains and plateaus.

C Hills have pointed tops.

D Hills are homes for animals.

12. Both weathering and erosion cause _____.

    F changes in Earth's surface

    G landforms to keep the same shape over time

    H new types of rocks to form

    J plants to grow

13. Hurricanes often cause _____.

    A earthquakes

    B rocks to break

    C soil to be washed away

    D caves to form

14. An earthquake is a sudden movement in the rocks that _____.

    F are inside glaciers

    G make up mountains

    H make up Earth's crust

    J rest along the bottom of Earth's lakes and oceans

15. Melted rock that flows out of the ground during a volcanic eruption is called _____.

    A dust

    B erosion

    C lava

    D limestone

Concepts and Skills

16. Reading in Science You see an old, crumbled stone wall. Why is it falling apart?

17. Critical Thinking Where do you think more erosion will happen—in a low-lying forest or on a mountainside? Why?

18. INQUIRY SKILL **Form a Hypothesis** How do you think a river and a valley could be related? Write a hypothesis.

19. Scientific Methods Would clay or sand be washed away more easily by rain? Design an experiment to find out.

20. Decision Making There is a sign that reads, "Keep Off the Dunes." Your friend wants to walk through the dunes. What do you do?

Did You Ever Wonder?

INQUIRY SKILL **Communicate** You have seen how landforms change. Explore one of the causes of change and report on how it has affected your environment.

LOG ON Visit www.science.mmhschool.com to boost your test scores.

Meet a Scientist

Cindy Lee Van Dover

Oceanographer

Cindy Lee Van Dover grew up near the ocean beaches of New Jersey. There she watched horseshoe crabs wash onto the shore. "They looked like they should be living on another planet," she says.

Watching those crabs steered Ms. Van Dover toward her career. She is an oceanographer—a scientist who studies the oceans. "I thought that the strangest animals might live deep in the sea." Years later she learned about some of those animals. She discovered "giant clams, giant worms, and lots of other cool stuff!" she says.

Van Dover travels to the sea floor in a tiny submarine called *Alvin*. At the ocean bottom, she studies vents, or openings, in the sea floor. The vents are hot-water springs. They give off chemicals from inner Earth. Creatures that live near these vents get their energy from the chemicals.

"Tiny organisms grow there. So it's possible they can grow without sunlight in other environments, such as Mars." Is there a connection between the deepest ocean and deepest space? According to Van Dover, there just might be!

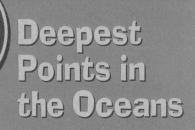

TOP 5 Deepest Points in the Oceans

Here are the deepest places in Earth's oceans.

1. Pacific Ocean: Mariana Trench, 36,198 feet
2. Atlantic Ocean: Puerto Rico Trench, 28,232 feet
3. Southern Ocean: South Sandwich Trench, 23,737 feet
4. Indian Ocean: Java Trench, 23,376 feet
5. Arctic Ocean: Eurasia Basin, 17,881 feet

Write About It

1. How did watching horseshoe crabs turn Van Dover into a scientist?
2. Why might there be a link between the deepest oceans and Mars?

LOG ON Visit www.science.mmhschool.com to learn more about oceanography.

RECYCLE and Reuse

Your goal is to demonstrate how a group of used objects can be reused to do something else.

What to Do

Look at a group of used items. Think of a way to use the items to do something different. For example you could reuse an old plastic bag as a waterproof liner for your book bag. You could reuse a soft drink bottle as a piggy bank. Write down your ideas. Pick one idea and try it.

Draw Conclusions

Why is recycling or reusing something better than throwing it away? Write a paragraph to answer this question.

• •

Form a Landform

Your goal is to make a model of three different kinds of landforms.

What to Do

Write down the name of three different kinds of landforms. Tell what you know about how each landform was formed. Draw pictures of the landforms, or use modeling clay or other art materials to model them.

Draw Conclusions

How might the three landforms change over time?

UNIT D

Cycles on Earth and in Space

Cycles on Earth and in Space

LOOK!

The Moon moves around Earth. How do you think Earth moves through space

Earth's Weather

Did You Ever Wonder?

How does snow form? Snow is not frozen rain. Snow forms when water in the gas state, called water vapor, changes directly into ice crystals. As the crystals fall to Earth, they combine to form snowflakes. No two snowflakes are alike.

INQUIRY SKILL Form a Hypothesis How does water get into the air?

D 3

The Weather

Vocabulary

atmosphere, D6
weather, D6
temperature, D8
air pressure, D9

Get Ready

Here's a puzzle to solve. The picture may help you. Name something that is matter but that you cannot see. Here's a hint. It's helping these kites fly. If you answered "Air," you are right. How do you know air is matter?

Inquiry Skill

You **communicate** when you share information.

D 4

Explore Activity

How Can You Show That Air Is Real?

Materials

plastic container

plastic cup

water

paper towels

Procedure

1. Fill the container about half full with water. Put a dry paper towel completely inside the cup.

2. Hold the cup upside down. Push the cup to the bottom of the container. Be careful not to tilt the cup.

3. **Observe** Remove the cup from the water. Remember to be careful not to tilt the cup. Look at the towel. Record your findings.

4. **Observe** Again, hold the cup upside down, and push it to the bottom of the container. This time slowly tilt the cup. Record your findings.

Drawing Conclusions

1. What happened to the towel in step 3? In step 4?

2. What keeps water from filling the cup?

3. Is air matter? How can you tell?

4. **FURTHER INQUIRY**
   Communicate How would this activity work on the Moon? Explain.

Main Idea Three characteristics of the weather are air temperature, air pressure, and wind.

Where Is Air?

You cannot taste, smell, or see air. So, how can you tell if air is matter? Wave a plastic sandwich bag around, and close it. There is something in the bag. That something is air.

Air is all around you. Air surrounds the entire Earth. The air that surrounds Earth is called the **atmosphere** (AT·muhs·feer). The atmosphere is made up of different gases and dust. Some of the dust comes from fires and volcanoes on Earth.

What do we know about Earth's atmosphere? It is made up of layers. Each layer has its own characteristics. The layer closest to the surface of Earth is called the *troposphere* (TRAHP·uh·sfeer). All life on Earth exists here. This is where **weather** (WETH·uhr) takes place. Weather is what the air is like at a given time and place.

▷ **What makes up the atmosphere?**

Layers of the Atmosphere

Thermosphere
The thermosphere is the top layer of the atmosphere. Light displays called the *northern lights* happen here.

Mesosphere
The mesosphere is between the stratosphere and the thermosphere.

Stratosphere
In the stratosphere the air is not still. Very strong winds called the *jet stream* are located here.

Troposphere
The troposphere is the layer of the atmosphere closest to Earth. In this layer clouds, rain, snow, and thunderstorms occur.

READING
Diagrams

1. Which layer is the airplane in?

2. Where does weather take place?

What Is Air Temperature?

What do you say when you go outside on a hot summer day? You say, "It is hot." The *it* is the air.

The Sun heats the air, so it feels hot. It has a high **temperature** (TEM·puhr·uh·chuhr). Temperature is a measure of how hot or cold something is. The Sun also heats Earth's surface—both the land and the water.

Air temperature is always changing. You know that it is usually warmer during the day than at night. The Sun heats Earth and the air.

How can you measure temperature? You need to use a *thermometer*. The diagram at the right shows you how to read a thermometer.

Does all the air around Earth get the same amount of heat from the Sun? Not really. Places near Earth's North and South Poles do not get as much sunlight as places near the equator. The Sun stays low in the sky near the poles. This is one reason why it is warmer near the equator than near the poles.

▷ **What heats the air?**

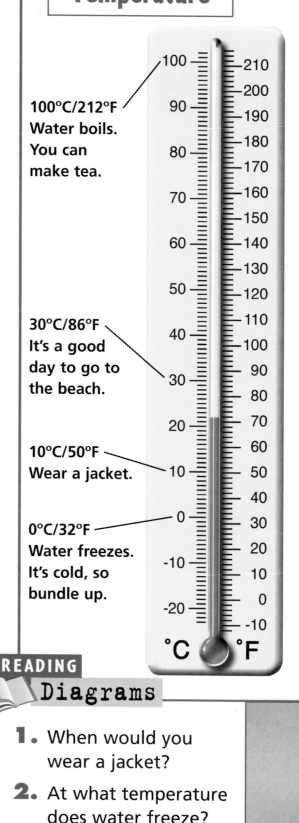

Measuring Air Temperature

100°C/212°F
Water boils. You can make tea.

30°C/86°F
It's a good day to go to the beach.

10°C/50°F
Wear a jacket.

0°C/32°F
Water freezes. It's cold, so bundle up.

READING Diagrams

1. When would you wear a jacket?
2. At what temperature does water freeze?

What Is Air Pressure?

The weight of the atmosphere presses on you all the time. It presses on everything on Earth. The pressing down force of the air on Earth is called **air pressure**.

Do you feel air pressure? Not usually. Your body is used to air pressure. You don't even notice it most of the time. However, you can notice when air pressure changes. What happens when you drive up mountain roads? Your ears "pop." This pop is caused by a change in air pressure pushing on your eardrum. You may also feel your ears pop if you ride in an elevator or fly in an airplane.

▶ **What is air pressure?**

As climbers scale a mountain, the air pressure changes.

QUICK LAB

Mighty Air

FOLDABLES Make a Two-Tab Book. (See p. R41.) Mark the book as shown.

1. Place a ruler on a desk. Half of the ruler should be hanging off the edge of the desk. Draw the set-up on the left tab.

2. **Observe** Carefully hit the edge of the ruler that is hanging off the desk with your hand. What happens? Record your answer under the left tab.

3. Cover the ruler with a page of newspaper. Draw the set-up on the right tab.

4. **Predict** What do you think will happen when the ruler is hit? Record your predictions on the right tab.

5. **Observe** Hit the ruler again. What happens? Write down your findings under the right tab.

What Happens When Air Moves?

Air moves from an area of high pressure to an area of lower pressure. This moving air is called *wind*.

What if you pour two cups of water toward each other in a sink? What happens when they meet? The water mixes and may even churn and bubble. When two different bodies of air meet, they also mix. Large bodies of air are called air masses. The place where different masses of air meet is where most weather changes happen. Here it may be cloudy or rainy or stormy.

A windsock is a common sight at an airport. It measures the direction of the wind.

READING **Summarize**
What happens when two different air masses meet?

The Movement of Air

A sea breeze blows from the water onto the shore. It occurs during the day when the air over the water is cooler than the air over the land. Cooler air has higher pressure. Air moves from an area of high pressure to an area of lower pressure.

A land breeze blows from the land onto the water. It occurs during the night when the air over the land is cooler than the air over the water. Cooler air has higher pressure. Air moves from an area of high pressure to an area of lower pressure.

D 10

L·I·N·K·S

Why It Matters

Weather changes from day to day. Weather also changes over the course of the seasons. Weather can be observed by measuring temperature. Weather can also be observed by describing cloud formations.

e-Journal Visit our Web site www.science.mmhschool.com to do a research project on weather.

Think and Write

1. Name two properties of air.

2. What do you use to measure temperature?

3. What is air pressure?

4. What is wind?

5. **Critical Thinking** How can changes in the weather affect your day?

Expository Writing Observe the weather in your area for a week. Measure the air temperature with a thermometer. Also, describe the cloud formations. Write down your notes in your journal. Use your findings to write a report.

Make a data chart. Use research materials or the Internet to find the average monthly temperature where you live. Record the information for each month of the year on a chart. What do you notice about the temperature patterns throughout the year?

Create a weather picture. People often say it is raining "cats and dogs" when it is raining very hard. Draw a picture of some strange weather. Write a few sentences to describe your picture.

LOG ON Visit www.science.mmhschool.com for more links.

Extreme Weather

Have you been through a hurricane? a flood? a tornado? If you have, you'll never forget it.

Tornadoes, hurricanes, and floods are natural disasters. They can destroy roads, bridges, homes, and schools. It is important to know when events like these are coming. They can be dangerous!

Tornadoes form on hot summer days. Thunderstorms whip air high up into the clouds. The rushing air spins rapidly as it rises. The spinning winds can reach 300 miles per hour! A tornado this strong will destroy anything in its path. It can pick up a car and throw it blocks away! The best way to protect yourself is to go below ground.

Hurricanes are the largest storms on Earth. Circular winds form over the ocean. As they move over warm water, they get stronger. Scientists can track a hurricane for weeks. That gives people several days to prepare.

Powerful winds can destroy everything in their path.

A hurricane's fierce winds can knock out electricity. Its heavy rains can turn roads into rivers. People should leave low lying areas. They should store bottled water, canned food, and fresh batteries for flashlights and radios.

Floods are the most common of all natural disasters. They can be caused by heavy rains or melting snow. Rivers and streams overflow their banks. Water rushes through low-lying areas. Sometimes floods can help by bringing rich soil to farmlands. But nobody wants to see homes washed away or buried under mud!

Weather satellite photos like this one can track hurricanes and give people time to get out of the way.

Write About It

1. How should you prepare for a hurricane?

2. Where is the safest place to go if a tornado is near?

LOG ON Visit www.science.mmschool.com to learn more about extreme weather.

The Water Cycle

Vocabulary

water vapor, D17

evaporation, D17

condensation, D17

water cycle, D18

precipitation, D19

Get Ready

Can you see all of the Golden Gate Bridge? Where do you think the fog that hides it came from? Fog is a cloud that forms near the ground. What are clouds made of?

Inquiry Skill

You make a model when you make something to represent an object or event.

Explore Activity

How Do Raindrops Form?

Materials

clear-plastic jar

plastic wrap

rubber band

marble

ice cubes

warm water

Procedure

1. Fill the jar one-fourth full of warm water.

2. Place plastic wrap over the top of the jar. Use a rubber band to seal the wrap to the jar.

3. Set a marble in the center of the plastic wrap.

4. **Make a Model** Place several small pieces of ice on top of the plastic wrap. You have made a model of Earth. The warm water represents a lake, and the air above it represents the air around Earth.

5. **Observe** Carefully watch the bottom of the plastic wrap. Record your observations.

Drawing Conclusions

1. What did you see inside the jar?

2. Where did the water come from to make the raindrops?

3. **Infer** Do you think water might go into the air faster during the day or the night? Why?

4. **FURTHER INQUIRY** **Infer** What do you think would have happened if you had poured cold water into the jar instead of warm water? Try it.

Main Idea The water cycle is the path water follows on Earth.

Where Does Water Go?

Have you ever seen tiny droplets of water on a bathroom mirror? Where did the droplets come from? Are you surprised to learn that they came from the air?

Everything around you is made up of something called *matter*. Air, water, and this book are all made of matter. Matter can be found in three different forms—solid, liquid, and gas.

A solid is a form of matter that has a definite shape and takes up a definite amount of space. A book is an example of a solid.

A liquid takes up a definite amount of space but does not have a definite shape. A liquid takes the shape of its container. This pitcher of juice is a liquid.

A gas has no definite size or shape. It spreads out to fill the container that holds it. Think of a balloon. The air inside the balloon spreads out to fill the entire balloon.

This journal is a solid.

The juice in this pitcher is a liquid.

Inside this balloon is helium. Helium is a gas.

Water is matter that can be a solid, a liquid, or a gas. How can you change the form of matter?

After it rains, there are puddles in the street. The next day they are gone. Where did the water go? The water went into the air above. When this happens, the water changes. It changes from a liquid into a gas. This gas is **water vapor**. The changing of a liquid into a gas is called **evaporation** (i·vap·uh·RAY·shuhn).

Have you ever seen water droplets on the inside of a window? These water droplets did not come from rain. They came from the air itself! When water vapor in the air cools, it changes back into liquid water. The change of a gas into a liquid is called **condensation** (kahn·den·SAY·shuhn).

Where did the water droplets on this web come from?

READING Summarize
What happens during the process of evaporation?

Where might the water in this lake go?

What Is the Water Cycle?

Animals and plants use water every day to survive. Where do they get the water they need? They get the water from one or more parts of the **water cycle**. The water cycle is the never-ending path water takes between Earth and the atmosphere.

The Water Cycle

Water condenses
As water vapor rises into the air, it cools. The cooled water vapor changes back into liquid water drops. The liquid water drops form clouds.

Water evaporates
The Sun heats the water in the oceans and on land. The water changes from a liquid into water vapor.

Water evaporates into the air, condenses into clouds, and returns to Earth as **precipitation** (pri·sip·i·TAY·shuhn). Precipitation is water that returns to Earth from the atmosphere. It can be in the form of rain, snow, sleet, or hail.

▶ **What is the water cycle?**

Precipitation
When enough water has condensed in clouds, the water falls to Earth as precipitation. Precipitation can be in the form of rain, snow, sleet, or hail. The form of precipitation depends mainly on the temperature.

Water on the ground
Some precipitation flows downhill into lakes, rivers, and oceans. Some falls directly into these bodies of water. Some precipitation soaks into the ground. This water is called *groundwater*.

READING
Diagrams

1. What part of the water cycle is easy to see?

2. Why is this path of water called a cycle?

Inquiry Skill
BUILDER

SKILL Make a Model and Infer

How Does Temperature Affect Evaporation?

Does the temperature of the air affect evaporation? How could you find out? In this activity you will make a model and then infer to investigate this question.

Materials

water

2 plastic cups

marker

Procedure

1 **Make a Model** Fill each cup half full with water. Use the marker to show where the water level is.

2 Place one cup in a warm place. Place the other cup in a cool place.

3 **Predict** In which cup will the water level change the most? Record your prediction.

4 **Observe** Look at the cups every day for one week. Measure the water depth in the cups. Record your measurements. How did the amount of water change?

Drawing Conclusions

1 **Infer** Where did the water go?

2 How did the amount of water differ after two days?

3 How does this compare with your prediction?

4 **Infer** How could you use this model to make seawater drinkable?

L·I·N·K·S

Why It Matters

Water is one of our most important resources. You need to drink fresh water every day. Plants and animals need water, too. The water cycle is nature's way of recycling. The continuous movement of water through the water cycle provides us with fresh, clean water.

e-Journal Visit our Web site www.science.mmhschool.com to do a research project on the water cycle.

Think and Write

1. What is water vapor?

2. Why does a puddle seem to disappear?

3. What determines whether precipitation is rain or snow?

4. INQUIRY SKILL **Make a Model** Draw a picture to show evaporation and condensation.

5. Critical Thinking What do you think might happen if there were no water cycle?

MATH LINK

Solve a problem. Ten inches of snow is approximately equal to one inch of rain. If it snowed five inches, how much rain would that be?

ART LINK

Create a poster. Make a list of the different ways you can use water. Then find or draw pictures of these ways. Use them to make a poster.

WRITING LINK

Writing a Poem Write the words *water cycle* in a word ladder down the side of a sheet of paper. Think of words that describe the water cycle and that begin with each letter in the two words. Arrange these words into a poem.

TECHNOLOGY LINK

LOG ON Visit www.science.mmhschool.com for more links.

Describing Weather

Get Ready

Look outside. Is it sunny? Is it raining? When you were outside, how did it feel? What is the weather like where you live? How do you measure the conditions of the air? For example, how can you measure air temperature?

Inquiry Skill

You measure when you find the temperature and air pressure.

Explore Activity

How Do You Measure Temperature?

Procedure

1 **Predict** Where do you think the air temperature in your classroom is the highest and the lowest? Record your predictions.

2 **Measure** Use a thermometer to find the air temperature at several places in the classroom. Then read and record the temperature. Remember to include the places in your predictions.

3 How did your measurements compare with your predictions?

Drawing Conclusions

1 What was the warmest spot in your classroom? What was the coolest spot in your classroom?

2 **Communicate** Use the measurements to make a bar graph.

3 FURTHER INQUIRY Predict What if you were doing this activity outside? Predict where you think the air temperature would be the highest and the lowest. Test your predictions.

Main Idea Temperature, air pressure, and wind speed can be measured.

How Do You Describe Weather?

When scientists describe weather, they measure temperature, air pressure, and amount of precipitation. They also measure the speed and direction of the wind.

You measure the temperature of the air with a thermometer. These pictures show the main weather instruments and what they measure.

A **thermometer** (thuhr·MAHM·i·tuhr) measures the temperature of the air. Indoor-outdoor thermometers give the air temperature both inside the house and outside at the same time.

A *rain gauge* measures how much precipitation has fallen.

A **barometer** (buh·RAHM·i·tuhr) measures air pressure. If the reading on the barometer is rising, it usually means fair weather is coming. A falling barometer reading usually means precipitation is on its way.

READING **Summarize**
What instruments do you use to describe weather?

A *weather vane* indicates the direction of the wind. The arrowhead tells you where the wind is coming from.

Make a Rain Gauge

FOLDABLES™ Make a Three-Tab Book. (See p. R43.) Mark the book as shown.

1. Use a plastic jar as a rain gauge. Tape a six-inch paper ruler to the jar. Make sure the ruler is straight up and down. Zero should be at the bottom of the jar.

2. When it is going to rain, place your jar in an open area where it can collect rain. Don't put the jar near or under trees or near buildings.

3. **Observe** After it rains, see how much rain fell. Try to measure to the nearest eighth of an inch.

4. **Measure** Record the amount of rainfall on your Foldables book. Do this for several rains.

An *anemometer* (an·uh·MAHM·i·tuhr) measures how fast the air is moving. It gives you the wind's speed.

How Do You Read a Weather Map?

What do you do when you make observations? You write them down. You might also share your data with other people.

Scientists gather data about the weather. They use symbols to show the data on a large weather map. The map shows weather conditions over a large area. Scientists then share this information with others and make weather forecasts.

Look at the weather map of the United States below. This weather map shows you cloud cover, temperature, and other current weather conditions. Some places, such as Phoenix, are having hot, sunny weather. Other places, such as New York City, are cooler and rainy. Each color band represents an area where the temperature falls in the same range.

▷ **What does a weather map show?**

READING

Maps

1. What is the current temperature for Phoenix, Arizona?

2. What is the current cloud cover for Atlanta, Georgia?

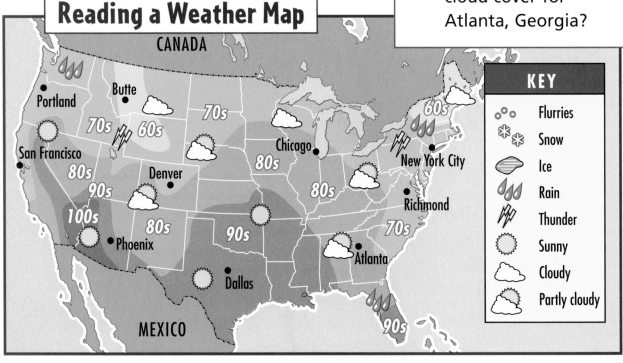

Reading a Weather Map

CANADA

Portland
Butte
70s
San Francisco
70s 60s
80s
Denver
90s
100s
80s
Phoenix
90s
Dallas
MEXICO
90s

Chicago
80s
80s
New York City
Richmond
70s
Atlanta

KEY

✿✿✿	Flurries
❄❄	Snow
🌫	Ice
💧💧	Rain
⚡	Thunder
☀	Sunny
☁	Cloudy
☁	Partly cloudy

L·I·N·K·S

Why It Matters

Weather patterns are constantly changing. That is why being able to read a weather map is important. For example, if you see that cities west of you are having rain, you'll probably have rain the next day. This can help you decide what to wear and what to do.

e-Journal Visit our Web site www.science.mmhschool.com to do a research project on weather pattern and changes.

Think and Write

1. How do you measure temperature?

2. What does a barometer measure?

3. Name two other weather instruments. What do they measure?

4. What information does a weather map provide?

5. **Critical Thinking** How might you use the information from a weather report?

LITERATURE LINK

Read *Stormy Weather* to learn about the weather. When you finish reading, list some of the kinds of weather in the story. Try the activities at the end of the book.

WRITING LINK

Expository Writing This weather-satellite photo shows a hurricane. Some areas of the United States have more hurricanes than others. Do research to find out which U.S. regions have the most hurricanes. Explain why in an essay.

MATH LINK

Make a bar graph. Use the Internet to gather data on the average annual rainfall for five different cities. Record the average annual rainfall for each city in a table. Use the table to make a bar graph.

TECHNOLOGY LINK

LOG ON Visit www.science.mmhschool.com for more links.

The Ups and Downs of Tides

If you live near the ocean, you probably know about tides. Tides are the rise and fall of the ocean's water level. Places along the ocean's shore usually have two high tides each day. The water level is high, and the edge of the ocean moves inland. In between high tides are low tides. The water level is low, and the edge of the ocean moves back out.

What causes tides? The answer comes from outer space! The Moon's gravity causes the oceans to bulge in some places and shrink in others. Because the Moon and Earth are always moving, tides rise and fall every day. Gravity from the Sun also affects tides.

At some places along the shore, you can find tide pools. Tide pools are puddles of water that a high tide leaves behind. It's fun to explore tide pools. You might find sea stars, crabs, or other sea creatures.

It is high tide. The water level is high.

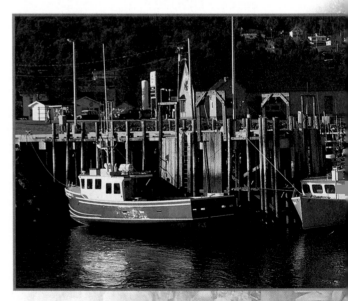

It is low tide. Look at what happened to the water level.

People can find shells and interesting sea creatures in tide pools.

Write **ABOUT IT**

1. What causes tides to rise and fall?
2. How might tides affect the lives of people who live by the ocean?

LOG ON Visit www.science.mmhschool.com to learn more about tides.

Chapter 7 Review

Vocabulary

Fill each blank with the best word or words from the list.

air pressure, D9 **precipitation,** D19
atmosphere, D6 **temperature,** D8
barometer, D24 **thermometer,** D24
condensation, D17 **water vapor,** D17
weather, D6
evaporation, D17

1. The air around Earth is a mixture of gases and dust called the _____.

2. The _____ of something measures how hot or cold it is.

3. The force of air pushing down on Earth is called _____.

4. Water in a gas form is called _____.

5. Rain, snow, hail, and sleet fall to Earth and are called _____.

6. A tool used to measure air pressure is a(n) _____.

7. The condition of the atmosphere at a given time and place is the _____.

8. To measure air temperature, you would use a(n) _____.

The water cycle is a never-ending process of precipitation,

9. _____

10. _____.

Test Prep

11. In which layer of the atmosphere does all weather take place?

    A troposphere

    B stratosphere

    C ozone

    D outer space

12. The change from a gas into a liquid is _____.

    F evaporation

    G condensation

    H precipitation

    J runoff

13. A weather map shows _____.

    A temperature ranges

    B cloud cover

    C precipitation

    D all of the above

14. A weather vane is used to measure _____.

    F wind

    G rainfall

    H temperature

    J air pressure

15. After it rains, some water soaks into the ground to become _____.

    A water vapor

    B groundwater

    C runoff

    D precipitation

Concepts and Skills

16. **Reading in Science** Study the drawing. Describe how water moves through the water cycle. Use the words *evaporation, condensation,* and *precipitation* in your answer.

17. **Critical Thinking** Air pressure is lower on mountains than in valleys. Why do you think this is so?

18. INQUIRY SKILL **Infer** If you pour lemonade into a cold glass, drops of water form outside the glass. What causes the drops to form?

19. **Scientific Methods** For the past two weeks, what was the average temperature in your town? Use the Internet to answer this question.

20. **Decision Making** Pretend you're a farmer. Fall has arrived and you need to harvest your crops. How does the weather affect you? What decisions might you make based on the weather?

Did You Ever Wonder?

INQUIRY SKILL **Predict** You have seen what causes weather to change. Gather information and predict your local weather for a week. Test your predictions.

LOG ON Visit **www.science.mmhschool.com** to boost your test scores.

CHAPTER

8

Earth in Space

Did You Ever Wonder?

How do scientists learn about space? One way is to look at the night sky through a telescope. Powerful telescopes are put in buildings called observatories. Observatories are often built on mountains or hilltops, away from the lights of cities.

INQUIRY SKILL Communicate What do we know about the objects in space?

How Earth Moves

Get Ready

Have you ever watched the Sun set and turn day into night? Have you watched the Sun rise? A dark sky brightens with just a peek of the Sun. What do you think causes night and day?

Inquiry Skill

You make a model when you make something to represent an object or event.

Explore Activity

What Causes Day and Night?

Materials

globe

medium self-stick notes

flashlight

Procedure

1 Write *I live here* on a self-stick note. Place the note over the United States on the globe. While one person holds the globe, shine the flashlight on the self-stick note.

2 **Observe** If the flashlight is the Sun, would it be day or night on the self-stick note? Is it day or night on the other side of the globe?

3 Think of two different ways to make it night at the place near the self-stick note.

4 **Make a Model** Use the globe and the flashlight to test your ideas.

Drawing Conclusions

1 How did you create day and night in the first model and in the second model?

2 Which idea do you think better explains what you know about day and night? Why?

3 FURTHER INQUIRY **Infer** You put your wet sneakers in sunlight to dry. An hour later they are in shade. How do you know what happened? Use your model to explain.

Main Idea Earth's rotation causes day and night, and its revolution causes the seasons.

What Causes Day and Night?

A long time ago, people thought that Earth stood still while the Sun traveled around it each day. It's easy to see why people once thought the Sun moved. Every day we see the Sun seem to come up, move across the sky, and go down. Today we know that the Sun does not move around Earth.

Better instruments have helped us observe the movements of Earth. It is the movement of Earth that causes day and night. Earth is shaped like a ball. This shape is called a **sphere** (SFEER). Earth **rotates** (ROH·taytz). To rotate means to turn. As Earth rotates, there is daylight where Earth faces the Sun and darkness where Earth is turned away from the Sun.

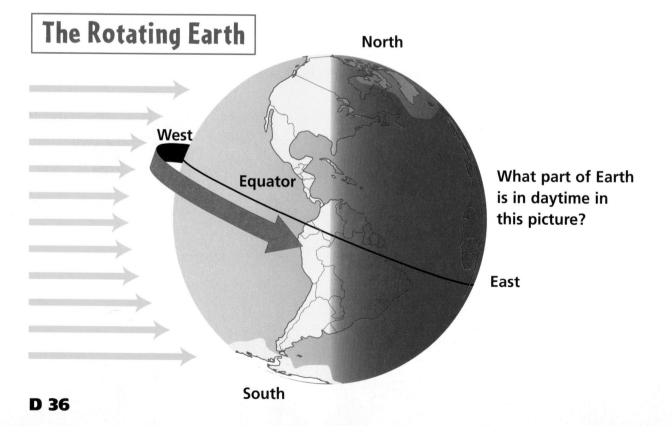

The Rotating Earth

North

West

Equator

East

South

What part of Earth is in daytime in this picture?

It takes 24 hours for Earth to make one complete rotation. One complete rotation is one day. A day is made up of the hours of light and the hours of dark.

Look at the illustration below. Notice the line drawn through the center of Earth. This imaginary line is called an **axis** (AK·sis). Earth spins, or rotates, around its axis. As you can see, Earth's axis is not straight up and down. It is slightly tilted. At the north end of Earth's axis is the North Pole. At the south end is the South Pole.

The tilt of Earth changes how the Sun's rays strike the surface. At the poles the Sun stays low in the sky during the day. Here the Sun's rays are weak. This is why it is cold at the poles. At the equator the Sun rises high in the sky during the day. These rays are stronger. Here the air temperature is higher.

▷ What is an axis?

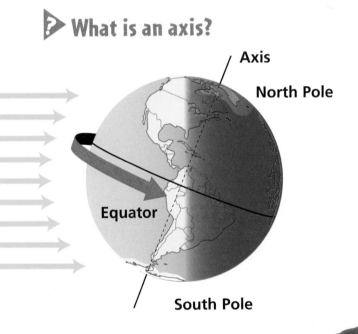

Axis

North Pole

Equator

South Pole

This tortoise lives near the equator. The temperature is warmer here.

These penguins live near the South Pole. The temperature is colder here.

What Causes the Seasons?

Rotation is only one way in which Earth moves. Earth also **revolves** (ri·VAHLVZ). An object that moves around another object revolves. Earth travels in a regular path around the Sun. It travels in an **orbit** (AWR·bit). An orbit is the path that an object follows as it revolves around another object. It takes one year, or $365\frac{1}{4}$ days, for Earth to make one complete revolution around the Sun.

In many parts of the world, the year is made up of four seasons—winter, spring, summer, and fall. Why do we have seasons? The answer has to do with Earth's tilted axis. Having a tilted axis means that Earth slants a little as it revolves around the Sun.

Look at the diagram. Notice that Earth is always tilted in the same direction. As Earth travels around the Sun, the part of Earth tilted toward the Sun changes. For part of the year, the North Pole tilts toward the Sun. During another part of the year, the North Pole tilts away from the Sun.

Summer
(begins June 21–22)
North America is tilted toward the Sun. The Sun is higher overhead, days are longer, and the temperature is warmer.

READING
Diagrams

If it is summer in the northern half of Earth, what season is it in the southern half?

When the North Pole is tilted toward the Sun, the Sun travels higher overhead in the sky. The Sun's rays shine straighter down on that part of Earth. It is then summer in that part of Earth. When the North Pole is tilted away from the Sun, the Sun stays lower in the sky. It is then winter in that part of Earth.

Earth Revolves Around the Sun

▷ **What is a year?**

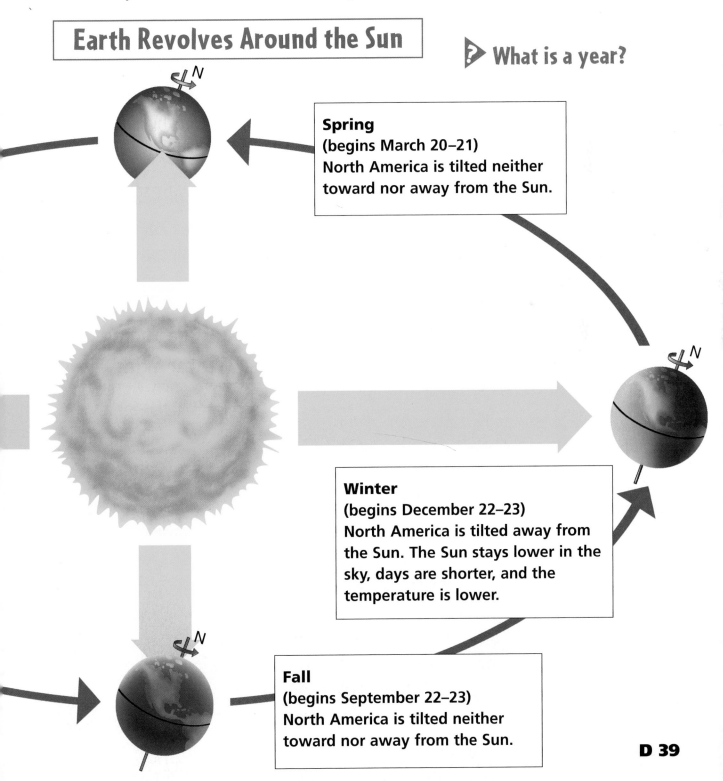

Spring
(begins March 20–21)
North America is tilted neither toward nor away from the Sun.

Winter
(begins December 22–23)
North America is tilted away from the Sun. The Sun stays lower in the sky, days are shorter, and the temperature is lower.

Fall
(begins September 22–23)
North America is tilted neither toward nor away from the Sun.

Sundial

FOLDABLES™ Make a Three-Tab Book. (See p. R43.) Mark the book as shown.

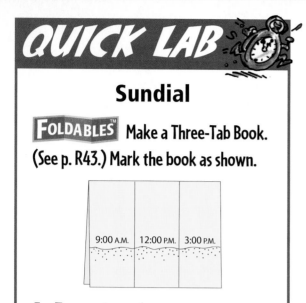

1. Tape a piece of paper to some cardboard. Use clay to anchor a pencil straight up at the center of the paper. Take your sundial outside at 9 A.M. on a sunny morning.

2. **Measure** Use a marker to draw a line through the middle of the pencil's shadow. Label the line with the time of day. Measure and mark the pencil's shadow again at 12 noon and 3 P.M.

3. On each tab of the Foldables book, draw the Sun's position.

4. How does the shadow's position change in one day? Is the Sun high or low in the sky when the shadows are the longest? Explain your answer on the back of your Foldables book.

How Does the Sun's Path in the Sky Change?

As the seasons change, so does the way the Sun appears to travel across the sky each day. In summer your part of Earth is tilted toward the Sun. The Sun's path appears higher in the sky. In winter your part of Earth is tilted away from the Sun. The Sun's path appears lower in the sky.

READING **Cause and Effect**
What causes the Sun to appear higher in the sky during the summer?

The Sun in the Summer and Winter Skies

June

December

Set   Rise

Why It Matters

The way Earth moves affects the way we lead our lives. Just think of all the things you do during the day and those you do at night. Also think about what you do throughout the year. Do you have a favorite season? Do you enjoy hot summer days, or do you like cooler ones?

e-Journal Visit our Web site www.science.mmhschool.com to do a research project on the changing seasons.

Think and Write

1. If it is nighttime at a certain place on Earth, is that place facing toward or away from the Sun?

2. Describe the motion of Earth that makes up one day.

3. How are rotating and revolving different?

4. What would happen to the seasons if Earth's axis were not tilted?

5. **Critical Thinking** How would your life be different if you lived in the southern half of Earth?

L·I·N·K·S

MATH LINK

Solve a problem. You learned that the revolution of Earth around the Sun causes the four seasons. If each season is about the same number of months, about how many months long is each season? How can you tell?

HEALTH LINK

Conduct an interview. Ultraviolet (ul·truh·VIGH·uh·lit) light (UV) from the Sun causes a suntan or sunburn. Interview adult family members to find out how they protect their skin. Write down what they tell you.

WRITING LINK

Writing That Compares Describe how your life would change if Earth made one complete rotation every 12 hours. Compare and contrast this with 24 hours in your real life on Earth.

TECHNOLOGY LINK

Science Newsroom CD-ROM Choose *Around the World* to learn how Earth's position affects the seasons.

LOG ON Visit www.science.mmhschool.com for more links.

Star Time

Can you tell time without a clock or a calendar? Yes, you can—by using the Sun and the stars!

Thousands of years ago, that's just what people did. Farmers used the position of the stars to tell the time of year.

Stargazers noticed that stars moved together across the sky. They also observed that stars were not evenly scattered. Some groups of brighter stars reminded people of familiar things – a lion, a hunter, a bull, a scorpion. We call these groups of stars constellations. As the seasons change, the constellations move across the sky.

Look at the sky at 8 p.m. one clear winter evening. Find the constellation Orion, the hunter. Check it again after one hour. Why is Orion moving? It's not! Earth is rotating, and you're on Earth. So you're the one who's moving!

The constellation Orion, the hunter.

Orion will be in a slightly different spot each night. This is because Earth is traveling around the Sun. As Earth moves, your view of the sky changes. In late spring, Orion disappears below the horizon. During the summer you'll see other constellations, such as Leo, the lion. But you won't see Orion again until late fall. In one year, Earth will circle the Sun once. Then Orion will be back in the same place in the sky.

Even today, our units of time are linked to the motions of our planet. The time it takes for Earth to rotate once is called one day. We break that day into parts—hours, minutes, and seconds. The time it takes Earth to revolve once around the Sun is called one year. The calendar is a daily reminder that we live on a planet!

Some stars are brighter than others.

What Did I Learn?

1. What did ancient people use to predict the seasons?

A rocks
B stars
C animals
D plants

2. Why do the stars appear to move across the sky at night?

F Earth is rotating.
G Orion, the hunter, is chasing them.
H The stars don't appear to move.
J The constellations are revolving around the Sun.

LOG ON Visit www.science.mmhschool.com to learn more about astronomy.

Phases of the Moon

Vocabulary

satellite, D46

phase, D46

crater, D49

Get Ready

Have you ever seen the Moon when it looked like this? Although the Moon is in the sky each day, it doesn't always look the same. Sometimes it is a full circle, and sometimes it is a thin slice. Why does the Moon seem to change shape?

Inquiry Skill

You **communicate when you share information.**

Explore Activity

Why Does the Moon's Shape Change?

Procedure

1 **Observe** From your seat, look at the ball closely. Draw the ball.

2 **Make a Model** Turn off the classroom lights. Turn on the lamp, and shine it on one side of the ball. Draw the shape of the ball where the light hits it.

3 **Infer** Compare all the drawings. What do you think caused the different shapes?

Drawing Conclusions

1 How did the ball look when you first observed it? How did it look in the darkened room?

2 Why did your classmates see different lighted shapes?

3 **Infer** In this model the ball is the Moon and the lamp is the Sun. What are you?

4 FURTHER INQUIRY
Infer Why does the Moon appear to change its shape? How do you know?

How Does the Moon's Shape Change?

Each day the Moon seems to change shape. On some days, you may see only a part of the Moon or not see it at all. Other times it is a big bright circle. The Moon is a **satellite** (SAT·uh·light) of Earth. A satellite is anything that orbits another, larger object in space. The same half of the Moon always faces Earth. The Moon's other side always faces away from Earth.

The Moon, like a ball, is a sphere. The Moon does not change shape. It only appears to change shape because you see different amounts of its lighted part as it orbits Earth. The positions of the Sun and the Moon make it seem to change shape.

As the Moon orbits Earth, our view of it changes. The Moon appears to have different shapes. These changing shapes are called the Moon's **phases** (FAYZ·uhz). It takes about 29 days for the Moon to pass through all of its phases. Then the phases repeat. The four main phases of the Moon are new Moon, first quarter, full Moon, and last quarter.

The Moon rises and sets almost an hour later each day. Because of this we sometimes see the Moon in the daytime sky as well as at night.

▷ **Why does the Moon appear to change shape?**

D 46

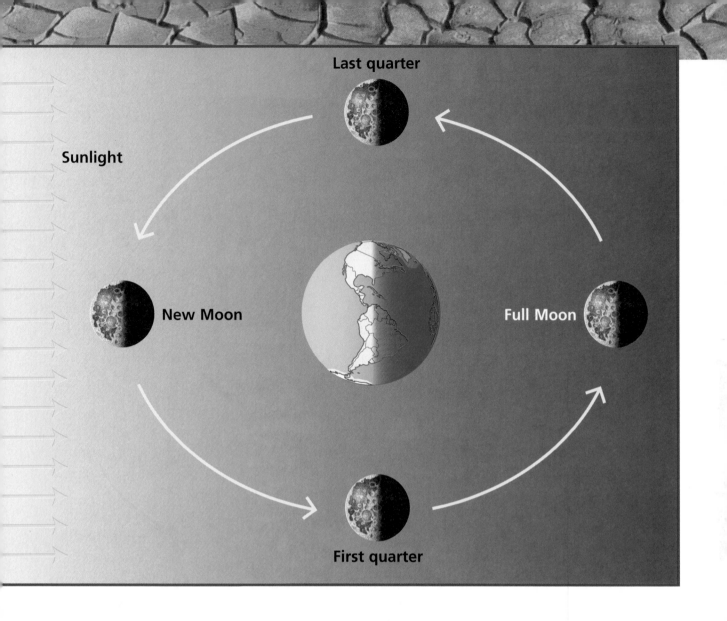

Last quarter

Sunlight

New Moon

Full Moon

First quarter

① New Moon   ② First quarter   ③ Full Moon   ④ Last quarter

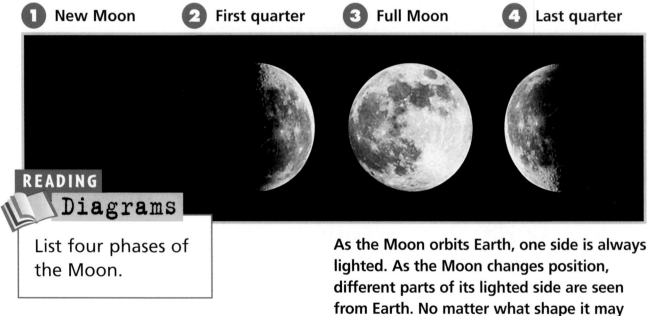

READING

Diagrams

List four phases of the Moon.

As the Moon orbits Earth, one side is always lighted. As the Moon changes position, different parts of its lighted side are seen from Earth. No matter what shape it may look like, the Moon is always a sphere.

D 47

The U.S. *Apollo 11* astronauts landed on the Moon on July 20, 1969.

How Are Earth and the Moon Different?

Both Earth and the Moon are spheres that rotate and revolve. They also receive light from the Sun. In most ways, however, Earth and the Moon are quite different. A day on Earth lasts 24 hours, while a day on the Moon lasts more than 27 Earth days.

The Moon is about one-fourth the size of Earth. The Moon has less mass than Earth. The Moon also has less gravity. The Moon's gravity is about one-sixth of Earth's gravity. If your mass were 30 kilograms, and your weight were 66 pounds on Earth, then you would weigh only 11 pounds on the Moon!

Craters (KRAY·tuhrz) cover most of the Moon's surface. A crater is a hollow area, or pit, in the ground. Some of the Moon's craters may have been formed by ancient volcanoes. Most, however, were caused by chunks of rock or metal from space that crashed into the Moon. Some of the Moon's craters are very large. Others are quite small.

Earth has few craters. Most objects from space burn up before they reach Earth. The air and water on Earth also cause craters here to erode, or wear away. The Moon has no air.

Water is found in many places on Earth. It is in the air. It is in oceans, rivers, lakes, and streams. Water is also found in the ground. The Moon has no liquid water. Water is needed by all living things. Because the Moon has no air or liquid water, there can be no life there. Astronauts were able to visit the Moon because their spacesuits provided air and protection.

READING **Cause and Effect**
What causes the craters on the Moon's surface?

Earth's surface is almost three-quarters water. There are few craters on Earth. Earth supports life.

Large and small craters cover the Moon's rocky surface. There is no liquid water on the Moon.

Inquiry Skill
B U I L D E R

Use Patterns

Rachel observed the Moon on different days during one month. She drew her observations on this calendar. There were some days she did not observe the Moon. Can you predict the shape of the Moon on the days she did not observe it?

Procedure

1 **Observe** Study the calendar shown here.

2 Look for similar shapes and patterns of the Moon.

Drawing Conclusions

1 **Predict** What do you think the Moon's shape was on Wednesday, January 9? Compare it with the shape of the Moon on January 8 and January 11. Draw your prediction.

2 **Predict** What was the Moon's shape on Friday, January 25? Compare it with the shape of the Moon on January 24 and January 26. Draw your prediction.

3 **Predict** Draw the shape of the Moon you would expect to see on January 29. What helped you decide on that shape?

4 **Observe** Observe the change in the shape of the Moon in the sky for one month. Draw the shape in a calendar like the one shown above. Describe how the pattern changes.

D 50

Why It Matters

Earth provides you with things you need to survive, such as water, air, and temperatures that aren't too hot or too cold. The Moon is Earth's nearest neighbor in space. However, the Moon cannot support life. It is very hot in some places and very cold in others. The Moon doesn't have any air or liquid water.

e-Journal Visit our Web site www.science.mmhschool.com to do a research project on the Moon.

Think and Write

1. What shape is the Moon? Why does it appear to change shape?

2. Explain what the term "a phase of the Moon" means. Identify the four main phases.

3. Why does the Moon appear to shine?

4. [INQUIRY SKILL] **Predict** Last night it was a new Moon. What will the next main phase be?

5. Critical Thinking Why is there no life on the Moon?

MATH LINK

Use a calculator. How much would you weigh on the Moon? It's easy to figure out. Weigh yourself at home. Your weight will probably be in pounds. Divide your Earth weight by six to find your Moon weight. Use a calculator to help you.

LITERATURE LINK

Read *Up, Up, and Away!* to learn about Mae Jemison, the first African American woman to go into space. When you finish reading this book, imagine a day on the space shuttle. Try the activities at the end of the book.

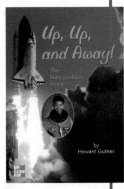

WRITING LINK

Writing a Story Write a science-fiction story about what it would be like to live on the Moon. Include characters, a setting, and a sequence of events with a problem that is solved at the end. Perform your story for an audience. Tape your story so you can watch it later.

TECHNOLOGY LINK

LOG ON Visit www.science.mmhschool.com for more links.

LESSON 6

The Sun and Its Planets

Get Ready

When you look at the night sky, you see many different objects. You can see the Moon and the stars. You can also see some of Earth's other neighbors—planets. What do you see when you look up at the night sky?

Inquiry Skill

You observe when you use one or more of the senses to identify or learn about an object or event.

Explore Activity

How Do Planets Move?

Materials

sign for each planet

2 signs for the Sun

Procedure

1 **Make a Model** Take turns with other groups of classmates. Model the motion of the planets around the Sun. When you are not doing the modeling, make as many observations as you can.

2 **Observe** Listen to the student who is modeling Earth. He or she will describe what can be seen from Earth in the night sky.

Drawing Conclusions

1 What planets were visible from Earth the first time you modeled the motions of the planets? What planets were visible the second time?

2 How did Earth's motion affect what planets could be seen from Earth? How did the motion of the other planets affect what planets could be seen from Earth?

3 Why does the position of the planets in the night sky change?

4 FURTHER INQUIRY Observe How would the position of Venus change in your model if that classmate moved faster or slower around the Sun? Use the model to test your ideas.

Read to Learn

Main Idea Our solar system includes the Sun, the nine planets, and their moons.

What Is the Solar System?

The Sun, Earth, and the Moon are part of a larger system called the **solar system** . The solar system is made up of the Sun and all the objects that orbit it.

Earth is one of nine **planets** (PLAN·itz) that orbit the Sun. A planet is a large body of rock or gas that orbits the Sun. Each planet is a different size. Some are smaller than Earth, and some are larger. Each planet rotates on its axis and revolves around the Sun as Earth does. Here is the order of the planets from the Sun: Mercury, Venus, Earth, Mars, Jupiter, Saturn, Uranus, Neptune, and Pluto. This sentence may help you remember the order: My Very Excellent Mother Just Served Us Nine Pizzas.

The Nine Planets Revolve Around the Sun

Venus

Mercury

Sun

Earth

Mars

The Sun is a **star**. A star is a hot, glowing ball of gases. The Sun is only a medium-sized star. It looks larger than any other star because it is the closest star to Earth.

The Sun is very big compared with Earth. It is so big that if it were hollow, more than one million Earths would fit inside it! The Sun looks small because it is very far from Earth. The Sun is so far away that it takes eight minutes for sunlight to make the trip to Earth.

Earth gets heat as well as light from the Sun. It's a good thing we live at this distance from the Sun. If we were much closer, Earth would be too hot to live on. If we were much farther away, Earth would be too cold for living things.

▷ **What is in our solar system?**

Jupiter

Uranus

Pluto

Neptune

Saturn

Mercury is the closest planet to the Sun. It looks a lot like Earth's Moon.

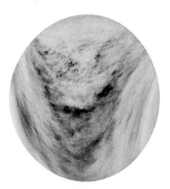

Space probes have visited cloud-covered **Venus** many times.

What Are the Nine Planets Like?

Like the Moon, planets have no light of their own. They reflect sunlight. Light reflected from the surface of the Moon and the planets shines steadily.

The name *planet* comes from a word meaning "wanderer." True to their name, planets appear to wander through the sky. Each planet moves in a different orbit and at a different speed. The planets are always moving and changing positions.

The planets are divided into two groups—the inner planets and the outer planets. The inner planets are the four planets closest to the Sun—Mercury, Venus, Earth, and Mars.

The inner planets are all small and made up of solid, rocklike materials.

Earth is our home. It is the only planet with liquid water.

Mars has some water, but most of it is frozen ice. Mars is known as the "red planet" because of its reddish rocks and soil.

Jupiter is the largest planet in our solar system. The Great Red Spot on Jupiter has been whirling around for 300 years.

Saturn is known for its thousands of beautiful rings. They are made up of different-sized bits of ice and rock that orbit the planet.

The outer planets are Jupiter, Saturn, Uranus, Neptune, and Pluto. All of the outer planets are made up mostly of gases, except for Pluto. Pluto is made up of a mixture of rocky materials and frozen gases. The outer planets are much colder than the inner planets. They are farther from the Sun.

READING **Cause and Effect**
What causes the outer planets to be colder than the inner planets?

Uranus is called the "sideways planet" because it rotates on its side.

Neptune is more than two billion miles from Earth. It has a Great Dark Spot similar to Jupiter's Great Red Spot.

Little is known about **Pluto** because it is so far away.

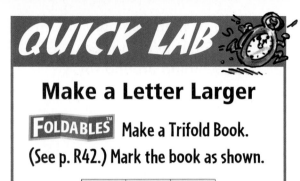

QUICK LAB

Make a Letter Larger

FOLDABLES Make a Trifold Book. (See p. R42.) Mark the book as shown.

Curved Lens | Both | Drop of Water

1. Cover a piece of newspaper with some wax paper.

2. **Observe** Put a small drop of water over a letter. How does it look?

3. **Experiment** Put water drops of different sizes over other letters. Observe.

4. How does the size of the drop affect the way the print looks?

5. **Infer** How is the curved lens in a telescope like the drop of water? Use the Venn Diagram on your Foldables book to record your answer.

The objects in our solar system are easier to see with a telescope.

How Do We Learn About Space?

The Sun, the Moon, and the planets are very far away. How do scientists learn about them? One tool they use is a **telescope** (TEL·uh·skohp). A telescope gathers light to make faraway objects appear larger, closer, and clearer. Telescopes gather light with mirrors and **lenses** (LENZ·uhz). A lens is a curved piece of glass.

▷ **What does a telescope do?**

Why It Matters

The solar system is Earth's "family" in space. Since early times people have wanted to know more about the other planets. Today telescopes and space probes give us a lot of important information. Do you like to look at the stars and planets at night? Now you know how to tell which objects are planets!

e-Journal Visit our Web site www.science.mmhschool.com to do a research project on the solar system.

Think and Write

1. What is the solar system?

2. What two things does Earth receive from the Sun?

3. How are the planets the same? How are they different?

4. How would life be different without the telescope?

5. **Critical Thinking** What if the outer planets were farther away from the Sun? How would this affect the planets' orbits around the Sun?

L·I·N·K·S

WRITING LINK

Personal Narrative Imagine yourself on a trip through space. What do you see as you pass by the planets? Write about an event that takes place. Use first-person point of view.

MATH LINK

Solve a problem. Jupiter has eight times as many moons as Mars. Mars has two moons. How many moons does Jupiter have? Explain how you found your answer.

LITERATURE LINK

Read *Mars Discovery* to learn about Mars. When you finish reading, make a list of the ways that Earth is similar to Mars. Try the activities at the end of the book.

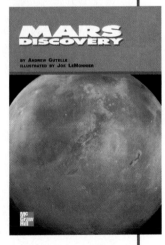

MARS DISCOVERY
BY ANDREW GUTELLE
ILLUSTRATED BY JOE LEMONNIER

TECHNOLOGY LINK

Science Newsroom CD-ROM Choose *Out for a Spin* to learn how Earth and Mars rotate and revolve.

LOG ON Visit www.science.mmhschool.com for more links.

Chapter 8 Review

Vocabulary

Fill in each blank with the best word from the list.

axis, D37   **revolve,** D38

crater, D49   **rotate,** D36

orbit, D38   **satellite,** D46

phase, D46   **star,** D55

planet, D54   **telescope,** D58

1. Earth revolves or travels in a(n) _____ around the Sun.

2. A new Moon and a full Moon are two of the Moon's _____.

3. Mercury, Mars, and Earth are three of nine _____ in our solar system.

4. A tool that makes faraway objects seem closer is a(n) _____.

5. Anything that orbits another larger object in space is a(n) _____.

6. When a meteorite slams into the Moon, it makes a hollow area called a(n) _____.

7. Earth spins on an imaginary line called a(n) _____.

8. The Sun is a medium-sized _____.

Two ways Earth moves are that it:

9. _____

10. _____.

Test Prep

11. There are days and nights because _____.

   A the Sun rotates

   B the Moon rotates

   C Earth rotates

   D the Moon revolves around the Sun

12. Earth revolves around _____.

   F the equator

   G the poles

   H the Moon

   J the Sun

13. The apparent changes in the Moon's shape are the Moon's _____.

   A craters

   B phases

   C orbits

   D seasons

14. The two planets closest to Earth are _____.

   F Mars and Venus

   G Mars and Jupiter

   H Mars and the Moon

   J Venus and Mercury

15. The largest planet is _____.

   A Earth

   B Saturn

   C Jupiter

   D Mars

Concepts and Skills

16. **Reading in Science** Why does the Moon appear to change shape when viewed from Earth? Use the diagram below to help you answer the question.

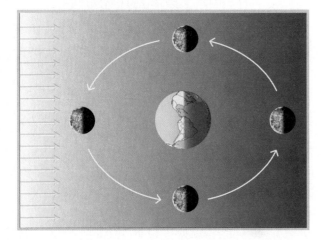

17. **Critical Thinking** Some places on Earth have 24 hours of daylight in the summer and 24 hours of darkness in the winter. Where are these places? Explain your answer.

18. INQUIRY SKILL **Predict** How would Earth's weather be different if Earth's axis was straight up and down, instead of tilted?

19. **Product Ads** Find ads for suntan lotion or sunscreen. Explain what the products claim to do. How do the ads try to interest people in the product?

20. **Scientific Methods** Scientists use tools to help them observe things. What tool has helped scientists to understand planets? How has it helped?

Did You Ever Wonder?

INQUIRY SKILL **Observe** You have learned about planets in our solar system. Explore the movement of a star or planet in the night sky. Explain what you see.

LOG ON Visit **www.science.mmhschool.com** to boost your test scores.

Dr. Renée Roberta Fair
Meteorologist

In January 1999, tornadoes ripped through Little Rock, Arkansas. Eight people lost their lives. "It could have been much worse," says Renée Roberta Fair. She is a meteorologist at the Little Rock office of the National Oceanic and Atmospheric Administration (NOAA)—the U.S. weather agency. Thanks to her office, people were warned and took cover from the dangerous winds.

Fair's team uses radar and other high-tech tools to do their job. Instruments record important data, such as wind speed, wind direction, and rainfall. NOAA also uses the Internet to keep track of weather—and to let people know about weather conditions.

Studying weather is an important job. "Absolutely everything and everyone depends on weather—and weather information," says Fair. And we all depend on meteorologists to tell us what the weather's going to be!

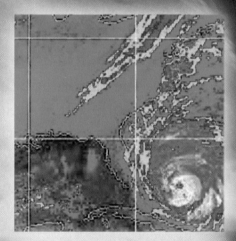
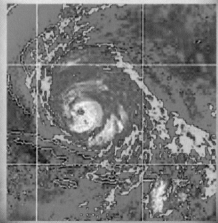

A hurricane roars toward the coast of Florida.

TOP 5 Most Expensive Hurricanes

Here's a list of the most expensive hurricanes in U.S. history. The costs are for rebuilding destroyed property.

1. Andrew, 1992: $26.5 billion
2. Hugo, 1989: $7 billion
3. Floyd, 1999: $4.5 billion
4. Fran, 1996: $3.2 billion
5. Opal, 1995: $3 billion

Write About It

1. Why is knowing about the weather important for everyone?
2. How did Dr. Fair and her team help save lives in 1999?

LOG ON Visit **www.science.mmschool.com** to learn more about meteorologists and weather prediction.

WATER CYCLE Story

Your goal is to write a story about the water cycle.

What to Do

Suppose you are a drop of water in a lake. What happens to you as you pass through each phase of the water cycle? How would you feel? Write a story about your adventures as a water drop.

Your story should explain the water cycle. Illustrate your pages with pictures and diagrams.

Moon Watch

Your goal is to make a chart. It will show how the Moon's position changes from day to day.

What to Do

Begin your observations when the Moon is crescent-shape. With a parent or guardian, look in the southwestern part of the sky just after sunset. Pick a point on the horizon directly under the Moon.

Hold your arm straight out and use your fist as a measuring tool. Measure how many fists above the horizon you see the Moon.

Record the Moon's position and elevation. Repeat the same measurements each day, at the same time, for one week.

Draw Conclusions

Describe the movement of the Moon in the sky over the week.

UNIT E

Forces and Motion

LOOK!

These windmills are using their motion to generate electricity. Why were they built at different heights?

Forces and Motion

How Things Move

Did You Ever Wonder?

How fast can a bobsled travel? The chart below
shows that a bobsled travels faster than a speeding
cheetah. It travels even faster than a car on a highway!

Speeds of Objects	Bobsled	Car on Highway	Cheetah
Kilometers per hour	150	105	97
Miles per hour	93	65	60

INQUIRY SKILL **Form a Hypothesis** What do you think
causes objects to move?

Motion and Speed

Vocabulary

position, E6

distance, E7

motion, E8

speed, E9

Get Ready

Have you ever been to a pond? Many animals live there. Each animal moves in a different way. A snake slithers along the ground. Fish swim in the water, while turtles crawl on shore. Frogs hop on lily pads, and birds fly overhead. Do you think this lizard moves faster than a fish? How do you know?

Inquiry Skill

You predict when you state the possible results of an experiment.

Explore Activity

How Fast Do You Move?

Materials

stopwatch

red crayon

blue crayon

graph paper

meter tape

Procedure

1. **Measure** Measure and mark 10 meters on the floor using the meter tape.

2. **Predict** Predict and record how long you think it will take each group member to walk 10 meters and to run 10 meters.

3. **Measure** Have each person walk 10 meters. Use the stopwatch to measure each person's time. Record each time.

4. Have each person run 10 meters. Measure and record each person's time.

Drawing Conclusions

1. Make a bar graph like the one shown. Use the blue crayon to show walking time. Use the red crayon to show running time. Make a key, and name your graph.

2. Repeat the activity. What is the difference, in seconds, between the first time you ran and the second?

3. **FURTHER INQUIRY** **Predict** How would the times change if you walked uphill and then downhill? How do you know?

Walking and Running 10 Meters

Stew	X X X X X X X X X X						
	X X						
Eumi	X X X X X X X X X						
	X X X						
Amir	X X X X X X X X X X X X						
	X X X X						
Tanya	X X X X X X X X X X X X						
	X X						
	2	4	6	8	10	12	14

Seconds

KEY: X = walking
X = running

Main Idea You can find out about speed.

How Do You Know If Something Has Moved?

Look at the two pictures of the snail. What has happened? How do you know that the snail has moved?

You know that something has moved because you can see that it has changed **position** (puh·ZISH·uhn). Position is the location of an object. The snail started out at one end of the leaf. It stopped at the other end of the leaf. It changed position.

Before

After

You can describe an object's position by comparing it with the positions of other objects. Words like *above* and *below, left* and *right, ahead* and *behind* give you clues about position.

Look at the pitcher's mitt in the pictures below. How has its position changed?

Before

After

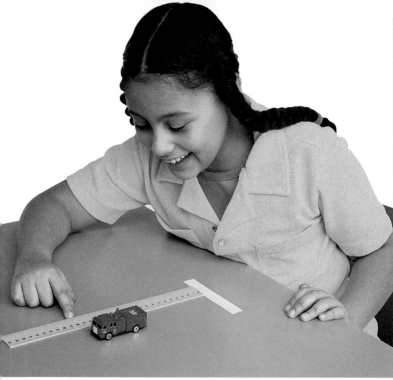

You can use a ruler to measure distance.

You can measure how far things move. **Distance** (DIS·tuhns) is the length between two places. When an object moves, it goes from a starting position to an ending position. Measuring the length between the starting and ending positions gives you distance. Knowing the distance tells you how far the object has moved.

READING **Main Idea**
What is distance?

QUICK LAB

Measuring Distance

FOLDABLES Make a Four-Row Folded Chart. (See p. R44.) Label the rows as shown.

Paper	1	2	3	4	5	6
Block	1	2	3	4	5	6
Pencil	1	2	3	4	5	6
Marble	1	2	3	4	5	6

1. Place one ruler on the floor to mark a starting line.

2. **Experiment** Set a crumpled piece of paper in front of the ruler. Take a breath and blow the paper as far as you can.

3. **Measure** Use another ruler to find the distance the paper moved. Record the number on your chart.

4. Repeat steps 2 and 3 using a block, a pencil, and a marble.

5. Use the Foldables chart to tell which object traveled the greatest distance.

How Do You Measure Motion?

Look again at the snails on page E6. You know the snail moved because it changed position. While an object changes position, it is in **motion** (MOH·shuhn). Motion is a change in position.

Look at the cheetah in the diagram. As it runs the cheetah is in motion. It travels a distance from the start to the finish. It changes direction. Finally, its motion stops. Some motions, such as those of a moving snail, are very slow. Other motions, such as those of a cheetah, are fast. Some motions are very fast.

1 Motion takes time to happen.

2 Motion can include a change in direction.

READING
Diagrams

1. How do you know motion has stopped?

2. How do you know that the cheetah moved?

A cheetah runs faster than a person. The cheetah has a greater **speed** (SPEED). Speed is how fast an object moves over a certain distance. Fast-moving objects go long distances in a short period of time. Slow-moving objects take longer to travel the same distance.

To measure speed, you need to measure time and distance. The distance an object travels in a period of time tells you its speed. Speed is the distance divided by the time. If a cheetah could run for one hour at its fastest speed, it would travel 96 kilometers (60 miles). That's as fast as a car!

4 Motion stops when the position no longer changes.

3 The distance is the space the cheetah traveled.

▷ **What two things do you need to measure speed?**

What Do Maps Tell You?

A map is a flat drawing. It shows the positions of things. To read a map, you need to use directions. Directions include north (N), south (S), east (E), and west (W). Directions are shown below. Every map shows which way is north. This helps you find places.

This map has a key. A key tells you what the symbols stand for. The symbol of the purple circle shows a picnic area.

This map also has a scale. The scale helps to measure the real distance between places.

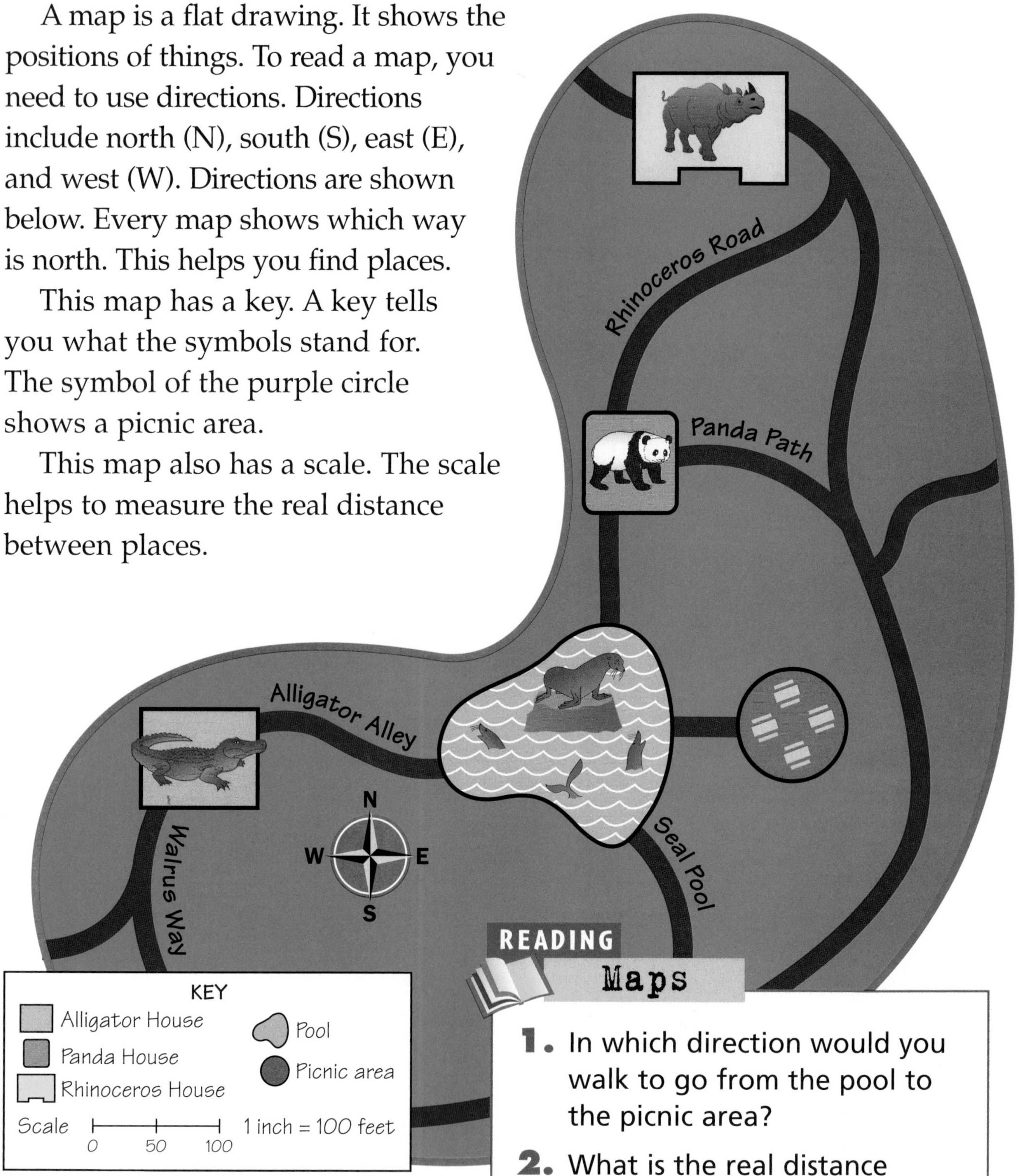

Rhinoceros Road

Panda Path

Alligator Alley

Walrus Way

Seal Pool

N
W E
S

KEY

Alligator House
Panda House
Rhinoceros House

Pool
Picnic area

Scale |———|———|———| 1 inch = 100 feet
       0   50   100

▷ **What does the map key show?**

READING **Maps**

1. In which direction would you walk to go from the pool to the picnic area?

2. What is the real distance between the Seal Pool and the picnic area?

Why It Matters

Every day your life is filled with motion. For example, you might go from home to school on the school bus. As it moves, the bus travels a distance. If you know the distance and the time the bus traveled, you can find its speed.

e-Journal Visit our Web site www.science.mmhschool.com to do a research project on speed and motion.

Think and Write

1. How would you describe an object that has changed position?

2. How is distance measured?

3. What is motion?

4. Three children live on the same street. Ann lives west of Peter. Peter lives east of Talia. Talia lives west of Ann. Draw a map of their street.

5. Critical Thinking Which moves faster—a cheetah running 96 kilometers in an hour or a bicycle traveling 24 kilometers in 30 minutes?

L·I·N·K·S

WRITING LINK

Writing That Compares Describe something that moves very slowly, such as a plant turning toward the light. Describe something that moves quickly, such as the fast motion of a tuning fork. Compare and contrast the two types of motion.

LITERATURE LINK

Read *There and Back, Then and Now* to learn about the history of travel. When you finish reading, think about your favorite way to travel. Try the activities at the end of the book.

There and Back, Then and Now by Patricia Baehr

MATH LINK

Solve a problem. If an adult runs 6 miles in an hour, how far will this person travel in 90 minutes? Show your answer. Explain how you solved the problem.

TECHNOLOGY LINK

 LOG ON Visit www.science.mmhschool.com for more links.

Forces

Get Ready

Every day, people use pushes and pulls to move things. In certain parts of the world, farmers use strong animals to pull heavy farm tools. You use a pull when you open a book. What are some other activities that use pushes and pulls?

Inquiry Skill

You measure when you find the weight of an object.

Explore Activity

Why Are Some Objects Harder to Pull?

Materials

spring scale

safety goggles

5 objects
of about the
same size

Procedure

BE CAREFUL! Wear goggles.

1 Observe What is the highest the spring scale can read?

2 Predict Which object will need the strongest pull to move it? Record your prediction.

3 Predict Which object will need the next strongest pull to move it? Record your prediction. Do the same for the rest of the objects.

4 Hook the scale on an object. Pull the scale and the object along a smooth, flat surface.

5 Measure Measure and record what the spring scale reads. Do the same for all the objects.

6 Compare your predictions with your measurements.

Drawing Conclusions

1 What did you feel when you pulled on an object with the spring scale?

2 Which objects made the scale read highest?

3 Why did you need a stronger pull to move some objects?

4 FURTHER INQUIRY **Experiment** How could you measure the size of the pull needed to move a lunchbox?

Main Idea You use forces to move things.

What Are Pushes and Pulls?

You push and pull on things every day to make them move. You push to open a door. You pull to put on your backpack.

All pushes and pulls are **forces** (FAWRS·uhz). Forces always work in pairs. When you push on something, such as a door, you can feel it pushing back.

Often a force can change an object's motion. It can make an object start moving, stop moving, or change direction. As you add force to a door, it moves. Sometimes an object doesn't move. No matter how hard you push, you can't push over a brick wall.

Heavier objects need more force to make them move. You have to push or pull a heavier object harder to make it move.

▷ **What do you feel when you push something?**

1 *All pushes and pulls are forces.* Pushes move away from you. Pulls move toward you.

2 *Forces may change the motion of an object.* The heavier an object, the more force you need to move it.

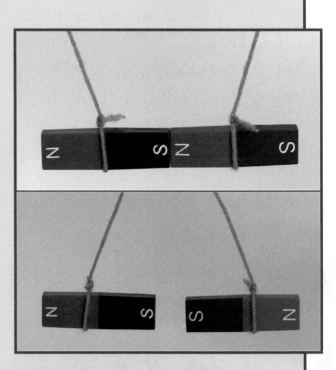

3 *Forces work in pairs.* Whenever you push or pull on something, it pushes or pulls on you. The push or pull that you feel is a force in the opposite direction.

4 *Many things can create forces.* Some forces push or pull on objects without even touching them.

READING Diagrams

1. What is a force?

2. Do you need more or less force to move a heavier object?

What Force Is Always Pulling on You?

One force is everywhere on Earth. It is even pulling on you right now. The force is **gravity** (GRAV·i·tee). Gravity is a pulling force between two objects, such as you and Earth.

This force keeps objects pulled toward Earth. Even when things go up, gravity pulls them down. Things fall to Earth because they are pulled by Earth's gravity.

Performing tasks in space is quite an experience for this astronaut.

READING Main Idea
When you jump up, why do you come down?

What Is Weight?

The pull of gravity is just about the same all over Earth. **Weight** (WAYT) is how much pull gravity has on an object.

That means an object's weight will be about the same anywhere on Earth. On other planets and the Moon, the pull of gravity is different. This is why objects have different weights away from Earth.

You can find out how heavy or light things are by measuring their weight. Some objects are heavy. Some are light. Scientists measure weight in *newtons*. A newton is the unit of force in the metric system. In the English system of measurement, the unit is the *pound*.

▷ **Would you weigh the same amount on the Moon?**

The pull of gravity is less on the Moon than on Earth.

These apples weigh nine newtons, or two pounds.

Inquiry Skill
BUILDER

SKILL Interpret Data

Read a Bar Graph

The graph below is a bar graph. Each bar gives you information, or *data*. This bar graph shows a dog's weight on different planets. Along the left side are the planet names. At the bottom are weights in pounds. Look at the end of the bar labeled *Earth*. It lines up with 40 pounds. The dog weighs 40 pounds on Earth. Look at the bar labeled *Jupiter*. What number does it line up with? You are interpreting data when you answer this question.

Interpret the data in this graph. Use the data to answer the questions.

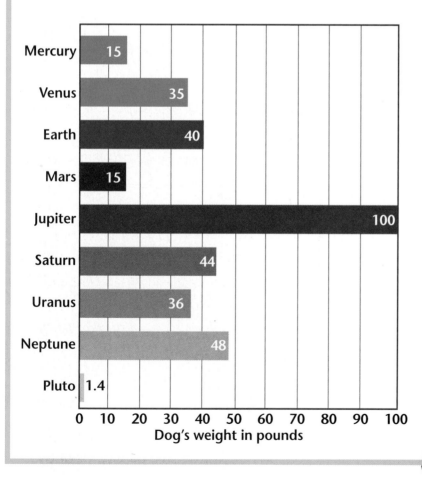

Procedure

1. **Interpret Data** How much does the dog weigh on Mars?

2. **Interpret Data** Where is the dog heavier than it is on Earth? Where is it lighter?

3. Compare the dog's weight on Jupiter with its weight on Venus. How much heavier is it on Jupiter?

Drawing Conclusions
Communicate How would your weight change if you visited the other planets?

Why It Matters

Forces are all around you. Whether you throw a ball, pull a wagon, or bump into things, you are using forces to move things. You use another kind of force when you use a magnet. The force of gravity holds things down on Earth. Gravity is pulling on you and everything else on Earth all the time.

e-Journal Visit our Web site www.science.mmhschool.com to do a research project on gravity.

Think and Write

1. How can you measure pushes and pulls?

2. List three forces that affect the motion of an object.

3. What is the name of the force that always pulls on you?

4. **INQUIRY SKILL** **Interpret Data** Look at the graph on page E18. How much does the dog weigh on Pluto?

5. **Critical Thinking** You drop a plate on Earth. It breaks. Would the same thing happen in space? Explain.

L·I·N·K·S

ART LINK

Make a mobile. Use buttons, beads, or anything else you find. Use string to attach these items to a plastic hanger. What do you have to do to get your mobile to balance? How does gravity affect your mobile?

LITERATURE LINK

Read _Get a Grip!_ to learn how a group of friends build a soapbox car. Try the activities at the end of the book.

Get a Grip!

WRITING LINK

Writing a Story How would a basketball game change if there were no gravity? Write a story about what the game would be like.

MATH LINK

Make an estimate. On Jupiter you weigh about two times what you weigh on Earth. If you weigh 100 pounds on Earth, would your weight on Jupiter more likely be 50, 100, 150, or 200 pounds? Explain.

TECHNOLOGY LINK

LOG ON Visit www.science.mmhschool.com for more links.

SHOW YOUR MUSCLES!

Let's hear it for your muscles! They're what help you move and stay on the go. They help you run and score that touchdown, climb trees, swim and dive, and so much more!

When you push or pull, you use muscles. Some of your muscles come in pairs. Your upper arm has biceps and triceps. Both muscles stretch between a bone in your upper arm and one in your lower arm.

Muscles contract, or get shorter. When your biceps contracts, it pulls on the lower bone. Your lower arm moves up so you can lift objects. How would you carry all your books without biceps?

You use your triceps to push things. When your triceps contracts, your biceps relaxes. Your arm becomes straighter, and you can push down.

How are these children using their muscles?

Want to run a little faster? Hit a ball a little harder? The more you push and pull, the stronger your muscles get.

Walking, jogging, and swimming build up muscles in your whole body. They make many muscles pull against gravity.

Here's how to use gravity to strengthen your muscles.

✓ Increase the amount of weight you pull or push.

✓ Increase the amount of time you push or pull that weight.

✓ Increase how often you push or pull that weight.

Remember that muscles need time to rest between exercise sessions!

Biceps

Triceps

What Did I Learn?

1. Which activity uses your biceps?

   A walking

   B sitting

   C lifting books

   D pushing down

2. What can you use to strengthen your muscles?

   F friction

   G energy

   H matter

   J gravity

LOG ON Visit www.science.mmhschool.com to learn more about your muscles.

Vocabulary

friction, E26

Changes in Motion

Inquiry Skill

You experiment when you perform a test to support or disprove a hypothesis.

Get Ready

Have you ever played a game of tug-of-war? In this game a flag is tied to the middle of a rope. Each team pulls on the rope. The team that pulls the rope hardest pulls the flag to its side. That team wins. Which team shown above do you think will win?

Explore Activity

What Causes a Change in Motion?

Materials

washers

2 paper clips

scissors

string

safety goggles

Procedure

BE CAREFUL! Wear goggles.

1. Cut two pieces of string that are slightly shorter than the width of your desk. Knot the strings together.

2. Lay the knot in the middle of your desk. Let the strings hang off the opposite sides of the desk.

3. Bend two paper clips into hooks. Tie a hook at the end of each hanging string.

4. Hold down the string at the knot.

5. **Predict** Hang two washers on one hook. Predict what will happen if you let go of the knot.

6. **Experiment** Test your prediction. Record the results.

7. **Experiment** Repeat steps 4, 5, and 6, this time hanging one washer on each hook.

Drawing Conclusions

1. **Communicate** Explain why the knot moved or did not move each time.

2. FURTHER INQUIRY
   Form a Hypothesis How could you move the knot in another direction?

Main Idea Forces can change an object's motion.

What Causes a Change in Motion?

When each person pulls on the rope, each applies a force. When the forces are equal, or balanced, there is no change in motion. The flag stays at rest.

What if one person pulls harder on the end of the rope? The forces are now unequal, or unbalanced. The flag moves to one side of the marker.

Equal forces: no motion

Unequal forces: motion

There is a change in its motion. A change in an object's motion comes from all the forces that are acting on it. Unequal forces cause a change in motion.

A change in motion occurs when an object starts moving or stops moving. It also occurs when a moving object speeds up, slows down, or changes direction. Here are some examples.

▷ **What causes a change in motion?**

Changes in Motion

1 A body at rest starts moving.

2 A moving body speeds up.

3 A moving body changes direction.

READING

Diagrams

What are five examples of a change in motion?

A moving body slows down.

4

5 A body stops moving.

How Can You Control Friction?

What happens when you roll a ball on the floor? It starts moving quickly but soon slows down. Then it stops. This means a force must be acting on the ball.

The force that slows the ball is called **friction** (FRIK·shuhn). Friction is the force that occurs when one object rubs against another. The ball rubbing on the floor creates friction.

Different materials produce different amounts of friction. Rough materials rub best. They produce a lot of friction. Many smooth materials don't rub well. They produce less friction. Other materials, such as rubber, are smooth but still produce a lot of friction.

Friction keeps the car's rubber tires on the road, even when the road is wet.

Ice reduces the amount of friction. The cars slide.

Friction slows things down. You can't get rid of it, but you can change the amount of friction you have.

People use slippery things to reduce friction. Oil is often put on moving parts of machines. To increase friction, people use rough or sticky things. In-line skates have a rubber pad that skaters use to slow down and stop.

READING Main Idea
How can you change friction?

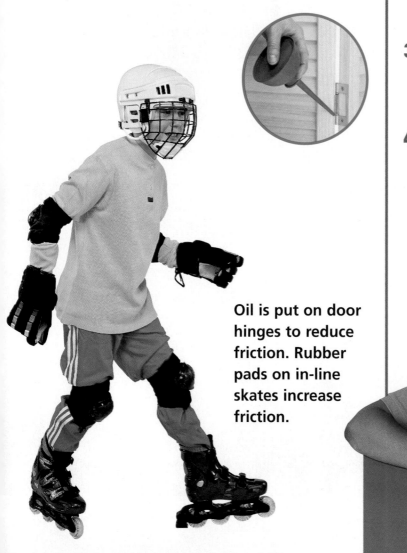

Oil is put on door hinges to reduce friction. Rubber pads on in-line skates increase friction.

QUICK LAB

Marbles in Motion

FOLDABLES Make a Four-Tab Book. (See p. R44.) Label as shown.

| Observe |
| Experiment |
| Observe |
| Explain |

1. **Observe** Push a wooden block across your desk. Describe how it feels under the tab of the Foldables book.

2. **Experiment** Place five marbles under a jar lid. Lay the block on top of the lid.

3. **Observe** Push the block across your desk again. Describe how it feels under the tab of the book.

4. On the back of your Foldables book, describe how the marbles helped reduce friction.

E 27

What Are Different Types of Motion?

Forces can cause objects to move in different ways. When you ride a bicycle, you pedal to move it forward. If you need to turn, you move the handlebars. You push on the one side and pull on the other. This pair of forces turns the wheel of the bicycle. Suppose you keep pedaling at the same speed and hold the handlebars so your bike travels in a circle. This is called circular motion. Circular motion changes the direction of an object so it goes in a circle and not in a straight line. Wheels, merry-go-rounds, and tops all move in circles.

Objects can move up and down. A *wave* is an up-and-down or back-and-forth movement. You may have seen water waves. Sound and light waves are not easy to see, but all waves have certain characteristics. The highest part of a wave is called the crest. The lowest part is the trough (TRAWF). A wave can be described and measured by its length. Length is the distance from one crest to another.

wavelength

crest

trough

What are three ways objects can move?

Why It Matters

You move objects—and your body—every day. To do so, you use forces. One force that you need and use is friction. Without friction you couldn't grip a doorknob or pick up a ball. You would slip when you tried to walk. Once you were moving, you might not be able to stop!

e-Journal Visit our Web site www.science.mmhschool.com to do a research project on motion.

Think and Write

1. What causes a change in motion?

2. What can you do to move a ball resting on the ground?

3. What is friction?

4. Would it be easier to roller-skate on a gravel road or a smooth road? How do you know?

5. **Critical Thinking** You are swinging on a swing. What must you do to swing higher? What must you do to stop?

L·I·N·K·S

MATH LINK

Make a bar graph. Use the information from the chart below to create a bar graph. Explain why it is easier to compare the data in a bar graph than in the chart. Share this discovery with your teacher.

Stopping Distances

Ice	Sand	Road
8 meters	1 meter	2 meters

WRITING LINK

Explanatory Writing Tell how to play this game. Use the words *motion*, *force*, and *friction* in your explanation.

TECHNOLOGY LINK

 Science Newsroom CD-ROM Choose *Roll Over* to learn more about friction and gravity.

 LOG ON Visit www.science.mmhschool.com for more links.

Windmills and Waterwheels

Have you ever felt a strong gust of wind? Wind can be powerful. Wind energy starts with the Sun. When the Sun shines on the Earth, it heats some places more than others. That means air in some places is warmer than in others. Warm air is lighter than cold air. So warm air rises, and cool air moves in to take its place. This moving air is wind.

The energy from wind lifts kites through the air. It moves sailboats across the water. It also turns the blades of windmills. The turning blades collect the wind's energy and put it to work. In the past, people used windmills to grind corn and pump water. Today, windmills turn generators to make electricity.

Another powerful energy source is moving water. Have you ever heard the roar of a waterfall? Rushing water is very powerful. People put waterwheels in fast-moving rivers or under waterfalls to capture this energy. Like windmills, waterwheels were once used to grind grain and pump water. Later they were used to generate electricity.

Today we still use water and wind to make electricity. What other forms of energy could be used to make electricity?

Windmills make electricity using wind energy instead of burning fuel.

Years ago waterwheels such as this were used to power grist mills.

Write About It

1. Often coal, natural gas, and oil are burned to make electricity. Why is it better to use water and wind to make electricity?

2. Write about different ways that you've seen water and wind move things.

LOG ON Visit **www.science.mmhschool.com** to learn more about wind and water power.

Chapter 9 Review

Vocabulary

Fill in each blank with the best word from the list.

distance, E7   **motion,** E8
force, E14   **position,** E6
friction, E26   **speed,** E9
gravity, E16   **weight,** E17

1. An object's location is its _____.

2. How fast an object moves is its _____.

3. When you throw a ball in the air, it falls down because of _____.

4. Snow and ice make the ground have less _____.

5. Unbalanced forces cause _____.

6. You can measure how heavy or light something is by measuring its _____.

7. _____ is the space between two objects.

8. A(n) _____ can be a push or a pull.

9. Two things you need to measure speed are time and _____.

10. _____ is a force that slows objects down.

Test Prep

11. You know you have moved if your _____.

   A speed is zero
   B position stays the same
   C position has changed
   D weight is the same

12. Which of the following measures the speed of a car?

   F 30 miles
   G 30 miles per hour
   H 30 hours
   J 30 meters

13. A goose travels 20 kilometers (12 miles) per hour. How many kilometers does it travel in 8 hours?

   A 40 kilometers
   B 80 kilometers
   C 160 kilometers
   D 460 kilometers

14. Which statement about forces is true?

  F All pushes and pulls are forces.

  G Forces work in pairs.

  H Gravity is a force that is always pulling on you.

  J All of the above.

15. Making a playground slide smoother _____.

  A decreases friction

  B decreases speed

  C decreases motion

  D decreases weight

Concepts and Skills

16. **Critical Thinking** Four people are pushing very hard on a large cardboard box. However, the box is not moving. Explain how this can happen.

17. **Reading in Science** List the different ways an object's motion can change. Write a few short sentences to explain your answer.

18. INQUIRY SKILL **Interpret Data** What is the difference in speed between the fastest and slowest runners?

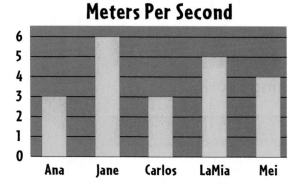

Meters Per Second

19. **Product Ads** Advertisements sometimes show people jumping very high in a certain type of sneakers. What force are these advertisements ignoring? Explain your answer.

20. **Scientific Methods** Your friend lives in a different country. How could you find out if your friend runs faster than you?

Did You Ever Wonder?

INQUIRY SKILL **Form a Hypothesis**

Forces cause objects to move, but what causes objects to stop moving? Investigate the different ways you can stop an object from moving.

LOG ON Visit www.science.mmhschool.com to boost your test scores.

CHAPTER 10

Work and Machines

Did You Ever Wonder?

Why is traveling on a bicycle faster than
walking? In both ways of traveling, you
work by moving your legs. A bicycle makes
work easier. It is a machine made of many parts.

INQUIRY SKILL **Infer** What are some other
machines, and how do they work?

Doing Work

Vocabulary

work, E38

energy, E39

Get Ready

People often say, "That's a lot of work!" What is work? Look at the picture. One person is doing work. The other person is not doing work. How can you tell who is doing work? Can you do a test to find out?

Inquiry Skill

You classify when you place things that share properties together in groups.

Explore Activity

Materials

4 books

pencil

What Is Work?

Procedure

1 Complete each action described below.
- Pick up one book.
- Pick up four books at one time.
- Put a book on your desk. Push down very hard on top of the book.
- Push against a wall with all of your strength.

2 **Classify** After each action, ask yourself, "Did I do work?" Decide whether the action was work. Record your decision in a data chart like the one shown.

Action	Work	Conclusion
Pick up one book	Work: Not work:	Why:

Drawing Conclusions

1 Evaluate your answers to the question "Did I do work?" Think about your answers. Is there a pattern? If so, what is it?

2 Explain why you classified each action the way you did.

3 FURTHER INQUIRY **Define Terms** Picking up one, four, or any number of books from your desk is work. Use this information and your chart to tell what work is.

Main Idea Work happens when there is a change in motion.

How Are Work and Energy Related?

How would you describe **work**? Scientists say that work is done when a force changes the motion of an object. This means that picking up books *is* work. You apply a force. The motion of the books changes. It takes work to move the books from the floor to the desk. However, pushing on a wall *is not* work. No matter how hard you push, the wall does not change.

Who's Doing Work?

READING

Diagrams

In which pictures is work being done?

To do work, you need **energy** (EN·uhr·jee). Energy is the ability to do work.

Energy exists in different forms. One form is the energy of motion. Moving things have energy of motion.

Another form is stored energy. Energy that can make an object move is called stored energy. A rock on top of a hill has stored energy. It can fall down the hill. Other examples of stored energy include fuel, batteries, and food. Different foods store different amounts of energy. The energy in foods is usually measured in calories.

Still other forms of energy include heat, light, sound, and electricity. What types of energy do you use every day?

READING **Compare and Contrast**
Compare and contrast stored energy and energy of motion.

Which rocks have energy of motion? Which rocks have stored energy?

QUICK LAB

Changing Energy

FOLDABLES™ Make a Folded Chart. (See p. R44.) Label the rows as shown.

Activity	Calories burned in 30 minutes

1. Your body needs energy. The table below shows the amount of energy in some of the foods we eat.

2. **Use Numbers** Using the table, plan a lunch. How many calories was your lunch? Record the information on the chart.

Food	Energy in Calories
2% chocolate milk	220
Tuna salad	190
Pizza	320

3. **Interpret data** Pick some of the activities you enjoy. How long would you need to do them in order to use the energy from your lunch? Record the information on your Foldables chart.

Activity	Calories Burned in 30 Minutes
Biking (slow)	35
Jogging	85
Listening to music	25

How Does Energy Change?

Energy can change from one form to another. Stored energy can change to the energy of motion when rocks roll down a hill. Another example is friction changing to heat. Try rubbing your hands together for 30 seconds. What do you feel?

Energy can also move from one object to another. Look at the diagram. It shows how energy of motion can move from one ball to another.

▷ **What is one example of how energy can change from one form to another?**

The green ball hits the yellow ball. The force of the green ball causes the yellow ball's motion to change. Now the yellow ball has energy of motion.

Why It Matters

Whether you have a job or not, you work every day. You work when you pedal a bike. You work when you jump rope. You even work when you do homework! Where do you get the energy to do work? You get it from the energy stored in the food you eat!

e-Journal Visit our Web site www.science.mmhschool.com to do a research project on how energy is stored.

Think and Write

1. Make a list of five things you did today that are examples of work. How do you know each is work?

2. What is energy?

3. How does energy change?

4. What energy change takes place when you hold a heavy box for ten minutes?

5. **Critical Thinking** You swing a baseball bat and hit the ball over the fence. Use the terms *work, energy, stored energy, energy of motion,* and *change of motion* to describe what happened.

L·I·N·K·S

WRITING LINK

Expository Writing Describe a job you would like to have someday. What would you do in this job? Would you be doing work the way a scientist would describe it?

MATH LINK

Order numbers. Use the table in the Quick Lab on the opposite page. Order the activities from fewest to most calories burned. Make an Energy Line: On a number line from 0 to 85, put each activity in its correct place.

SOCIAL STUDIES LINK

Research Habitat for Humanity. Habitat for Humanity is a group that helps people work together to build houses. What kinds of work would you do when building a house? Find out about Habitat for Humanity efforts in your area. Share the information with your class.

ART LINK

Make a poster. Think of the foods you eat that give you the most energy. Make a poster of these foods. Label your drawing. Display the posters about the classroom.

TECHNOLOGY LINK

LOG ON Visit www.science.mmhschool.com for more links.

Levers and Pulleys

Get Ready

How many machines have you used today? Probably many more than you think. Every day you use machines as you play and work. Machines make our lives easier. Some machines are complex. Others are simple. How do you think machines make work easier?

Inquiry Skill

You **experiment** when you perform a test to support or disprove a hypothesis.

Explore Activity

How Can You Make Work Easier?

Materials

roll of masking tape

safety goggles

building materials

Procedure: Design Your Own

BE CAREFUL! Wear goggles.

1. Invent a way to get the roll of tape from the floor to your desk. Your hands can help provide the lift, but you can't just pick up the tape.

2. **Communicate** Think of as many ways as you can to lift the tape. Share your ideas with your group members.

3. As a team, choose two plans and write them down. Remember to listen to each person's ideas.

4. **Experiment** Place the roll of masking tape on the floor. Try to lift it. Write down what happens. Does the plan work well?

5. **Experiment** Try another plan.

Drawing Conclusions

1. Which plan worked better?

2. What materials did you use in your most successful invention?

3. What forces did you use? What force did you work against?

4. **FURTHER INQUIRY**
   Experiment Would your plan work for lifting a small book? Explain your answer.

Main Idea Levers and pulleys are machines that make work easier.

How Can You Make Work Easier?

You need to move something. Often you move things with your hands. Sometimes you might need to use a **machine** (muh·SHEEN).

What is a machine? A machine is a tool that makes work easier to do. Remember, work is done when a force changes the motion of an object. How do machines make it easier for forces to move objects? This diagram will help you find out.

A **simple machine** (SIM·puhl muh·SHEEN) is often used to make work easier. Machines with few or no moving parts are called simple machines. A **lever** (LEV·uhr) is an example of a simple machine. A lever is a straight bar that moves on a fixed point. All levers have three important parts—the load, the fulcrum, and the force.

A lever makes moving a load easier in two ways. It lets you change the direction of a force. It may change the amount of force needed to move something.

Look at the girl on page E45. She presses down on one end of the lever. The rock is lifted at the other end. By using the lever, she makes lifting the rock easier.

The load is the object being lifted or moved. The force is the push or pull that moves the lever. The fulcrum is the point where the lever turns.

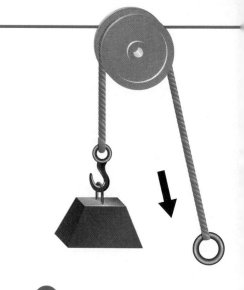

1 A machine can change the direction of the force you need to do work.

▷ **What is a simple machine?**

What Machines Do

2 Some machines change both the direction and the amount of force you need to do work.

3 A machine can change the amount of force you need to do work.

How Levers Work

READING Diagrams

1. How do levers make work easier?

2. Draw a lever. Label the force, load, and fulcrum.

Force

Fulcrum

Load

QUICK LAB

Make a Lever

FOLDABLES™ Make a Trifold Book. (See p. R42.) Label the rows as shown.

2. Experiment
3. Experiment
4. Draw and Label

1. Use clay to hold a pencil in place on your desk. Place a ruler over the center of the pencil.

2. **Experiment** Put two blocks on one end of the ruler. Add pieces of clay to the other end of the ruler. How much clay does it take to lift the blocks? Write your answer on the Foldables book.

3. **Experiment** Change the position of the ruler on the pencil. Repeat step 2. How does the new position change your results? Write your answer on the Foldables book.

4. Draw your lever on the book. Label the force, load, and fulcrum.

Are There Different Kinds of Levers?

All the levers in the world fall into three types. Each type is set up differently. The force, fulcrum, and load can change places. How the force, fulcrum, and load are arranged tells you what type of lever it is. Take a look at how each lever works.

▷ **What three parts must every lever have?**

Different Kinds of Levers

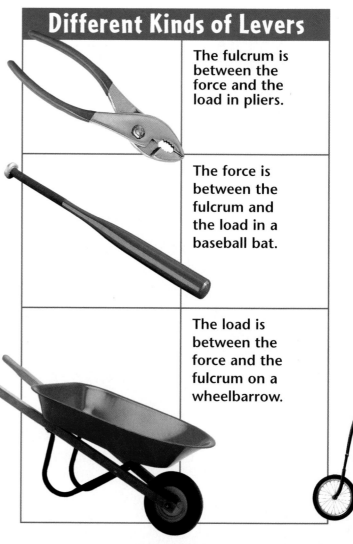

The fulcrum is between the force and the load in pliers.

The force is between the fulcrum and the load in a baseball bat.

The load is between the force and the fulcrum on a wheelbarrow.

What Are Some Other Simple Machines?

Another kind of lever is the **wheel and axle** (HWEEL AND AK·suhl). This simple machine has a wheel that turns on a post. The post is called an axle.

A wheel and axle makes work easier. It changes the strength of a turning force. The wheel turns a long distance. The axle turns a short distance.

A *windlass* (WIND·luhs) is used to raise water from a well. A bucket is tied to a rope. The other end of the rope is tied to the axle. At the end of the axle is the handle. When you turn the handle in a large circle, the axle turns in a small circle. The bucket moves up.

What kind of simple machine is a windlass?

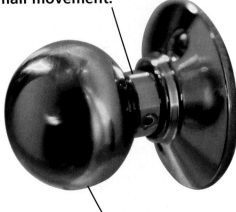

The axle makes a small movement.

The wheel makes a large movement.

> ▷ **How does a wheel and axle make work easier?**

Turning the pedals turns the axle. That turns the wheel. When the wheel makes a circle, it goes a long distance.

What Goes Down to Go Up?

A **pulley** (POOL·ee) is another kind of lever. It uses a wheel and a rope to lift a load. There are different kinds of pulleys. The diagram helps you compare two kinds of pulleys you may have seen. In both kinds of pulleys, you pull down to lift up.

One-wheel pulley   **Two-wheel pulley**

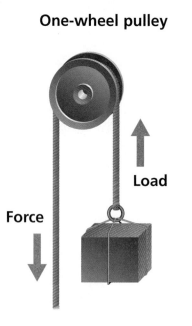

Load

Force

The force and load are equal.

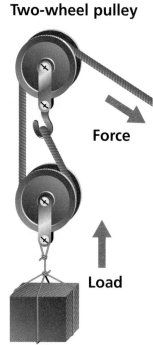

Force

Load

Less force is needed to move the load.

READING **Compare and Contrast**
Compare two different kinds of pulleys. How are they the same? How are they different?

L·I·N·K·S

Why It Matters

You are surrounded by machines. If you don't believe it, take a look around. A spoon is a type of lever. A bottle opener is a type of lever, too. Even your arms, legs, and fingers are levers!

ⓔ-Journal Visit our Web site www.science.mmhschool.com to do a research project on simple machines.

Think and Write

1. How do machines make work easier?

2. What is a simple machine?

3. What kind of simple machine will help you raise a sail on a sailboat?

4. How do your arms, legs, and fingers help you to lift things during the day?

5. **Critical Thinking** What if you are trying to lift a toy car using a lever? Where can the fulcrum be moved to lift the load most easily?

WRITING LINK

Expository Writing How do modern tools, such as cars and computers, affect your daily life? Brainstorm ideas with a group. List how such tools have had a good or bad effect on you. Then use your list to write a newspaper article.

MATH LINK

Make a bar graph. List what types of things you lifted in two days. How many times a day did you lift each? Make a bar graph to show your findings. Share this with your classmates.

LITERATURE LINK

Read *Machines That Build* to learn about simple machines at a construction site. When you finish reading the book, draw your favorite piece of construction equipment. Try the activities at the end of the book.

Machines That Build
by Whit Fisher
illustrated by John Rice

TECHNOLOGY LINK

LOG ON Visit www.science.mmhschool.com for more links.

What Is a System?

Your digestive system has many parts that work together.

Could you digest food without a stomach? Could a flashlight shine without a battery? No! You need those parts to make things work.

Your stomach is part of a system—the digestive system. A system is made up of parts that interact with each other. All the parts work together to do a job. Take a bite of pizza. Your digestive system gets to work! Your mouth chews the food. The food slides down your esophagus. Next, your stomach mixes chemicals with the food to break it down. Then the food moves into your small intestine. There the nutrients from the food pass into your bloodstream. That's how nutrients get to your cells.

Look inside this flashlight. Name the parts of the system that are working together.

A flashlight is a system, too. The parts of a flashlight work together to make a beam of light. The parts of a flashlight are the battery, the light bulb, wires, and the switch. The battery provides the power. The light bulb provides the light. And the switch connects the battery and the light bulb. When these parts work together, you can find your way in the dark!

Take a bite of pizza. Turn on a flashlight. What other systems can you describe?

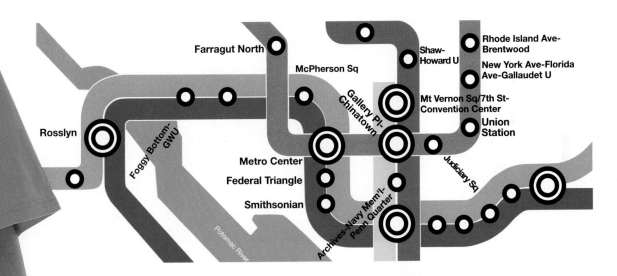

City transportation systems take people where they want to go. The circles show where trains make stops.

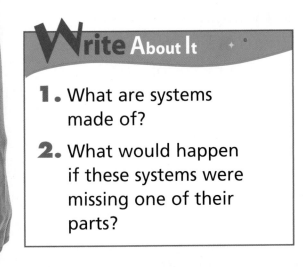

Write About It

1. What are systems made of?

2. What would happen if these systems were missing one of their parts?

LOG ON Visit www.science.mmhschool.com to learn more about systems.

More Simple Machines

Vocabulary

ramp, E54

inclined plane, E54

wedge, E55

screw, E56

compound machine, E57

Get Ready

This pyramid is called the Pyramid of the Sun. It was built more than one thousand years ago. It is made from mud, dirt, and large pieces of stone. It stands more than 200 feet tall!

One thousand years ago, there were no bulldozers, tractors, or trucks. People built this huge pyramid. How did they do it?

Inquiry Skill

You infer when you form ideas from facts or observations.

Explore Activity

How Can a Ramp Make Work Easier?

Materials

1-m wooden board

spring scale

thin spiral notebook

10-cm piece of string

chair

meterstick

safety goggles

Procedure

BE CAREFUL! Wear goggles.

1. Can you design a plan to find out if lifting an object straight up takes less force than pulling it up a ramp?

2. Tie one end of the string around the bottom of the spring scale. Tie the other end to the middle of the spiral wire of the notebook.

3. **Measure** Measure the pull needed to lift the notebook straight up to the height of the chair's seat. Then measure the distance you pulled the book. Record your measurements.

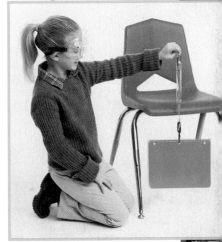

4. **Measure** Lean one end of the wooden board on the chair. Measure the pull needed to move the notebook up the board to the seat of the chair. Then measure the distance you pulled the book. Record your measurements.

Drawing Conclusions

1. Look at your measurements. Which method of moving the notebook required more force? Which method required moving the notebook a greater distance?

2. **FURTHER INQUIRY** **Infer** What happens if you change the angle of the board? How does this affect the amount of force needed to move the object?

Main Idea Simple machines make work easier.

What Is an Inclined Plane?

How might the people who built the Pyramid of the Sun have lifted the blocks of stone? They might have used a **ramp**. A ramp is a flat surface that is higher at one end. A ramp is also called an **inclined plane** (in·KLIGHND PLAYN). Inclined planes are simple machines that make work easier.

How does an inclined plane make work easier? To go up a hill, you have two paths. The path that goes straight up is shorter. However, it takes more effort. The ramp is a longer distance, but it takes less effort.

Which way should you go? When the load isn't heavy, you may choose to go straight up. When the load is heavy, you must use a ramp. The stone blocks used to build the pyramid were too heavy to move straight up. Scientists think that they may have been moved using an inclined plane.

Where have you seen ramps used in your community?

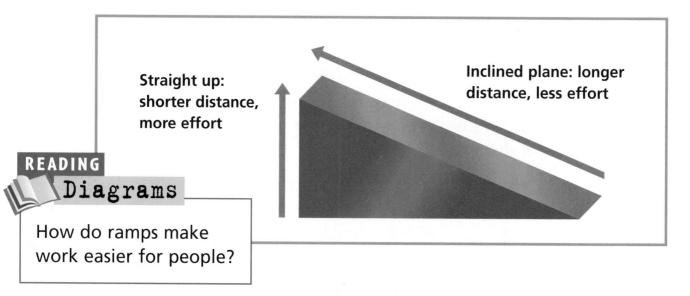

Straight up: shorter distance, more effort

Inclined plane: longer distance, less effort

READING Diagrams

How do ramps make work easier for people?

A **wedge** (WEJ) is another simple machine. A wedge is made of two inclined planes placed back to back. A wedge uses force to raise an object or to split objects apart.

An ax is a wedge. When an ax is swung, the downward force is changed into a sideways force. The sideways force pushes, or splits, the wood apart.

Another example of a wedge is a plow. A plow is a machine used by farmers. As the plow is dragged through the soil, it cuts through the ground. The soil is pushed aside.

▷ **What kind of simple machine is a plow?**

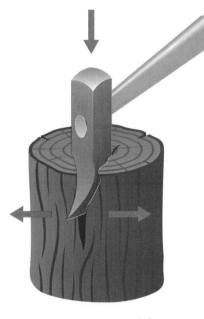

The downward force of the ax changes to the sideways force that splits the wood.

A plow helps a farmer prepare the ground for planting.

What Is a Screw?

What happens when you wrap an inclined plane around a pole? You have a **screw**! A screw is an inclined plane wrapped into a spiral. The ridges of the screw are called *threads*.

It takes less force to turn a screw than to pound a nail. That is because the screw is moving a longer distance. Remember, the longer the distance, the less force you need to do work. When you turn the head of a screw once, the threads travel a long way. You apply force over a longer distance, just like any other inclined plane.

▷ **What simple machine is wrapped around a screw?**

This machine is called an auger. An auger is a screw. It can drill into soil.

READING Diagrams

1. How do a nail and a screw compare?

2. Which screw has a longer inclined plane?

A screw with a longer inclined plane has more threads. A screw with a shorter inclined plane has fewer threads.

What Happens If You Put Two Simple Machines Together?

You can make work easier by using a **compound machine**, too. When you put two or more simple machines together, you make a compound machine.

A pair of scissors is a compound machine. Part is a lever. Part is a wedge.

A water faucet is also a compound machine. Part is a wheel and axle. Part is a screw.

READING **Compare and Contrast**
How are simple machines and compound machines alike? How are they different?

A bicycle uses wheels and axles, and a lever. There are several sets of wheels and axles.

Inquiry Skill
BUILDER

Which Screw Makes Work Easiest?

You know that a screw is a simple machine. It makes work easier, just like any other inclined plane. It lets you use less force over a longer distance. Screws come in many shapes and sizes. Some screws make work easier than others.

The diagram here shows three screws. In this activity you will use numbers to evaluate how each screw is different. Then you will use that information to infer which screw makes work easiest.

Procedure

1. **Measure** What is the width of each screw's head? What is the length of each screw?

2. Record your measurements in a table.

3. **Use Numbers** Count the number of threads on each screw.

4. Record the information in a table.

Drawing Conclusions

1. How does the number of threads on each screw compare?

2. Explain how the number of threads on each screw relates to the length of its inclined plane.

3. **Infer** Which screw makes work easiest? How do you know?

Materials
ruler

Why It Matters

Simple and compound machines help you do many of your everyday activities. They help you cut an apple and wrap a present. You use them to travel from place to place.

e-Journal Visit our Web site www.science.mmhschool.com to do a research project on simple and compound machines.

Think and Write

1. How does an inclined plane make work easier?

2. What is a compound machine?

3. Which is easier—turning a screw or pounding a nail of the same size? Why?

4. **INQUIRY SKILL** **Use Numbers** You have two screws. Each measures 2 inches long and has a 1-inch head. One screw has 20 threads. The other screw has 30 threads. Which screw will make work easier? Why?

5. **Critical Thinking** You see a bird flying by with grass in its beak. Explain how the bird is using its beak as a simple machine.

L·I·N·K·S

SOCIAL STUDIES LINK

Take a survey. What simple machines are in your neighborhood? Make a list of the simple machines you find and where they are located. For example, you might find a seesaw in the playground.

WRITING LINK

Persuasive Writing Pick a product of technology such as the zipper, paper clip, or computer. Find out more about the technology of the product. Write about how this technology contributes to solving problems. Share this information with your class.

MATH LINK

Compare numbers. Find the simple machines in your classroom. Make a tally chart of the different kinds of simple machines. Compare to tell which kind has more.

TECHNOLOGY LINK

Science Newsroom CD-ROM Choose *Machines in Motion* to learn about six simple machines.

LOG ON Visit www.science.mmhschool.com for more links.

Chapter 10 Review

Vocabulary

Fill in the blank with the best word or words from the list.

compound machine, E57

energy, E39

inclined plane, E54

lever, E44

pulley, E48

screw, E56

simple machine, E44

wedge, E55

wheel and axle, E47

work, E38

1. A ramp is a type of _____.

2. A(n) _____ is made up of at least two simple machines.

3. When you use a force to change the motion of an object, you do _____.

4. The ability to do work is called _____.

5. The simple machine with a fulcrum, load, and force is a(n) _____.

6. A machine with few or no moving parts is a(n) _____.

Two types of inclined planes:

7. _____

8. _____.

Two types of levers:

9. _____

10. _____.

Test Prep

11. Which is a true statement about work?

A Work takes money.

B Work takes a long time.

C Work changes an object's size.

D Work changes an object's position.

12. A lever moves back and forth on a(n) _____.

F fulcrum

G straight bar

H axle

J ramp

13. What simple machine is shown in the diagram?

A wheel and axle

B screw

C inclined plane

D lever

14. Which simple machine lets a roller skate roll?

    F a screw

    G a pulley

    H an inclined plane

    J a wheel and axle

15. A pair of scissors is a compound machine. What two simple machines make up a pair of scissors?

    A wheel and axle, and lever

    B lever and wedge

    C lever and pulley

    D pulley and wedge

Concepts and Skills

16. **Reading in Science** Look at the two different types of pulleys below. How are they alike? How are they different?

One-wheel pulley

Two-wheel pulley

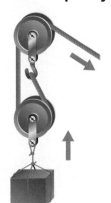

17. **Critical Thinking** Amanda can lift 10 kilograms with a single pulley. Will a two-pulley system make lifting easier? Explain your answer.

18. INQUIRY SKILL **Use Numbers** You want to pry a big rock out of your garden. You have a 1-meter board and a 2-meter board. Which board will help you move the rock more easily? Explain.

19. **Scientific Methods** You need to find a way to hold down paper in the wind. Describe how you would test your ideas.

20. **Decision Making** There is a meeting in your school to discuss plans to install ramps for people with disabilities. Write a speech explaining what you would say.

Did You Ever Wonder?

INQUIRY SKILL **Communicate** Explain how you could combine several simple machines to make work easier.

LOG ON Visit www.science.mmhschool.com to boost your test scores.

Dr. Ellen Ochoa

Engineer and Astronaut

Astronaut Ellen Ochoa has made four trips in the space shuttle. Her main job was to control a robotic arm to move large objects in space.

"The robotic arm is like a human arm. It has joints that make it move," Dr. Ochoa explains. Two hand controllers tell each joint how to move. A team of scientists and engineers spent years developing the arm.

In 2002, Dr. Ochoa used the arm to set up a big frame on the International Space Station (ISS). The frame holds solar panels that power the station.

The ISS is a laboratory in space. Teams of astronauts from many countries will live on it. They do experiments to learn more about space. "Without the arm, we wouldn't have been able to build the station as it is today," explains Dr. Ochoa.

LOG ON Visit www.science.mmhschool.com to learn more about the work of space engineers.

TOP 5 International Space Station Facts

1. The Space Station is the most expensive single object ever built.
2. The Space Station circles Earth every 90 minutes.
3. When completed, the Space Station will be visible to more than 90 percent of the world's population.
4. The Space Station's electric power system is connected with eight miles of wire.
5. If lined up end to end, the batteries used on the Space Station would measure 2,900 feet.

Write About It

1. What is the International Space Station?
2. How does the robotic arm work?

Gravity Games

Your goal is to build a toy or game that uses gravity.

What to Do

Gravity causes things to fall to Earth. You can roll a marble down a ramp. You can toss a ball into the air and it comes back down. Invent a toy or game that uses gravity. Write down your invention. Have your teacher approve it. Try to build it. You can use materials such as marbles, construction paper, modeling clay, or shoe boxes.

Draw Conclusions

Identify the forces that are used in your toy or game. Write them down.

Machines Make an Amusement Park Fun!

Your goal is to make a model of a ride at an amusement park.

What to Do

Remember the rides at an amusement park? Use what you've learned about machines and forces to build your own ride. Use materials such as rubber bands, paper plates, milk cartons, and crayons.

Draw Conclusions

Write a short paragraph to explain what type of machine you built and what type of force it uses.

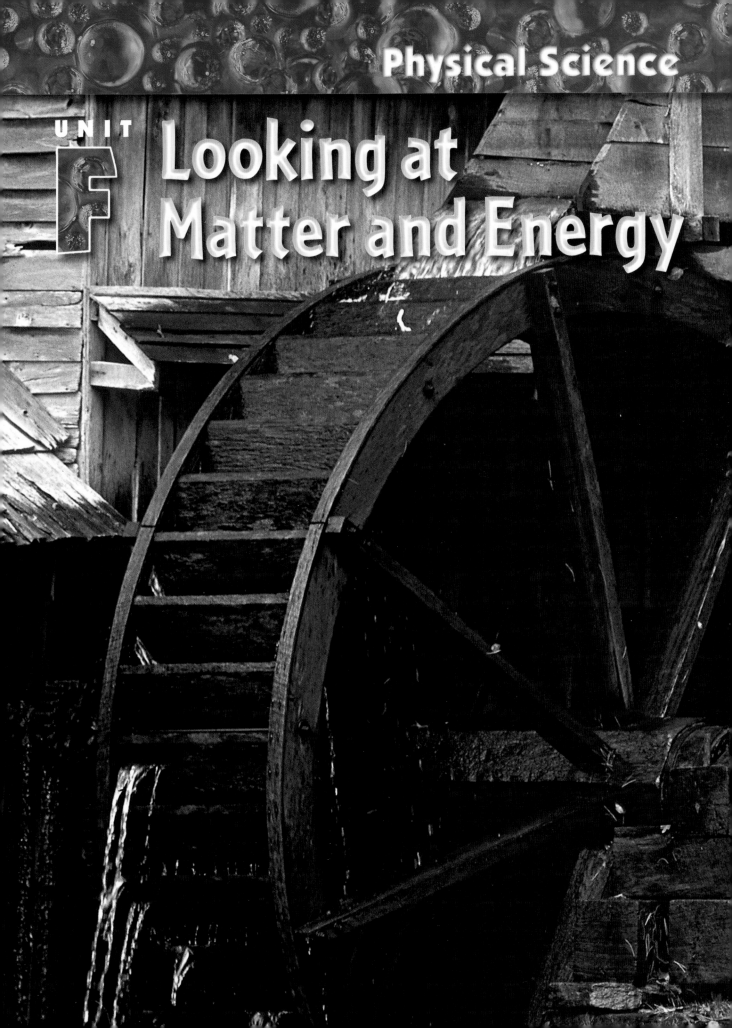

UNIT F

Looking at Matter and Energy

Looking at Matter and Energy

LOOK!

At a water mill, the flow of water turns a large wheel. Why do people build water mills?

CHAPTER

11

Matter

Did You Ever Wonder?

How can you tell different vegetables from one
another? Each vegetable has its own color, shape,
feel, and taste. Some even have a certain smell.
You can describe objects by their properties.

INQUIRY SKILL Measure What property do you think
a scale measures?

Properties of Matter

Get Ready

Have you ever tried to stuff too many books into your book bag? The book bag has only so much room. Books take up space. Papers and pencils do, too. Do all objects take up space?

Inquiry Skill

You experiment when you perform a test to support or disprove a hypothesis.

Explore Activity

Which Object Takes Up More Space?

Materials

plastic cup

water

markers

piece of clay

classroom objects

Procedure

1 **Predict** Look at the photograph. What will happen to the water level when you put the clay in the cup?

2 **Measure** Half-fill the cup with water. Use a marker to mark the water level on the outside of the cup.

3 **Observe** Place the clay in the cup. What happens? Mark the new water level. Use a different color.

4 **Predict** Look at other objects. Which one will raise the water level most? Record your prediction.

5 **Experiment** Add one object at a time to the cup. Mark the new water level each time. Use a different color.

Drawing Conclusions

1 **Infer** Which object takes up the most space? How do you know?

2 FURTHER INQUIRY **Experiment** What will happen to the water level in the cup if you change the shape of the clay?

Main Idea Matter is anything that takes up space and has mass.

How Do We Describe Matter?

Water, clay, rocks, and trees are all examples of **matter** (MAT·uhr). Matter is anything that takes up space and has mass. You are made of matter. This book and your pencil are, too. Every object you can name is made of matter.

The world is full of many kinds of matter. How do we tell them apart? Matter can be described by **properties** (PRAHP·uhr·teez). A property is any characteristic of matter that you can observe.

You can observe some properties with your sense of sight. You can observe color, size, and shape. You can also observe texture and luster. *Texture* (TEKS·chuhr) is how an object feels when you touch it. *Luster* (LUS·tuhr) is how an object shines in the light.

Observations of Matter

Object	dime
Color(s)	silver
Shape	a circle
Texture	hard and bumpy
Flexibility	does not bend
Luster	shiny
Diameter	1.9 millimeters
Weight	2 grams

READING Charts

1. What are some properties shown in the chart?

2. How could you make a chart like this for the other objects shown here? Try it.

Volume and Mass

Some objects take up more space than others. An object that takes up more space has a greater **volume** (VAHL·yewm). Volume is how much space an object takes up. The beach ball has a greater volume than the bowling ball. The bowling ball has a greater volume than the small rubber ball.

Another way to describe objects is by their **mass** . Mass is how much matter is in an object. An object with a large mass feels heavy. An object with a small mass feels light. The bowling ball has more mass than the beach ball.

▶ **Which object has the most volume? The most mass?**

How Do You Measure Mass and Volume?

Larger objects do not always have more mass than smaller ones. The bowling ball is smaller than the beach ball. However, the bowling ball has a greater mass. How is that possible?

Matter is made of very tiny particles. In some objects the particles are close together. In other objects they are farther apart. The particles inside the bowling ball are packed together tightly. They are packed more tightly than those inside the beach ball. The bowling ball is made of more particles than the beach ball. It has more mass. Matter with tightly packed particles is called dense matter. Matter that is dense usually sinks in water. Matter that is less dense than water will float.

Particles of air are inside the beach ball. They are loosely packed. The beach ball floats in water.

Tightly packed particles make up the bowling ball. The bowling ball sinks in water.

This juice carton has a volume of two liters.

One unit used to measure mass is called the *gram*. One gram is the mass of about two small paper clips. A nickel has a mass of about five grams. You can use the letter *g* to stand for the word *gram*.

You can measure more massive objects in *kilograms*. One kilogram equals 1,000 grams. An eight-year-old has a mass of about 30 kilograms. You can use the letters *kg* to stand for this word.

One unit used to measure volume is the *liter*. You can use the letter *L* to stand for the word *liter*.

READING Draw Conclusions

Why does a bowling ball have more mass than a beach ball?

QUICK LAB

Measuring Mass

FOLDABLES™ Make a Folded Table. (See p. R 44.) Label the table as shown.

Object	Predicted Order	Mass	Order by Mass

1. **Predict** Gather five small objects. Predict the mass of the objects. Record your predictions in the table.

2. **Measure** the mass of each object. Place the object on one side of a balance. Add paper clips to the other side until the two sides balance. Record the number of paper clips in the table.

3. **Use Numbers** What is the mass of each object in grams? (Two paper clips equal about one gram.)

4. Record the objects from most mass to least mass. How do your results compare with your predictions? Explain on your table.

5. What is the mass of all of the objects combined? Explain your answer on the back of the table.

How Are Mass and Weight Related?

The more mass an object has, the more it weighs. How are mass and weight different?

A good place to look for the answer is the Moon! If you visited the Moon, your mass would stay the same. The matter inside you would not change. However, you would weigh much less. This is because the weight of an object depends on the pull of gravity. Gravity is the force pulling two objects together. Your weight is the pull of gravity between you and Earth. The pull of gravity on the Moon is weaker than on Earth. Your weight here would be less.

Weight is an example of a force. Remember, a force is a push or a pull. Forces can be measured in units called *newtons*. If your mass is 25 kilograms, then your weight on Earth is 245 newtons.

▷ **How do mass and weight compare?**

Earth		
	Boy	**Cat**
Weight	235 N	58 N
Mass	24 kg	6 kg

Moon		
	Boy	**Cat**
Weight	40 N	9 N
Mass	24 kg	6 kg

Why It Matters

Matter takes up space and has mass. That's why two objects cannot be in the same place at the same time. You can describe matter by naming its properties. You might describe your new sneakers to a friend. Knowing an object's properties is important when you need to find a lost item.

e-Journal Visit our Web site www.science.mmhschool.com to do a research project on properties of matter.

Think and Write

1. List at least four physical properties of your favorite food.

2. What is the difference between mass and volume?

3. Does the largest object always have the greatest mass? Explain.

4. If your mass is 25 kilograms on Earth, what is your mass on the Moon? Explain your answer.

5. **Critical Thinking** Tanya has a rock, a measuring cup, and some water. How can she measure the volume of the rock?

L·I·N·K·S

WRITING LINK

Writing That Compares Mass and weight are related. Yet they are also different. Write an essay that compares mass and weight. Organize your facts. For example, give all the details about mass in one paragraph, and all the details about weight in another. Use words that compare and contrast.

MATH LINK

Compare and order fractions. Make a number line. Place a 0 and a 1 on the number line. Locate the following fractions on the number line: $\frac{2}{3}$, $\frac{3}{4}$, and $\frac{5}{6}$. Which fraction is closest to 0? Which fraction is closest to 1? Think of three other numbers. Add them to the number line. Is there any number that cannot be added to the number line?

ART LINK

Draw a picture. Draw a picture of something you saw on your way to school. Label all of its properties.

TECHNOLOGY LINK

 LOG ON Visit www.science.mmhschool.com for more links.

Comparing Solids, Liquids, and Gases

Get Ready

Do you see different kinds of matter all around you? Some matter is solid, like these flowers. What are some properties of solids? Some matter is liquid, like the drops of water on the flowers. What are some properties of liquids? The air is also matter. The air is a gas. What are some properties of gases?

Inquiry Skill

You **classify** when you place things that share properties together in groups.

Explore Activity

How Can You Classify Matter?

Materials

plastic
container of
Oobleck

investigation
tools

newspaper

safety goggles

Procedure: Design Your Own

BE CAREFUL! Wear goggles.

1. In your own words, define solids and liquids.

2. **Observe** Use your senses to describe Oobleck. How does it look? What does it feel like? Record your observations.

3. **Experiment** Use the tools given to you to experiment with Oobleck. What new things do you observe? Record your observations.

4. **Classify** Review your definitions of solids and liquids. Would you classify Oobleck as a solid or a liquid? Explain your answer.

Drawing Conclusions

1. **Communicate** What observations did you make about the properties of Oobleck?

2. How did you decide to classify Oobleck? What helped you make your decision?

3. **FURTHER INQUIRY** **Form a Hypothesis** Does Oobleck have different properties at different temperatures? Design an experiment to find out.

Main Idea Matter exists as solids, liquids, and gases.

How Can You Classify Matter?

Solids and liquids are two forms of matter. A third form of matter is gas. The forms of matter are also called states of matter. All states of matter take up space and have mass.

A sneaker is a **solid** (SAHL·id). A solid is matter that has a definite size and shape. *Definite* means it stays the same. Put a sneaker into a jar or box. It stays the same.

Juice is an example of a **liquid** (LIK·wid). A liquid is matter that has a definite volume. It does not have a definite shape. Pour juice into a glass. It will take on the shape of the glass.

A **gas** is matter that has no definite shape or volume. Gases take the shape of whatever container they are in. The air all around us is a gas.

This balloon is filled with a gas. The gas is helium.

The juice in this glass is a liquid.

This sneaker is a solid.

Remember that matter is made of particles. These particles are very, very small. In a solid the particles are packed closely together. They form a certain pattern. The pattern gives a solid its definite shape.

The particles in a liquid are close together. However, they do not form a pattern. The particles in a liquid have more energy. They are able to slide past one another. That is why liquids change shape.

The particles in a gas have even more energy. They spread out to fill a large container. They squeeze together to fit into a small container.

▶ **What do solids and liquids have in common?**

READING ▢▢ **Diagrams**

1. How do the particles in a solid compare with the particles in a gas?

2. How would you describe the particles in a liquid?

Particles in Different States of Matter

Solid

Liquid

Gas

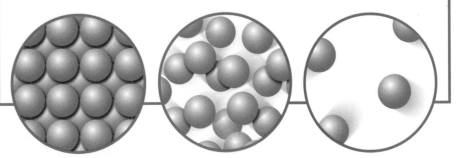

How Can Matter Change?

Matter can change but still remain the same kind of matter. What happens when you cut a piece of paper? The paper looks different, but it is still made of the same particles. Cut paper into as many pieces as you like. It will still be paper!

The same is true when you make a wooden model. As you cut and sand the wood, its size and shape change. The wood is still wood. It is still made of the same particles.

A **physical change** (FIZ·i·kuhl CHAYNJ) is a change in how matter looks, but not in the kind of matter it is. The kind of matter stays the same. Sifting, sanding, and pounding are examples of physical changes.

Wood is still wood when it is cut.

When the paper is folded, its shape changes. It is still paper.

Matter can change state. You can find water in the solid state, liquid state, or gas state. Water looks very different in each state, but it is still the same kind of matter.

Ice is the solid state of water. The particles in ice are close together. They do not move very much. When ice is heated, it *melts*. Melting is the change from solid to liquid. The particles gain energy and move faster.

Water can also change from a liquid to a gas. This happens when water *evaporates* (i·VAP·uh·rayts). The gas state of water is called water vapor. You cannot see water vapor. It is part of the air around you.

When water vapor cools, it loses energy and *condenses*. It becomes a liquid. When liquid water cools enough, it *freezes* into ice. Ice is a solid. Melting, freezing, condensing, and evaporating are also examples of physical changes.

▶ **What is a physical change?**

READING

Charts

1. How can liquid water change to a solid?

2. How can liquid water change to a gas?

Changes of State

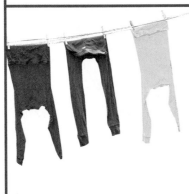

Melt
When ice melts, water changes from a solid to a liquid.

Freeze
When water freezes, liquid water changes to a solid.

Evaporate
When water evaporates, it changes into water vapor. You cannot see water vapor.

Condense
When water vapor in the air touches the cold glass, it condenses. You see the water drops on the outside of the glass.

Can You Mix Different Kinds of Matter Together?

When you mix different kinds of matter together, you may get a **mixture** (MIKS·chuhr). In a mixture the properties of each kind of matter do not change. Lemonade is a mixture of lemon juice and water.

Fruit salad is a mixture of many kinds of fruit. Pick out a piece of orange from a fruit salad. It will be just like any other orange piece.

Mixtures can be any combination of solids, liquids, and gases. Air is a mixture of different gases. Pour milk in your breakfast cereal. You have made a mixture of a liquid and a solid.

▷ **What is a mixture?**

What kinds of fruit make up this mixture?

How can you separate the rice, marbles, and paper clips in this mixture?

What Is a Solution?

Salt and water mix well together, forming a solution.

Sand and water do not mix well. Sand does not dissolve.

There are many kinds of mixtures. One kind of mixture is a **solution** (suh·LEW·shuhn). A solution forms when one or more kinds of matter are mixed evenly in another kind of matter. Making a solution is an example of a physical change.

Salt water is an example of a solution. Mix salt with water, and you cannot see the salt anymore. The salt is still there.

If the water evaporates, the salt will be left behind.

Not all solids form solutions in water. Try to mix sand with water. The sand will just sink to the bottom. Some things fall to the bottom no matter how long you stir.

Some solutions contain no liquid at all! Air is a solution of different gases. Steel is a solution of several solids. Steel is used to make cars, bridges, and buildings.

READING Draw Conclusions
What do you need to make a solution?

When you make lemonade with water, lemon juice, and sugar, what happens to the sugar?

Inquiry Skill
BUILDER

SKILL Communicate

Making a Table

When you communicate, you share information with others. Scientists communicate what they learn from an experiment. They might tell people how they think the new information can be used. You can communicate by talking or by creating a drawing, chart, table, or graph.

Communicate what you know about the properties of solids, liquids, and gases. Look at the photograph on this page to help you answer the questions at right.

Procedure

1 Observe What states of matter do you see in the photograph?

2 What properties do these states have?

3 Draw a table like the one shown on this page.

4 Communicate Fill in the table with your observations.

Drawing Conclusions

Communicate Give an example of a solid, a liquid, and a gas. Write a sentence that tells about the shape and volume of each one.

Properties of Matter	
States of Matter	**Properties**

L·I·N·K·S

Why It Matters

You eat many mixtures every day! Foods such as salad, pizza, and tacos are mixtures. You eat and drink solutions, too. Orange juice and hot cocoa are two examples of solutions. Can you think of other solutions you eat or drink?

e-Journal Visit our Web site www.science.mmhschool.com to do a research project on solids, liquids, and gases.

Think and Write

1. Name three states of matter. Give an example of each.

2. What is a physical change?

3. How is sugar different from lemonade?

4. INQUIRY SKILL Communicate How many ways can matter change state? Make a table.

5. Critical Thinking How would you separate salt from water?

WRITING LINK

Expository Writing What happens when oil and water mix? In 1989 a ship spilled oil into the water off the coast of Alaska. Research the *Exxon Valdez* oil spill. Write a news article describing what happened. Also, write about the clean-up efforts. Find facts that answer these questions: *What* took place? *Who* took part in it? *When*, *where*, and *why* did it happen?

MATH LINK

Select appropriate measuring units. Irene fills her thermos with lemonade for lunch. Does the thermos hold 1 liter or 1 milliliter of lemonade? Explain your answer.

LITERATURE LINK

Read *A Ride Over the Serengeti* to learn how a boy and a girl used their knowledge of matter to make a safe landing. Try the activities at the end of the book.

TECHNOLOGY LINK

LOG ON Visit www.science.mmhschool.com for more links.

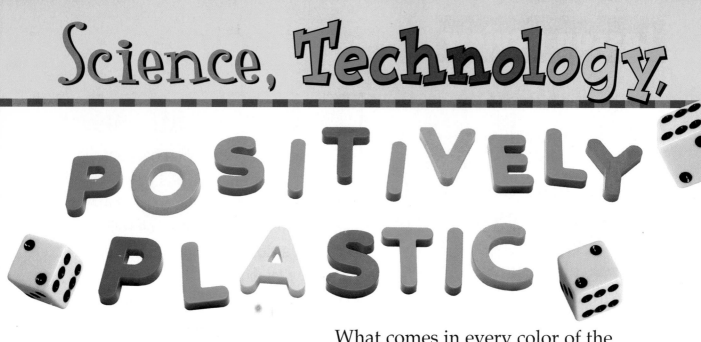

Science, Technology,

POSITIVELY PLASTIC

What comes in every color of the rainbow and can be found in almost every home in America? Plastic! We use plastic wrap to protect our foods. We put our leftovers in plastic containers. We put our garbage in plastic bags or plastic cans. We sit on plastic chairs, play with plastic toys, drink from plastic cups, and wash our hair with shampoo from plastic bottles! We know how useful it is, but exactly what is it?

Plastic doesn't grow in nature. It's made by mixing certain things together. We call it a produced or manufactured material. Plastic was first made in the 1850s from plants such as wood and cotton. However, the plastic was often soft and burned easily.

In the late 1920s, scientists began making usable plastics. Many modern plastics were invented in the 1930s.

Plastic is being rolled up at this factory.

and Society

What are the compass and sail boat made of?

Today plastics are made from oil and natural gas. It's true! Most clear plastic starts out as thick, black oil. That hard plastic coating inside a cooking pan begins as natural gas!

Over the years hundreds of different plastics have been developed. Some are hard and strong. Some are soft and bendable. Some are clear. Some are many colored. There's a plastic for almost every need. Scientists continue to experiment with plastics. They hope to find even more ways to use them!

What Did I Learn?

1. Plastic was first made from

A plants.

B animals.

C oil.

D natural gas.

2. According to the passage, plastics can be

F hard and strong.

G soft and bendable.

H clear or many colored.

J all of the above.

LOG ON Visit **www.science.mmhschool.com** to learn more about plastics.

Building Blocks of Matter

Get Ready

This large magnet is being lowered into a pile of junk. The magnet picks up some objects but not others. If you used a magnet, what objects could you pick up?

Inquiry Skill

You **predict** when you state possible results of an event or experiment.

Explore Activity

Materials

magnet

several objects

What Do Magnets Attract?

Procedure

1 **Observe** Look at your objects. What properties of the objects do you observe? Record your observations.

2 **Predict** Which objects will the magnet attract? Record your predictions.

3 **Experiment** Get a magnet from your teacher. Test your predictions. Hold a magnet over each object. Record the results.

Drawing Conclusions

1 **Classify** Use a table like the one below to identify objects the magnet attracts and those objects it does not attract.

2 What do the objects that a magnet attracts have in common? What do the objects that a magnet does not attract have in common?

3 FURTHER INQUIRY **Experiment** How can magnets be used to separate objects? Test your ideas.

Magnet attracts	Magnet does not attract

What Objects Do Magnets Attract?

Magnets attract some objects but not others. Objects that a magnet attracts are made of certain **metals** (MET·uhlz). A metal is a hard, shiny material found in Earth's ground. There are many kinds of metals. Magnets attract the metal called iron, and some other metals, too.

Anything that attracts metals has the property of *magnetism* (MAG·ni·tiz·uhm). Magnetism is the property that holds a magnet to your refrigerator.

Magnetism is very useful. Visit a junkyard. You can see magnetism at work. It is used to sort certain metals from other objects.

What Is a Magnet?

A magnet is an object that attracts iron and some other metals.

A rock called magnetite acts as a weak magnet.

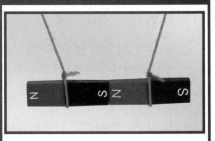

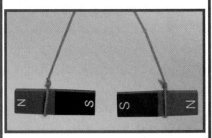

Magnets have two poles called North and South. Unlike poles attract each other. Like poles repel each other.

Do you need iron in your body? The answer is yes! You need to eat iron every day to stay healthy. You get iron from meats and dark green vegetables, such as spinach.

Iron is often mixed with other materials to make steel. Steel is strong and lasts a long time. It is used to build things such as bridges, railroads, and cars.

Other metals include gold, silver, copper, and aluminum (a·LEW·muh·nuhm). Each metal has its own properties. Copper and aluminum are light and soft. We use copper to make pipes. We use aluminum to make airplanes. Gold is soft, yellow, and very shiny. Silver is shiny, too. We often use gold and silver to make jewelry.

Spinach contains the metal iron, which is important to good health.

▷ **What properties do metals have?**

Gold is used to make jewelry because it is soft and shiny.

Aluminum is strong and light, so it is used to make canoes.

What Are the Building Blocks of Matter?

The metals iron, gold, silver, and copper are **elements** (EL·uh·muhnts). Elements are the building blocks of matter. There are more than 100 different elements. They make up all the matter in the world. Some elements, such as iron and copper, are solids. Other elements are found as liquids. Still others, such as helium (HEE·lee·uhm), are gases.

Each element has its own properties. Elements join together in different ways. They form everything on Earth.

All elements are made of **atoms** (AT·uhmz). An atom is the smallest particle of matter. It is too small to see with your eyes. The atoms that make up one element are all alike. They are different from the atoms of other elements.

Long ago, people thought the only elements were air, water, fire, and earth. Today we know these are not elements.

The element neon is used to light signs. Neon is a gas.

The element helium is used to fill these balloons.

For example, water can break apart into two gases. These gases are hydrogen and oxygen. Both of these gases are elements.

Do you think wood is an element? If wood is heated, it gives off gases. It also produces a solid, black substance. This substance is called carbon. Carbon is an element. If carbon is heated, it only gets hotter.

What is an element?

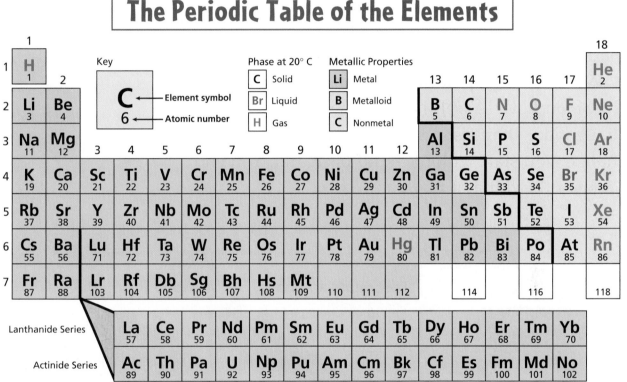

The Periodic Table of the Elements

This is the periodic table. It lists all the elements. The letter or letters in each box stand for the name of the element.

The tusks of a walrus contain calcium. Calcium is an element.

What Happens When Elements Join Together?

How do about 100 elements form all the materials on Earth? Elements can join together to form **compounds** (KAHM·powndz). A compound may form when you put two or more elements together. Compounds have very different properties from the elements they are made of.

Some compounds are made of just two elements. Have you seen rust on an old fence? Rust is a compound made of the two elements iron and oxygen.

When a compound forms, a **chemical change** (KEM·i·kuhl CHAYNJ) has taken place. Chemical changes are changes in the matter itself. In a chemical change, you start with one kind of matter. You end with another kind of matter.

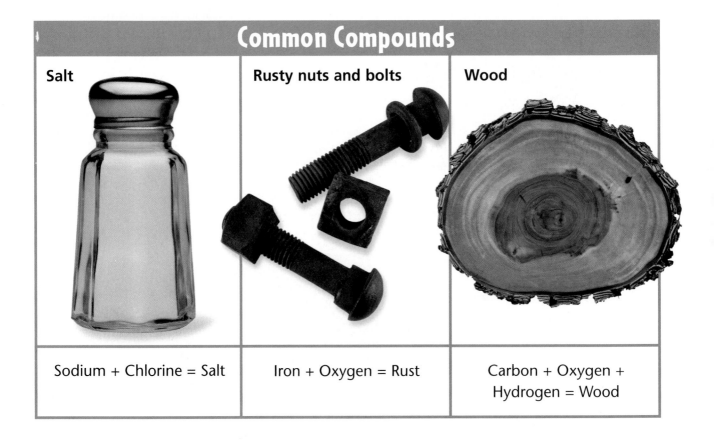

Common Compounds

Salt	Rusty nuts and bolts	Wood
Sodium + Chlorine = Salt	Iron + Oxygen = Rust	Carbon + Oxygen + Hydrogen = Wood

You observe chemical changes every day. When wood burns, it produces gases and ash. This is a chemical change. Iron changing into rust is also a chemical change. Rust is very different from iron. It is softer, and it peels.

Cooking uses lots of chemical changes. Cake batter changes when you bake it. You know it has changed because it feels and tastes different. When you eat the cake, your body breaks it down. Then your body uses its energy. These, too, are chemical changes.

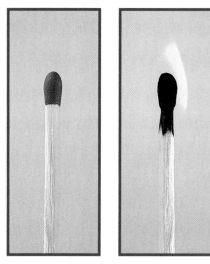

A chemical change is happening in the lighted match. The wood is combining with oxygen in the air to form new kinds of matter.

Chemical changes happen when plants make food. They change water and carbon dioxide into food.

▷ **What are two common chemical changes?**

Heat causes a chemical change in the dough. It changes into bread.

How Do Chemical Changes and Physical Changes Compare?

Remember that folding and tearing are physical changes. Freezing and melting are, too. Matter looks different after a physical change, but the kind of matter stays the same.

In a chemical change, the kind of matter changes. Look for one material going away and a new material forming. That is a sign of a chemical change. Other signs are burning, forming bubbles, and forming new colors. When a new material is formed, it has changed its chemical properties. The ability to burn, change color, and form bubbles are all examples of chemical properties.

Toasting a marshmallow is a chemical change.

READING **Draw Conclusions**
How can you tell a chemical change from a physical change?

Chemical changes happen when a tomato becomes ripe.

Melting is a physical change.

Cutting paper is making a physical change.

Lesson Review

Why It Matters

Everything in the world is made of elements. Elements are the building blocks of matter. You need some elements and compounds to live and grow. Others make life easier or more fun. Some can be dangerous!

Your body changes as you grow. Both physical changes and chemical changes take place inside you every day.

e-Journal Visit our Web site www.science.mmhschool.com to do a research project on physical and chemical changes.

Think and Write

1. What kinds of objects does a magnet attract?

2. What is an element?

3. What is the difference between a physical change and a chemical change?

4. How are elements different from compounds?

5. **Critical Thinking** Two clear liquids are mixed together. Bubbles and a green powder form. What kind of change is this? Explain.

L·I·N·K·S

WRITING LINK

Writing a Story In the 1840s gold was discovered in California. Many people headed west to dig for gold and to become rich. This event was called the gold rush. Research how it changed California. Write a story that takes place in the gold rush.

MATH LINK

Make a bar graph. Scientists discovered elements over the years. The chart shows the number of known elements in different years. Make a bar graph that shows this information.

Year	1800	1850	1900	1950	2000
Known elements	33	57	81	96	109

LITERATURE LINK

Read *I Can't Believe My Eyes* to see some extraordinary photographs of ordinary things. Create a picture like those in the book. Try the activities at the end of the book.

TECHNOLOGY LINK

 LOG ON Visit www.science.mmhschool.com for more links.

GLASS is GREAT!

Why is this speedboat made of fiberglass?

What can be spun into threads finer than a spider's web? What can be molded into huge mirrors that weigh as much as five elephants? What can be stronger than steel or crumble like a cracker? The answer is glass!

The simplest glass is made of a mixture of sand and small amounts of other materials, such as soda ash and limestone. The mixture is melted, then shaped. The glass hardens as it cools.

We use many kinds of glass. One kind is very strong glass, called safety glass. It is used in car windows. Safety glass is hard to break.

When it does break, it shatters into small pieces with dull edges. Another kind of glass, called fiberglass, is made of thin glass fibers. Each fiber is many times thinner than a human hair. Some boats are made of fiberglass because it is strong and light. Fiberglass is also used in firefighters' suits because it does not burn and it washes easily.

Glass is amazing for another reason. It can be recycled. Americans recycle 13 million glass bottles and jars every day. They are melted and formed into new glass products.

Objects made from glass

A glassblower shapes soft, hot glass.

This is where glass is stored when it is waiting to be recycled.

What Did I Learn?

1. Glass can be

A spun into threads.
B stronger than steel.
C molded into huge mirrors.
D all of the above.

2. Thin glass fibers are used in

F fiberglass.
G safety glass.
H recycled glass.
J molded glass.

LOG ON Visit **www.science.mmhschool.com** to learn more about glass.

Chapter 11 Review

Vocabulary

Fill in each blank with the best word or words from the list.

chemical change, F30
compound, F30
element, F28
gas, F14
liquid, F14
mass, F7

metal, F26
physical change, F16
physical property, F6
solid, F14
volume, F7

1. The amount of space an object takes up is its _____.
2. Size and color are examples of a(n) _____.
3. Grams are one unit of measurement for _____.
4. A shiny material found in Earth is a(n) _____.
5. A building block of matter is a(n) _____.
6. No new kinds of matter are formed in a(n) _____.
7. New kinds of matter are formed in a(n) _____.

The states of matter are:

8. _____
9. _____
10. _____.

Test Prep

11. What does NOT describe the physical properties of your science book?

    A smooth
    B hard
    C soft
    D rectangular shape

12. Matter that does not have a definite shape or volume is a(n) _____.

    F gas
    G solid
    H liquid
    J element

13. Which is an example of a solution?

    A marbles and paper clips
    B salt mixed in water
    C fruit salad
    D sand and water

14. Which of the following is a physical change?

    F a cake baking
    G ice melting
    H metal rusting
    J wood burning

F 36

15. One example of an element is _____.

   A wood

   B fruit salad

   C rust

   D hydrogen

Concepts and Skills

16. Reading in Science How can you tell the difference between a mixture and a compound?

17. INQUIRY SKILL **Communicate** Draw diagrams that show the differences among solids, liquids, and gases. Write a brief explanation of each diagram.

18. Critical Thinking One element that makes up salt is a poisonous gas. Why do you think that salt does not poison us?

Salt

Chlorine gas—a poisonous green gas

19. Product Ads You may have seen ads on television that show people sitting on clouds. What properties of matter have the advertisers ignored? Write a sentence to explain your answer.

20. Scientific Methods Metals are good carriers of heat. They heat up quickly. Do metals also cool off quickly? Write a hypothesis. Describe how you would test your idea.

Did You Ever Wonder?

INQUIRY SKILL **Classify** How do you classify things? You sort them into groups according to their characteristics. Choose a group of items, such as fruits or vegetables. Design and test a classification system for the group. What properties did you use to classify the items? Explain your answer.

LOG ON Visit www.science.mmhschool.com to boost your test scores.

Energy

Did You Ever Wonder?

People depend on energy. During an electrical power
outage, lights go dark and computers shut down. Electricity
is only one of the forms of energy we depend on.

INQUIRY SKILL **Classify** What other forms of energy
do we use?

How Heat Travels

Vocabulary

heat, F42
temperature, F43
degree, F43
conductor, F46
insulator, F46

Get Ready

Could you fry an egg on the sidewalk? In Oatman, Arizona, they try! Oatman has a sidewalk egg-frying contest every year on the Fourth of July. Sidewalks can get very hot in the sunlight. Sand at the beach and metals can, too. Other things, such as water, stay cooler. Why do some things warm up more than others?

Inquiry Skill

You experiment when you perform a test to support or disprove a hypothesis.

F 40

Explore Activity

How Does Heat Affect Different Materials?

Materials

soil

water

2 foam cups

2 thermometers

heat source (sunlight or lamp)

Procedure

1 **Predict** Which will heat up faster—a cup of soil or a cup of water?

2 Fill one cup with water. Fill the other cup with an equal amount of soil.

3 **Measure** Use two thermometers to measure the temperature of the soil and the water. Record the measurements.

4 **Experiment** Place the soil and water near a heat source. Make sure each cup is the same distance from the heat source. Record the temperature every 5 minutes for 15 minutes in a chart.

5 **Use Numbers** Find the difference between the first and last readings of each thermometer. To do this, subtract the first measurement you made from the last measurement you made.

Drawing Conclusions

1 Which cup warmed up more? Were your predictions correct?

2 **Infer** Why is it important to place the soil and water an equal distance from the heat source?

3 **FURTHER INQUIRY** **Experiment** Try this activity using gravel, sand, or salt.

Main Idea Heat is a form of energy that makes things warmer.

How Do Things Get Warmer?

Rub your hands together quickly. What happens? Your hands warm up. Why did this happen? The energy from your moving hands changed to **heat** . Heat is a form of energy that makes matter warmer.

The Sun is Earth's main source of heat. Fire and light bulbs also produce heat. The coils inside an oven or toaster produce heat, too.

Heat can move in different ways. It can move through solids, liquids, and gases. Heat can even move through space. This helps us because space lies between Earth and the Sun.

READING Diagrams

How does the soup in the pot get warmer?

Wood — Metal

Wood — Metal

4:00 PM   4:10 PM

The coils in a toaster get very hot. Heat moves into the food to toast it.

A thermometer measures **temperature** (TEM·puhr·uh·chuhr). Temperature is a measure of how warm or cold something is. The units of temperature are called **degrees** (di·GREEZ). The symbol for degree is °. It is a tiny, raised circle.

Some materials need more energy to cause the same change in their temperature. At the beach you will find sand and water. Both are under the same heat source, the Sun. The sand gets very hot, but the water stays much cooler. The water needs more energy to cause the same change in temperature.

▶ **What is temperature?**

Why would you go for a swim on a hot day?

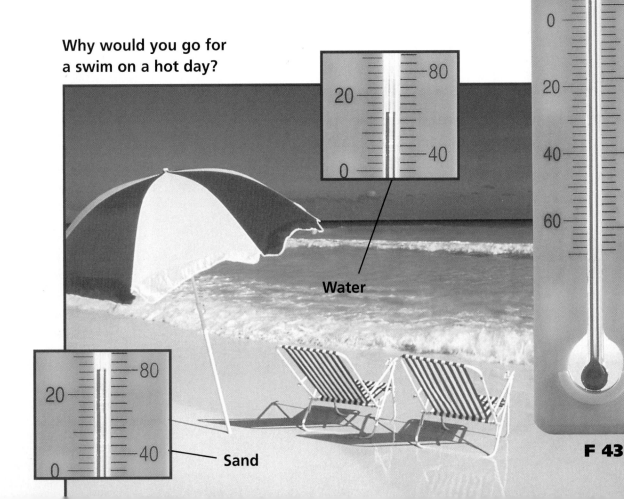

Water

Sand

How Does Heat Change Matter?

You can't see heat. You cannot hold it in your hand, either. However, you can see how heat changes matter.

Look at the road. The Sun heated it day after day. This made the road expand. To expand means to get bigger. The road expanded so much that cracks formed.

Why did this happen? Remember that matter is made of particles. Adding heat makes the particles move faster. It also causes them to move farther apart. This raises the temperature and makes the matter expand.

When matter loses heat, its particles slow down. They also move closer together. Losing heat is the same as cooling. Matter contracts as it cools. To contract means to get smaller.

You learned that a thermometer measures how warm or cold something is. How does it do this? A thermometer is a glass tube filled with a liquid. The liquid expands and contracts to show different temperatures.

When heat makes the liquid expand, the liquid rises up the tube.

Roads may expand and crack in hot weather.

When a thermometer is in a warm place, the liquid in the thermometer rises. When the air around the thermometer loses heat, the liquid in the thermometer falls. The level tells you the temperature.

Heat always flows from warmer objects to cooler ones. Heat flows from a warm table to a cold ice pop. The table loses heat and the ice pop gains heat, until they are the same temperature.

READING **Sequence of Events**
What happens to an ice pop when you take it from a freezer and later put it back?

QUICK LAB

Expand and Contract

FOLDABLES™ Make a Shutter Fold. (See p. R42.) Label as shown.

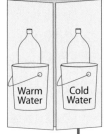
Warm Water   Cold Water

1. Stretch the opening of a balloon over a plastic drink bottle.

2. **Observe** Place the bottle in a bucket of warm water. What happens to the balloon? Make a diagram on the left side.

3. **Observe** Move the bottle to a bucket of cold water. What happens to the balloon? Make a diagram on the right side.

4. **Communicate** Under the tabs, explain the changes in the balloon.

How Can You Control the Flow of Heat?

Why are cooking pots made of metals such as iron and aluminum? The answer is that heat moves quickly through metals. The heat moves from the stove to the metal pot. The pot gets warm.

Materials such as metals are good **conductors** (kuhn·DUK·tuhrz). A conductor is a material that heat moves through easily.

Heat does not move quickly through some other materials, such as wool, cotton, and fur. These materials are called **insulators** (IN·suh·lay·tuhrz). An insulator is a material that heat does not move through easily.

Cooking pots are made of conductors.

Insulation keeps heat inside the house.

In cold weather people need to stay warm. This boy is wearing clothing that traps heat.

Winters in the north get very cold. How do animals that live there stay warm? Good insulators cover their bodies. Animals such as the walrus have layers of fat under their skin. Fat is an excellent insulator. Bears have very thick hair that helps trap heat inside the animal's body.

This red-eyed treefrog can live only in warm places, such as the rain forest. In the cold its thin skin would lose heat. It would die.

▷ How are conductors and insulators used?

Walruses

Brown bears

Insulators help these animals stay warm in cold places.

How Can Energy Change?

Heat is a form of energy. Energy changes from one form to another. Many forms of energy can change into heat. For example, rub your hands together. Some of the energy of moving your hands changes into heat. For the same reason, sawing wood or bending wire produces heat. Fuel, such as wood or gasoline, has energy locked in it. When fuel is burned, heat is given off.

Food is fuel for your body. As your body uses food, heat is produced. That's why your body has a certain temperature.

▷ **What is an example of energy changing form?**

Burning wood gives off heat.

Cutting wood makes the saw hot. Some of the energy moving the saw changes to heat.

It is very warm inside your body. Your body heat comes from the energy in your food.

L·I·N·K·S

Why It Matters

Your body uses energy from food to keep the same body temperature. Not all animals can do this. Some animals get heat from outside their bodies. Their body temperature changes with the temperature of the surroundings. Snakes warm themselves in the sunlight.

e-Journal Visit our Web site www.science.mmhschool.com to do a research project on heat.

Think and Write

1. What is heat? Give an example of an object that gives off heat.

2. How does a thermometer work?

3. Name a good conductor. Name a good insulator.

4. What happens to the particles of matter when matter is heated? Draw a diagram.

5. **Critical Thinking** Why do people use foam cups when they drink hot chocolate?

WRITING LINK

Personal Narrative
Sometimes the weather stays very hot for many days. This is called a heat wave. Recall an experience or ask adults about the worst heat wave they remember. Write about what you or they did to cool off.

MATH LINK

Solve a problem. The temperature outside is 25 °C. Would you go outside in shorts or a jacket? Explain your answer. Use a thermometer to help answer the question.

ART LINK

Make a model. Make a model that shows what happens when matter is heated. Use clay, felt, or cotton balls as the particles of matter. Present your model as a poster or diorama.

TECHNOLOGY LINK

LOG ON Visit www.science.mmhschool.com for more links.

SAVING ENERGY

Why is it important to save energy? Most of the energy we use comes from fossil fuels. Fossil fuels are burned to make electricity, heat buildings, and power cars. Burning destroys these fuels. Once they are gone, they are gone forever.

You can help! You can save energy and reduce your use of fossil fuels. This will make Earth's supply of fossil fuels last longer. It will decrease air pollution. You will save money, too.

There are many ways to save energy. Some are surprising. All are simple to do.

Solar calculator

- Turn out lights when you are not using them.
- Clean dust off light bulbs. Clean light bulbs work better than dirty ones.
- Don't use batteries when other choices are available. Try a solar calculator that runs on light. A solar calculator changes light energy to electrical energy.

and Society

- Saving hot water saves both water and energy. Don't waste water when you take a bath, wash your hands, or do the dishes.
- Don't keep refrigerators open for a long time. Think about what you want before you open the door.
- Don't turn the heat in your house too high in the winter. Stay warm by wearing a sweater.
- Use cars wisely. Take buses or trains when you can, or walk, or ride a bike.

It is up to everyone to use energy wisely. How many ways can you save energy?

How are these children saving energy?

What Did I Learn?

1. What can you conserve by saving electricity?

   A aluminum
   B trees
   C fossil fuels
   D batteries

2. Which of the following is a reason to save energy?

   F decrease air pollution
   G save money
   H reduce use of fossil fuels
   J all of the above

LOG ON Visit www.science.mmhschool.com to learn more about saving energy.

How Light Travels

Vocabulary

opaque, F54
reflect, F55
refract, F56

Get Ready

You depend on light every day. Sunlight in the morning tells you a new day has begun. Light allows you to see people and objects. Look at the picture shown here. Some things, such as the window and the vase, let light shine through. Other things, such as the wall, block the light.

What materials let light pass through them?

Inquiry Skill

You predict when you state the possible results of an event or experiment.

Explore Activity

What Does Light Pass Through?

Materials

flashlight

classroom materials, such as paper, wax paper, plastic wrap, aluminum foil, large balloon

Procedure

1 **Predict** Look over your materials. Which materials will light pass through? Which materials will form shadows?

2 **Experiment** Hold each material in front of the lighted flashlight. Does light shine through the material? Do any shadows form? Record your observations.

3 **Experiment** Try changing the materials in some way. You may try folding the papers to make them thicker, or crumpling the plastic wrap. Repeat step 2 with the changed materials.

Drawing Conclusions

1 **Classify** Which materials did the light pass through? Which materials formed shadows? Make a list.

2 Did changing the materials change the results? Explain any changes you observed.

3 FURTHER INQUIRY
Predict How might the brightness of the light affect your results? How do you know?

Main Idea Light travels in straight lines.

How Does Light Travel?

You see and use light every day. What is light? Light is a form of energy. Light is not matter, but it can make matter move or change.

Light comes from many different sources. The Sun and other stars, lightning, and fires are natural light sources. Light bulbs and candles are made by people.

Light travels in straight lines from its source. A beam of light is called a light ray.

Some materials let light rays pass through them easily. Air, glass, and some plastics are examples. Other materials block light rays. These materials are called **opaque** (oh·PAYK). Bricks, wood, metals, and many other materials are opaque. An opaque material will make a shadow when light is shined on it.

How does this photograph show that light travels in a straight line?

Rays of light travel in straight lines from the Sun to Earth.

Put two or three mirrors together. You can see more reflections.

When light hits an object, some light **reflects** (ri·FLEKTS) off the object. *Reflect* means "bounce." You see an object because light reflected from the object enters your eye.

Mirrors reflect light very well. That's because mirrors are smooth and shiny. A light ray reflects off a mirror just like a table tennis ball bounces off a smooth table. Look at a mirror, and you will see your face. This is your reflection.

Most objects are not as smooth and shiny as a mirror. A light ray that hits something dull or rough bounces in lots of different directions. This is why you don't see your reflection when you look at most things.

A curved mirror reflects light in a different way from a flat mirror. It might stretch your reflection or turn it upside down.

READING Sequence of Events

Why do you see your reflection when you look in a mirror?

F 55

Why Does Light Bend?

Look at the spoon in the water. It looks as if the bottom was cut away from the top! In fact this spoon is not cut at all.

Why does the spoon look broken? The light **refracts** (ri·FRAKTS) as it passes from air into water. To refract means to bend. The bending light rays make the spoon look as if it is broken.

Light also refracts as it passes between air and glass. This can be very useful. People can see better by looking through a piece of glass shaped the right way.

▷ **Why does the spoon look broken in the water?**

Try putting a spoon into a glass with different amounts of water. What happens?

A camera uses a lens to bend light and focus the light on the film.

Eyeglasses help people see better. Lenses work by refracting light.

Why Do You See Colors?

You might think that light from the Sun is yellow or white. In fact it is a mixture of many colors! To show this, you can use a *prism* (PRIZ·uhm). A prism is a thick piece of glass that refracts light. The prism bends each color a different amount.

We see objects when light reflects off them. Most objects reflect some colors better than other colors. The colors that are not reflected are absorbed. A leaf reflects green light and absorbs most of the other colors. A red apple reflects red light. Blue paint reflects blue light. This is why we see colors.

▷ **What does a prism do to light?**

READING
Diagrams

Why does a leaf look green?

Tiny drops of water in the air act like a prism. This forms a rainbow!

Sunlight

When a light ray enters a prism, the colors are bent in different amounts and break apart.

Controlling an Experiment

Variables are things in an experiment that can be changed to find answers to questions. For example, what if you wanted to answer the question "What affects how light bends in a liquid?" Here are some variables that could be changed.

- the kind of liquid
- the shape of the container
- the position of an object in the liquid

For a fair test, all of the variables in the experiment must remain the same except for one. The one variable that does not change is called the control.

Variable	Control

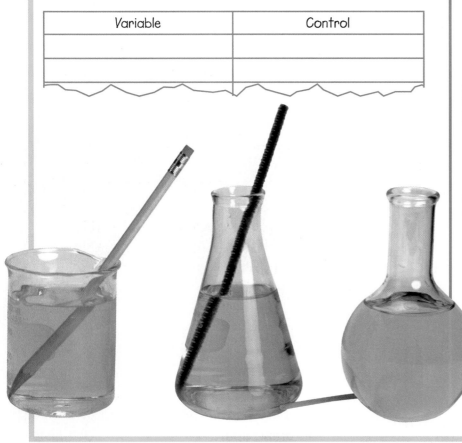

Procedure

1 Communicate Take a close look at the containers in the picture. What differences do you see? These differences are variables. List all the variables you can. Use a table.

2 Use Variables Describe a fair test for each variable. For example, how would you test the shape of the container?

Drawing Conclusions

1 How many variables can you change in a fair test?

2 Use Variables Which one variable would you change to see its effect on the bending of light? Why?

Why It Matters

Light is a form of energy that is everywhere in your world. It travels in straight lines at 300,000 kilometers (186,000 miles) per second! Light can even travel through a vacuum—a space without matter. That's how light from the Sun and distant stars can travel through space to Earth.

e-Journal Visit our Web site **www.science.mmhschool.com** to do a research project on light.

Think and Write

1. Name three things that make light.

2. What kinds of objects make shadows?

3. When you look at an object that reflects light very well, what do you see?

4. INQUIRY SKILL **Use Variables** You want to know if sunlight fades paper. List the variables in the experiment.

5. **Critical Thinking** A magician says that she can bend a wand. She dips the wand in water. The wand looks bent. Explain how this trick works.

L·I·N·K·S

WRITING LINK

Explanatory Writing Make a sculpture using crayons, tissue paper, wax paper, and other materials. Use some opaque materials and some that let light through. Explain in a paragraph how to make the sculpture, and include the steps in the order you used them.

MATH LINK

Measure length. Turn off the lights. Shine a flashlight on a ruler. Use another ruler to measure the length of the shadow. Measure shadows with the flashlight in different positions. Use the table to record your measurements. How does the flashlight position affect the shadow?

Position of flashlight	Length of shadow

TECHNOLOGY LINK

Science Newsroom CD-ROM Choose *Time to Reflect* to learn how mirror reflections and light are related.

 LOG ON Visit **www.science.mmhschool.com** for more links.

Energy Everywhere

Do you listen to music? make popcorn? ride to school? Then you use energy! We all use energy to run our televisions, computers, and refrigerators. It powers our cars, buses, and airplanes.

Most of our energy comes from burning oil, coal, or natural gas. These are called fossil fuels. It takes millions of years to make fossil fuels. They are formed from dead plants and animals far below the ground. Everyone needs energy. But burning fossil fuels pollutes our environment.

There are other sources of energy, though, that will never run out. Wind energy can turn windmills to make electricity. The energy in flowing water can provide electricity, too. Energy in sunlight can power calculators and space satellites! And these energy sources don't pollute the environment.

Some cars today can run on electricity.

Some calculators run on solar power.

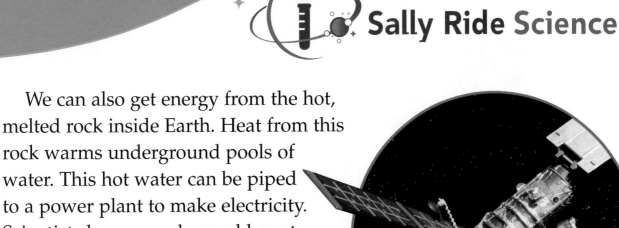

We can also get energy from the hot, melted rock inside Earth. Heat from this rock warms underground pools of water. This hot water can be piped to a power plant to make electricity. Scientists have even learned how to make fuel from wastes such as corn stalks, grass clippings, and chicken feathers!

Look around. Everywhere you see things that use energy. And now you'll see sources of clean energy that won't run out!

Solar panels power satellites in space.

What Did I Learn?

1. Which of these are fossil fuels?

   A coal and oil
   B sunshine and water
   C wind and rain
   D TV sets and refrigerators

2. Which is a source of energy that won't run out?

   F natural gas
   G sunlight
   H oil
   J coal

LOG ON Visit www.science.mmhschool.com to learn more about alternative fuels.

Properties of Sound

Get Ready

Everyone waits quietly. There isn't a sound. Soon you hear the drums drumming. Then you hear the flutes singing. The band is here! At a parade you hear lots of music. What makes all of these sounds?

Inquiry Skill

You experiment when you perform a test to support or disprove a hypothesis.

F 62

Explore Activity

How Can You Make Sounds?

Materials

paper strips, 10 cm (4 in.) wide

tape

scissors

straws

plastic rulers

Procedure: Design Your Own

1. **Observe** Hold a strip of paper at an end. Wave it. Describe what you hear.

2. **Observe** Flatten a straw. Cut a point on one end of the straw. Blow hard through that end. Describe what you hear.

3. **Observe** Hold a ruler on a desktop. Let half of the ruler reach over the edge. Tap that end. Describe what you hear.

4. **Experiment** Test ways to change the sound you made with each object. Try to make the sounds louder or softer, higher or lower. For example, try using strips of paper of different lengths.

Drawing Conclusions

1. What makes sounds?

2. How can you make a sound change?

3. **FURTHER INQUIRY** **Experiment** Make more sound makers out of other materials, such as string and paper cups. How can you change the sounds?

Main Idea Sounds can travel through all kinds of matter.

How Are Sounds Made?

To make a sound, you need to make something move. Put your hand to your throat, and speak. You can feel something moving inside. Tap the end of a ruler that you are holding over a desk. You hear it and see it move. Sound is a form of energy.

Sounds are made when an object **vibrates** (VIGH·brayts). To vibrate is to move back and forth quickly. Sometimes you can see an object vibrate. Pluck a guitar string. You might see it vibrate. Other times it may vibrate so fast you can't see it moving.

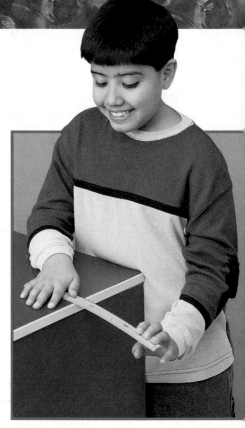

You hear the ruler, and see it move.

When a guitar string vibrates, it makes the air around it vibrate, too. Particles in the air move back and forth quickly.

When someone plays a trumpet, air vibrates inside it. Touch the trumpet, and you can feel it vibrate.

The sound moves through the air. You hear the sound when the back-and-forth motion of the air reaches your ear.

If there were no air around you right now, would you hear anything? No. Sounds travel through air. Particles in the air vibrate. That's how air carries sounds.

You can also hear sounds underwater. Sounds travel through water and other liquids. Sounds can travel through solid objects, too. Put your ear on a desk. Tap the other end of the desk. You can hear the tapping noise through the desk.

Sounds can move through solids, liquids, and gases. Sounds move better through some kinds of matter than others.

READING **Sequence of Events**

How do sounds from a guitar reach your ears?

Dolphins send sounds to each other through water.

QUICK LAB

String Phone

FOLDABLES Make a Folded Table. (See p. R44.) Label the table as shown.

String	Speak	Listen

1. Make a hole in the bottom of a paper cup. Thread 3 meters of string through the hole. Tie the end of the string to a paper clip. Tape the paper clip to the inside of the cup bottom.

2. Repeat step 1. Tie a second paper cup to the other end of the string.

3. **Experiment** Find a partner. Pull the string tight and have your partner listen. Speak softly into the cup. Record your observations on the table.

4. **Make a Hypothesis** How well will your telephone work if you use a different type of string? Test your ideas. Record your observations on the table.

How Do Sounds Get Higher and Lower?

Tap the key at the far left of a piano keyboard. The sound is very deep, or low. Now move your finger along the keys to the right. The sound becomes higher and higher. You are changing the **pitch** (PICH) of the sound. A sound's pitch is how high or low it is.

What causes a change in pitch? Length is sometimes the answer. Shorter strings vibrate faster than longer ones. The faster a string vibrates, the higher the pitch of the sound.

Other times, thickness changes pitch. Thinner strings vibrate faster. Thinner strings have higher pitches.

Did you ever notice that guitars and pianos have screws on strings? Twist a screw, and the string becomes tighter. Tighter strings vibrate faster, making the pitch higher.

Notice the different lengths and thicknesses of the piano strings. Which string makes a higher pitch, 1 or 2?

▷ **What causes pitch to change?**

Pull the slide out. The air inside has a longer path. The pitch gets lower.

What Makes Sounds Loud or Soft?

Tap your desk. Then pound it harder. How has the sound changed? The pitch is the same. However, pounding the desk makes a louder sound than tapping it. **Volume** (VAHL·yewm) means how loud or soft a sound is.

Why do sounds have different volumes? Try whispering softly. Now call out loudly through a window. How did you make the different sounds? You had to take a deep breath to make the loud sound. You used more energy. Making loud sounds takes more energy than making soft sounds.

▷ The sounds of a rocket launch are louder than the sounds kittens make. Why?

F 67

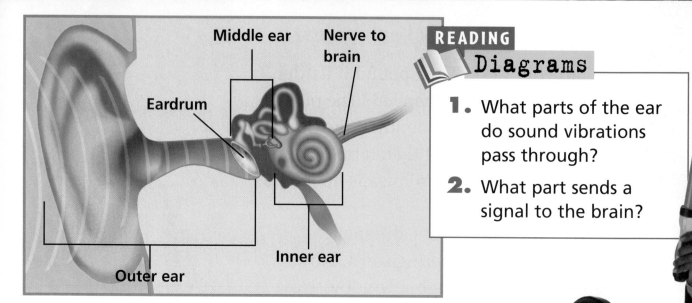

Middle ear

Nerve to brain

Eardrum

Inner ear

Outer ear

READING

Diagrams

1. What parts of the ear do sound vibrations pass through?

2. What part sends a signal to the brain?

How Do You Hear Sounds?

A sound takes less than a second to travel across a room to your ear. Then the sound must pass through your ear. A signal from the ear travels to the brain. This is how you hear sounds.

Never put a finger or pencil in your ear. You may damage the parts inside. Loud sounds can damage your ear as well. Loud sounds have a lot of energy. They can damage the way parts inside the ear vibrate. In time they can cause a loss of hearing.

▷ **What happens when sound reaches your ears?**

Hearing aids can help people who hear poorly. The hearing aid makes sounds louder.

Ground-crew workers must protect their ears.

Why It Matters

You depend on sounds in many ways. A buzzer sounds. It's time for school to begin. After school you listen to your favorite songs on the radio.

Animals use sounds, too. Sounds can warn animals of danger or help them find food. Many animals call to one another, just like humans do!

e-Journal Visit our Web site www.science.mmhschool.com to do a research project on sounds.

Think and Write

1. What do you need to do to make any sound?

2. Why can you hear sounds underwater?

3. How will the sound change when you loosen a guitar string?

4. Why might you cover your ears when a plane flies overhead?

5. **Critical Thinking** You hear nothing. Your dog jumps. Explain what happened.

L·I·N·K·S

MATH LINK

Make a chart. Volume is measured in units called decibels.

Kind of Sound	Decibels
Whisper	20
People talking	50
Heavy traffic	80
Thunder	110
Jet plane (30 meters away)	140

List sounds that you hear. Check to see if any of these sounds are shown on the chart above. Write down the decibel levels of these sounds. Then use research materials or the Internet to look up the remaining sounds on your list. Record this information in a chart.

WRITING LINK

Writing a Poem Listen to the sounds around you. Write down how you hear the sounds. For example, you might hear a drip or a beep. Use these or other sound words to write a poem. Share your poem with your classmates.

TECHNOLOGY LINK

LOG ON Visit www.science.mmhschool.com for more links.

Paths for Electricity

Vocabulary

cell, F72

circuit, F72

electric current, F72

switch, F73

Get Ready

Have you ever played with an electric train set? The set has lots of parts. You need to put the parts together in the right way for the train to work. How do the parts need to be set up to make the train move?

Inquiry Skill

You **predict** when you state possible results of an event or experiment.

F 70

Explore Activity

What Makes the Bulb Light?

Materials

D-cell battery

small light bulb

20-cm wire

Procedure

1 **Predict** Look at the bulb, wire, and battery. How might you put them together to make the bulb light? Work with a partner to record your ideas.

2 **Experiment** Try to light the bulb. Draw a picture of each setup that you try. Record which ones work and which ones don't.

Drawing Conclusions

1 How many ways did you find to light the bulb?

2 **Interpret Data** How were the ways that made the bulb light alike? How were they different from the ways that did not make the bulb light?

3 What is the job of the wire?

4 **FURTHER INQUIRY** **Predict** How could you light the bulb with two pieces of wire?

Main Idea Electricity is a form of
energy. It travels in a path called a circuit.

What Makes a Bulb Light?

A **cell** (SEL) is a source of electricity.
A battery is made up of two or more cells.
With a bulb, wires, and a cell, you can use
electricity to light the bulb. However, you
need to put the parts together in the right way.

READING
Diagrams

Why is the second
bulb unlit?

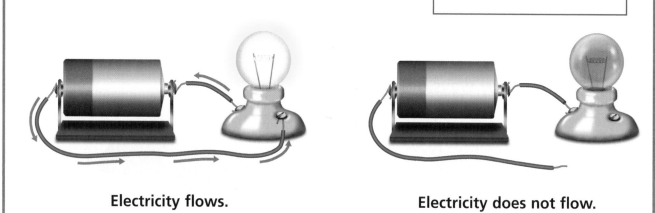

Electricity flows.   Electricity does not flow.

Electricity is a form of energy that travels in a
circuit (SUR·kit). A circuit is a path in which
electricity goes around and around. For the bulb to
light, wires must connect it to the cell to form a circuit.

Electricity flowing through a circuit is called
electric current (KUR·uhnt). Electric current can light
a bulb, power a toy train, and do many other things!

These women are using cables to
power a car battery. What part of
the circuit are the cables?

How can you control the flow of electricity? One way is to use a **switch** (SWICH), such as the switch on a flashlight. A switch opens or closes an electric circuit.

When a flashlight switch is off, there is a gap in the circuit. The circuit is open. Electricity does not flow. Turn the switch on, and the gap is no longer there. The circuit is closed. Electricity flows, and the bulb lights.

Switches such as this one control the flow of electricity in your home.

READING **Sequence of Events**

What happens when you turn on a switch?

QUICK LAB

Flashlight

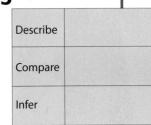

FOLDABLES™ Make a Folded Chart. (See p. R44.) Label the chart as shown.

Describe	
Compare	
Infer	

1. Use two D cells, a paper tube, 30 centimeters of wire, masking tape, and a flashlight bulb to make a model flashlight.

2. How does your model flashlight work?

3. Describe the electric circuit in the flashlight. Record your answer on the chart.

4. How does our model flashlight compare with a real flashlight? Record your answer on the chart.

5. Infer How might you improve your model? Record your answer on the chart.

How Do You Use Electricity?

How many ways do you use electricity at home? Almost everyone uses electric lights. You may also use electricity to heat your home. Electric machines include refrigerators, hair dryers, televisions, and vacuum cleaners.

▷ **What electric machines do you use?**

Electricity is changed to sound.

Electricity runs the motor in a vacuum cleaner.

Electricity changes to heat as it flows through coils in a toaster.

Electricity lights the tiny dots that make up the picture on a computer screen.

Lesson Review

Why It Matters

Electricity helps you do all sorts of things. Telephones use electricity to carry sound. You use electricity to cook your food and wash your clothes. You need electricity to run your computer and listen to the radio.

e-Journal Visit our Web site www.science.mmhschool.com to do a research project on electricity.

Think and Write

1. What is a cell?
2. What is a circuit?
3. How does a switch control the flow of electricity in a circuit?
4. Name four ways that you use electricity in your life.
5. **Critical Thinking** You turn the switch on a flashlight. The light does not come on! List three things that might be wrong with the flashlight.

L·I·N·K·S

MATH LINK

Solve a problem. Harvey has five flashlights. Each flashlight takes three D cells. How many batteries does he need to power all five flashlights?

WRITING LINK

Explanatory Writing Think of an invention that has more than one purpose. For example, a radio gives information and entertains. Then write a letter to your classmates. Explain the invention and how it can be used in two different ways.

LITERATURE LINK

Read *Electrical Inventions* to learn about inventions that use electricity. When you finish reading the book, think about creating an invention of your own. Try the activities at the end of the book.

Electrical Inventions
by Lisa Benjamin
Illustrated by Mike Dammer

TECHNOLOGY LINK

 Science Newsroom CD-ROM Choose *Let's Join the Circuits* to learn how circuits must be set up for electricity to flow through them.

 LOG ON Visit **www.science.mmhschool.com** for more links.

Chapter 12 Review

Vocabulary

Fill in each blank with the best word from the list.

cell, F72   **reflect,** F55

heat, F42   **refract,** F56

insulator, F46   **switch,** F73

opaque, F54   **vibrate,** F64

pitch, F66   **volume,** F67

1. A form of energy that makes things warmer is _____.

2. A material that heat doesn't flow through easily is called a(n) _____.

3. An object that does not allow light to pass through it is _____.

4. Sound is made when an object _____.

5. A flashlight gets electricity from a(n) _____.

6. To open or close an electrical circuit, you use a(n) _____.

   When light hits a surface, it can:

7. _____

8. _____.

   Two properties of sound are:

9. _____

10. _____.

Test Prep

11. Heat can travel through _____.

    A solids

    B liquids

    C gases

    D all of the above

12. It is cold outside. You put on a warm jacket. The jacket is a(n) _____.

    F mixture

    G conductor

    H insulator

    J switch

13. Light travels _____.

    A in straight lines

    B in curvy lines

    C slowly

    D around objects

14. Objects that vibrate slowly make sounds with _____.

    F a high volume

    G no volume

    H a high pitch

    J a low pitch

15. Heat, light, sound, and electricity are all forms of
_____.

A motion

B energy

C work

D friction

Concepts and Skills

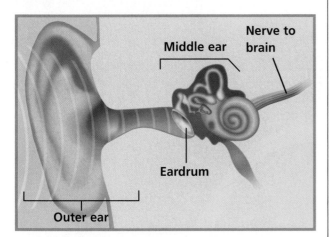

Middle ear

Nerve to brain

Eardrum

Outer ear

16. **Reading in Science** List the sentences in correct order. Use the diagram above to help you.
1. The middle ear vibrates.
2. A special nerve carries messages about sound to the brain.
3. A sound reaches your ear.

17. **Critical Thinking** How could you use mirrors and a light to signal your friend across the street? Explain in a paragraph.

18. INQUIRY SKILL **Use Variables** Which freezes faster—salt water or fresh water? Describe how you would test your ideas. What variable changes in the experiment?

19. **Scientific Methods** How could you find out if there is electrical energy in a cell? Write a hypothesis. Describe how you would test your idea.

20. **Safety** Are people in danger from very loud sounds in your community? Write some rules that would protect people from harmful noises.

Did You Ever Wonder?

INQUIRY SKILL Interpret Data
We use many different forms of energy. Think of a question about how we can conserve energy. Research ways we can reduce the amount of energy we use.

LOG ON Visit www.science.mmhschool.com to boost your test scores.

Meet a Scientist

Dr. John Oaks

Bioscientist

John Oaks has an unusual job. He studies worms that live inside rat intestines. The worms are parasites called tapeworms. They may give Oaks information to help medicine work better in people.

Like human intestines, rat intestines have muscles that push waste out of the body quickly. Tapeworms, however, don't get pushed out along with everything else. Oaks wanted to know why.

Through many experiments, he found that tapeworms make a special chemical. It slows down muscle movement in the intestine. So tapeworms hang around for a long time.

Oaks thinks the tapeworm's chemicals may help keep medicine in the human body longer. And that's a good thing. Many drugs get pushed out of the intestine quickly. If they do, some of the medicine is not absorbed. Oaks may test the tapeworm's chemical on people. That will take a long time. But thanks to his work, doctors may be able to give patients smaller amounts of drugs. Patients may also feel better quicker. That's good news for everyone!

TOP 5 Careers in Medicine

If you want to study medicine, but don't want to be a doctor, here are some jobs to check out:

1. Biomedical engineer: Develops tools to solve health problems.
2. Biochemist: Studies drug and chemical actions.
3. Microbiologist: Studies strains of microorganisms.
4. Pharmacologist: Researches the effect of drugs on humans and animals.
5. Virologist: Grows viruses and develops vaccines.

Write About It

1. How might the chemicals in tapeworms help humans?
2. Why do scientists get as much information as possible before trying out their ideas on people?

Visit **www.science.mmhschool.com**

A Question of BALANCE

What to Do

Find two objects that you think have the same mass. Cut three pieces of string that are 10 cm long. Use the string to tie each object to the ruler as shown. Tie the third piece of string to the center of the ruler. Hold the center string with your hand. Try to have the two sides balance. Try different objects until you are able to balance the ruler.

Draw Conclusions

Were you able to have the two sides of the ruler balance? Write a short paragraph to explain what happened.

SAND DANCE

Your goal is to make sand move without touching it.

What to Do

Stretch the plastic wrap over one end of the cardboard tube. Fasten it with the rubber band, as shown. Put a pinch of sand on the plastic wrap. Bring the tube near the radio. Turn the radio on. Watch what happens to the plastic wrap. Strike the tuning fork near the tube. Again, watch what happens to the plastic wrap.

Draw Conclusions

How did you make the sand move most? Which way of moving the sand produced the most sound energy? Explain why you think so.

Exploring
New York

The sugar maple is the
New York state tree.

White pine

Oak leaf

Lake Ontario

Rochester 📷 Syracuse

Buffalo

Lake Erie

Genesee River

NEW YORK

Binghamton

Sugar maple

Red maple seed wings

SYLVANIA

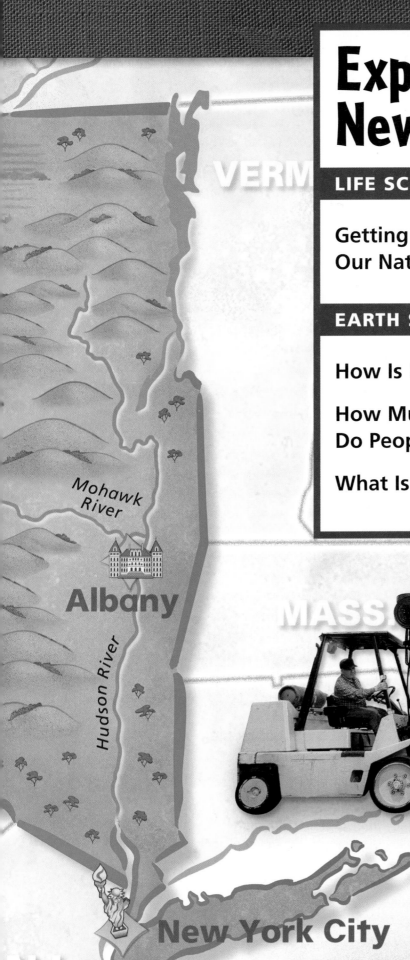

Exploring New York

LIFE SCIENCE

EARTH SCIENCE

VERM

MASS.

Mohawk River

Albany

Hudson River

New York City

Atlantic Ocean

NJ

Getting to Know Our Native Trees

What do you need to know to help identify trees? Location is important. You can find trees on mountaintops, in wet areas, in dry areas, and near your school. What is the shape and size of the tree? Is it triangular or more rounded? Does it grow very large or stay small?

White pine

Sugar maple

Coniferous or Deciduous?

Most coniferous trees keep their leaves year round. Deciduous trees lose their leaves in the fall.

Oak

White pine

Sugar maple

Leaves

Leaves help us identify trees. Leaves grow in different shapes, sizes, and colors.

Bark

Observe the bark. Bark can be smooth and gray like American beech. It can be yellow and peel off in strips like yellow birch. Bark can be rough, dark, and deeply ridged as on chestnut oak.

ACTIVITY

INQUIRY SKILL Classify Collect different leaves. Sort the leaves as many ways as you can. Into what different categories did you sort your leaves?

■ Find two leaves from the same tree that are most different and draw them. Label your drawing with the tree name.

Witch hazel

Buds, flowers, fruits, and seeds

These help us identify trees. Look for their many different colors, shapes, and sizes.

Crab apple

The Function of Tree Parts

What are the different parts of
a tree and what do they do?

Leaves

All plants including trees are
producers. **Producers**
make food from water,
air, and the Sun's
energy. Most of this
food-making process
takes place in the leaves.
Leaves also give off oxygen.

Red maple leaf

Stem

The stem, or trunk, supports the
tree so it can stand upright. The
stem carries water and minerals
up the tree from the roots. It
carries food from the leaves to
the other tree parts. Branches
are part of the stem.

Bark

The bark protects the tree from insects,
disease, fire, and other things that might
harm it.

Roots

Roots anchor the tree in the ground. Roots bring
water and minerals into the tree from the soil.

Red maple

Buds

Buds are unopened packages of next year's leaves and flowers. Scales cover buds. They protect these precious packages from drying out or from getting too cold in the winter.

Red maple buds

Flowers and Seeds

Most trees flower in the spring. Seeds develop later. These seeds can grow into new trees.

Red maple flowers and seed wings

BE CAREFUL!

- Be careful not to harm the roots of a tree. Without healthy roots, trees will die.

- Do not peel bark or remove it from trees. Trees need this protective layer to stay alive and healthy.

- Be careful when you are looking at buds. For every bud that is removed, the tree loses some of next year's flowers and leaves.

- Look at leaves, but don't pick them. A tree needs these food-producing parts in order to grow and survive.

- Take care of trees and their parts. Trees need all of their parts to be healthy, to stay alive, and to produce new trees.

ACTIVITY

INQUIRY SKILL **Make a Model**
Trees that grow in different places can have different shapes.

- Design a tree whose parts would help it grow in a swampy environment.

Why Are Trees Important?

All living animals, including humans, depend on trees and other plants. Plants produce the oxygen animals need in order to survive. Let's take a look at how trees are used.

Birds

Birds eat insects that live on trees. Birds also eat the fruits, seeds, and nuts provided by trees. Birds use trees for nesting, as singing perches, and as resting and hiding places.

Northern mockingbird eating a berry

Barn owl

Cicada

Insects

Insects use trees for cover. They can live under the bark and in the leaves. Insects feed on tree parts, and they eat other insects living there.

Black bear napping

Mammals

Some mammals use trees for nesting, hiding, resting and feeding. Some, like black bears and squirrels, depend heavily on food provided by trees.

Beaver

Another mammal, the beaver, cuts down trees to build dams across streams. Beavers also use the cut trees to build their nests, called *lodges.*

Why Are Trees Important to People?

Trees are important to people in many ways. People eat the nuts, fruits, seeds, and other parts of the tree. Trees provide shade for the environment. They enrich the soil. The roots of trees soak up water and help to control flooding. They protect soil from washing away. Trees provide the raw materials for thousands of products. Wood is used for building materials and furniture. Wood fiber is made into paper.

Most houses built today are constructed with wood frames.

Even the chemicals that come from trees are important. These chemicals are used to make products we rely on. These products include detergents, vitamins, soap, roofing shingles, and toothpaste! They also include medicines, such as aspirin and cough syrup.

Trees help make our streets, schools, and towns more beautiful. People use forests for hiking, camping, photography, and animal watching. Trees are fun to climb and play in.

WE CAN HELP!

- By preserving trees, we are caring for other plants and many animals, including people.

- We can plant new trees in our yards and in our towns.

How Is Paper Made?

Most trees used to make paper come from forests called managed timberlands. These trees are grown as a crop, like vegetables on a farm. Only trees smaller than 20 centimeters in diameter are used for paper. When these trees are cut, the limbs are removed and the trunk is sent to a paper mill. At the mill, the bark is removed and burned for fuel or turned into garden mulch.

First the wood is chopped into very small pieces. Then, chemicals are added to the chopped wood.

The wood chips are cooked in a big pressure cooker until the pieces turn into pulp.

Wood pulp

The pulp is pressed onto a large screen, and water is drained from the pulp.

Then the pulp is dried flat and thin and rolled onto huge rolls.

Now the paper is ready to be used.

How Much Paper Do People Use?

The average American uses about 350 kilograms (750 pounds) of paper each year. Did you know that it takes more than six trees to make that much paper? We throw most of that paper away.

Fortunately, more paper is recycled in America than is sent to landfills. To **recycle** is to treat something so that it can be used again. When we use recycled paper, we save trees and energy.

WE CAN HELP!

- Look for a statement that says a product is "made from recycled material."
- Recycle paper products that have not been soiled.
- Use cloth napkins and towels rather than paper ones.
- Don't buy over-packaged products that waste our resources.

These bales of paper are ready to be recycled.

ACTIVITY

For one week save all waste paper created by the class. Every day, separate the papers into two stacks. Put paper that has been used on both sides in one stack. Put paper that could be used again in the other stack.

INQUIRY SKILL **Measure** Use a scale to weigh each stack of paper. Record the information in a chart. Use the chart to create a bar graph. You can use a computer to help.

Compare the amount of paper in the stacks used during the week. Is the class wasting paper? Think of some ways you can use less paper.

What Is the Best Buy?

People buy many products made from paper. There are many different brands and packages to choose from. When you compare brands and packages, consider the following:

- How much can you afford to spend?
- How much does the product cost per ounce or per gram?
- Do people you know like and use this brand?

Smart shoppers know how to save money. They can buy products at discount stores. They can also clip and use coupons. You can often save money by buying store brands or **generic** (juh•NAYR•ik) products. Generic brands are products sold in plain packages.

ACTIVITY

To compare the value of these packs of paper you need to compare the cost per unit. To do this, find out how many sheets of paper are in each package. Have an adult divide the price of the package by the number of sheets. The result is the unit price. Compare the unit prices. Which is the best value?

Evaluating Ads

You buy many different products. Sometimes choosing products can be confusing. You may have many thoughts before deciding to buy a product. You might buy a marker because your friend really likes that brand. Or you might buy a brand of crayons because it is cheaper.

Ads are messages used to get people to buy certain products. They do not always provide useful information. If a message sounds too good to be true, it probably is not true. Ask your parent or guardian if you need help deciding which product to buy.

- Madeline's -
Art Supplies

- Good for crayons and markers!
- Comes in many different colors!
- Helps you draw the best pictures!

Which claims sound true? Which claim sounds false? Find an ad that has false claims. Send a friend an e-mail that tells about the ad.

Glossary

bark (bärk) A tree part that protects the tree from insects, disease, fire, and other things that might harm it. (p. G 4)

buds (budz) Unopened packages of next year's leaves, flowers and buds. (p. G 4)

generic brand (jə ner'ik brand) A brand or product sold in plain packages. (p. G 12)

leaf (lēf) A plant part that grows from the stem and helps the plant get air and make food. (p. G 4)

recycle (rē sī'kəl) To treat something so that it can be used again. (p. G 10)

seed (sēd) A tiny capsule that contains a baby plant. (p. G 5)

stem (stem) A plant part that supports the leaves. (p. G 4)

Illustrations: Karen Minot: p. Gl.

Photography Credits:
All photographs are by Macmillan/McGraw-Hill (MMH) except as noted below:

Unit Opener: JIM Zipp/ Photo Researchers, Inc.

Contents: Gl: (bl) Clyde H. Smith/Peter Arnold, Inc.; (blr) Patti Murray/Earth Scenes; (br) Lester Lefkowitz/Corbis; (tl) C. Milkins/Earth Scenes; (tlc) Color Pic/Animals Animals; (tr) Breck P. Kent/Animals Animals.

Unit G: G2: (c) Clyde H. Smith/Peter Arnold, Inc.; (l) Color Pic/Animals Animals. G2-G3 (br) Patti Murray/Earth Scenes; (tr) C. Milkins/Earth Scenes. G3: (bcl) Elizabeth A. Domingue; (bcr) William Harlow/Photo Researchers, Inc.; (br) Gilbert S. Grant/Photo Researchers, Inc.; (tc) DK Images; (tr) Breck P. Kent/Animals Animals. G4: (tl) Michael P. Gadomski/Photo Researchers, Inc. G4-G5: Glenn Oliver/Visuals Unlimited, Inc. G5: (br) Patti Murray/Earth Scenes; (cr) Stephen G. Maka/DRK Photo; (tr) Ed Reschke/Peter Arnold, Inc. G6: (c) Martin Harvey/Corbis; (l) Richard Day/Animals Animals. G6-G7: (b) Harry Engels/Photo Researchers, Inc. G7: (tl) Gary Meszaros/Photo Researchers, Inc.; (tr) Gary W. Carter/Visuals Unlimited, Inc. G8: (l) Tony Freeman/Photo Edit; (tr) Patrick Johns/Corbis. G8-G9: (b) Steve Terrill/Corbis. G9: (tr) David Buffington/Photodisc. Gl0: (inset) Richard Ashley/Visuals Unlimited; (l) Morton Beebe/Corbis; (r) Peter Vadnai/Corbis. Gll: (b) Lester Lefkowitz/Corbis; (tl) Chris Close/Getty; Images; (tr) Firefly Productions/Corbis. Gl2: (bc) David Young-Wolff/Photo Edit; (bl) C-Squared Studios/Getty Images; (c) Siede Preis/Getty Images; (t) Felicia Martinez/Photo Edit. Gl2-Gl3: Thomas Firak Photography/Stockfood America. Gl3: (bcr) Photodisc; (tr) David Sailors/Corbis.

For Your Reference

Science Handbook

Health Handbook

Units of Measurement

Temperature

1. The temperature is 77 degrees Fahrenheit.

2. That is the same as 25 degrees Celsius.

3. Water boils at 212 degrees Fahrenheit.

4. Water freezes at 0 degrees Celsius.

Length and Area

1. This classroom is 10 meters wide and 20 meters long.

2. That means the area is 200 square meters.

Mass and Weight

1. That baseball bat weighs 32 ounces.

2. 32 ounces is the same as 2 pounds.

3. The mass of the bat is 907 grams.

Measurement

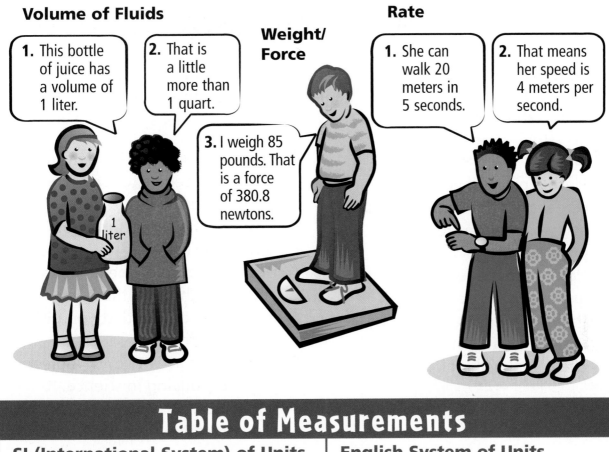

Volume of Fluids

1. This bottle of juice has a volume of 1 liter.

2. That is a little more than 1 quart.

Weight/Force

3. I weigh 85 pounds. That is a force of 380.8 newtons.

Rate

1. She can walk 20 meters in 5 seconds.

2. That means her speed is 4 meters per second.

Table of Measurements

SI (International System) of Units	English System of Units
Temperature Water freezes at 0 degrees Celsius (°C) and boils at 100°C.	**Temperature** Water freezes at 32 degrees Fahrenheit (°F) and boils at 212°F.
Length and Distance 10 millimeters (mm) = 1 centimeter (cm) 100 centimeters = 1 meter (m) 1,000 meters = 1 kilometer (km)	**Length and Distance** 12 inches (in.) = 1 foot (ft) 3 feet = 1 yard (yd) 5,280 feet = 1 mile (mi)
Volume 1 cubic centimeter (cm³) = 1 milliliter (mL) 1,000 milliliters = 1 liter (L)	**Volume of Fluids** 8 fluid ounces (fl oz) = 1 cup (c) 2 cups = 1 pint (pt) 2 pints = 1 quart (qt) 4 quarts = 1 gallon (gal)
Mass 1,000 milligrams (mg) = 1 gram (g) 1,000 grams = 1 kilogram (kg)	**Weight** 16 ounces (oz) = 1 pound (lb) 2,000 pounds = 1 ton (T)
Area 1 square kilometer (km²) = 1 km x 1 km 1 hectare = 10,000 square meters (m²)	**Rate** mph = miles per hour
Rate m/s = meters per second km/h = kilometers per hour	
Force 1 newton (N) = 1 kg x 1m/s²	

Use a Hand Lens

You use a hand lens to magnify an object, or make the object look larger. With a hand lens, you can see details that would be hard to see without the hand lens.

Magnify a Piece of Cereal

1. Place a piece of your favorite cereal on a flat surface. Look at the cereal carefully. Draw a picture of it.
2. Hold the hand lens so that it is just above the cereal. Look through the lens, and slowly move it away from the cereal. The cereal will look larger.

3. Keep moving the hand lens until the cereal begins to look blurry. Then move the lens a little closer to the cereal until you can see it clearly.
4. Draw a picture of the cereal as you see it through the hand lens. Fill in details that you did not see before.
5. Repeat this activity using objects you are studying in science. It might be a rock, some soil, a seed, or something else.

Use a Microscope

Hand lenses make objects look several times larger. A microscope, however, can magnify an object to look hundreds of times larger.

Examine Salt Grains

1. Place the microscope on a flat surface. Always carry a microscope with both hands. Hold the arm with one hand, and put your other hand beneath the base.

2. Look at the drawing to learn the different parts of the microscope.

3. Move the mirror so that it reflects light up toward the stage. Never point the mirror directly at the Sun or a bright light. Bright light can cause permanent eye damage.

4. Place a few grains of salt on the slide. Put the slide under the stage clips on the stage. Be sure that the salt grains are over the hole in the stage.

5. Look through the eyepiece. Turn the focusing knob slowly until the salt grains come into focus.

6. Draw what the grains look like through the microscope.

7. Look at other objects through the microscope. Try a piece of leaf, a strand of human hair, or a pencil mark.

8. Draw what each object looks like through the microscope. Do any of the objects look alike? If so, how? Are any of the objects alive? How do you know?

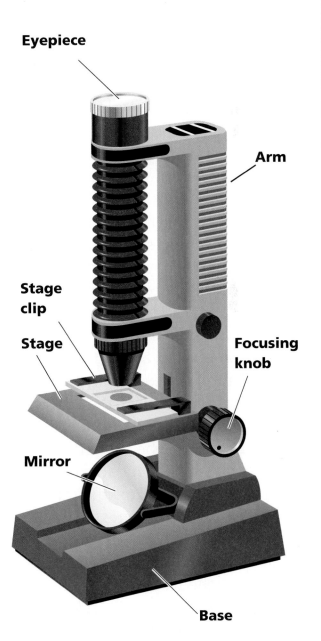

Eyepiece

Arm

Stage clip

Stage

Focusing knob

Mirror

Base

Measure Time

You use timing devices to measure how long something takes to happen. Some timing devices you use in science are a clock with a second hand and a stopwatch. Which one is more accurate?

Comparing a Clock and a Stopwatch

1. Look at a clock with a second hand. The second hand is the hand that you can see moving. It measures seconds.
2. Get an egg timer with falling sand. When the second hand of the clock points to 12, tell your partner to start the egg timer. Watch the clock while the sand in the egg timer is falling.
3. When the sand stops falling, count how many seconds it took. Record this measurement. Repeat the activity, and compare the two measurements.
4. Look at a stopwatch. Click the button on the top right. This starts the time. Click the button again. This stops the time. Click the button on the top left. This sets the stopwatch back to zero. Notice that the stopwatch tells time in hours, minutes, seconds, and hundredths of a second.
5. Repeat the activity in steps 1–3, but use the stopwatch instead of a clock. Make sure the stopwatch is set to zero. Click the top right button to start timing. Click the

button again when the sand stops falling. Make sure you and your partner time the sand twice.

0 minutes   **25 seconds 72 hundredths of a second**

More About Time

1. Use the stopwatch to time how long it takes an ice cube to melt under cold running water. How long does an ice cube take to melt under warm running water?
2. Match each of these times with the action you think took that amount of time.

a.   b.   c.

1. A Little League baseball game
2. Saying the Pledge of Allegiance
3. Recess

Measure Length

You measure length to find out how long something is or how far away something is.

Find Length with a Ruler

1. Look at this section of a ruler. Each centimeter (cm) is divided into 10 millimeters (mm). How long is the paper clip?
2. The length of the paper clip is 3 centimeters plus 2 millimeters. You can write this length as 3.2 centimeters.
3. Place a ruler on your desk. Lay a pencil against the ruler so that one end of the pencil lines up with the left edge of the ruler. Record the length of the pencil.
4. Measure the length of another object. What unit of measure did you use?
5. Ask a partner to measure the same object. Compare your answers. Explain how measurements can be slightly different even if the item measured is the same.

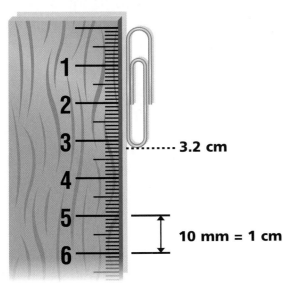

3.2 cm

10 mm = 1 cm

Measuring Area

Area is the amount of surface something covers. To find the area of a rectangle, multiply the rectangle's length by its width. For example, the rectangle here is 3 centimeters long and 2 centimeters wide. Its area is 3 cm x 2 cm = 6 square centimeters. You write the area as 6 cm^2.

1. Find the area of your science book. Measure the book's length to the nearest centimeter. Measure its width.
2. Multiply the book's length by its width. Remember to put the answer in cm^2.

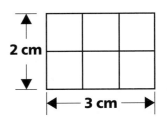

2 cm

3 cm

More About Length

Another tool that measures length is called a caliper. It measures distances and thicknesses. It has two movable, curved legs on a hinge. Try measuring a baseball with a caliper. How wide is it from one side to the other?

Measure Mass

Mass is the amount of matter an object has. You use a balance to measure mass. To find the mass of an object, you balance it with objects whose masses you know.

Measure the Mass of a Box of Crayons

1. Place the balance on a flat, level surface.
2. The pointer should point to the middle mark. If it does not, move the slider a little to the right or left to balance the pans.
3. Gently place a box of crayons on the left pan. Add gram masses to the right pan until the pans are balanced.
4. Count the numbers on the masses that are in the right pan. The total is the mass of the box of crayons, in grams.

5. Record this number. After the number, write a *g* for "grams."

More About Mass

What would happen if you replaced the crayons with a paper clip or a pineapple? You may not have enough masses to balance the pineapple. It has a mass of about 1,000 grams. That's the same as 1 kilogram, because *kilo* means "1,000." Measure other objects and record your measurements.

Measure Volume

Have you ever used a measuring cup? Measuring cups measure the volume of liquids. Volume is the amount of space something takes up. In science you use special measuring cups called beakers and graduated cylinders. These containers are marked in milliliters (mL).

Measure the Volume of a Liquid

1. Look at the beaker and at the graduated cylinder. The beaker has marks for each 25 mL up to 200 mL. The graduated cylinder has marks for each 1 mL up to 100 mL.

2. The surface of the water in the graduated cylinder curves up at the sides. You measure the volume by reading the height of the water at the flat part. What is the volume of water in the graduated cylinder? How much water is in the beaker?

3. Pour 50 mL of water from a pitcher into a graduated cylinder. The water should be at the 50-mL mark on the graduated cylinder. If you go over the mark, pour a little water back into the pitcher.

4. Pour the 50 mL of water into a beaker.

5. Repeat steps 3 and 4 using 30 mL, 45 mL, and 25 mL of water.

6. Measure the volume of water you have in the beaker. Do you have about the same amount of water as your classmates?

beaker

graduated cylinder

Measure Weight/Force

You use a spring scale to measure weight. An object has weight because the force of gravity pulls down on the object. Therefore, weight is a force. Like all forces, weight is measured in newtons (N).

Measure the Weight of an Object

1. Look at your spring scale to see how many newtons it measures. See how the measurements are divided. The spring scale shown here measures up to 10 N. It has a mark for every 1 N.

2. Hold the spring scale by the top loop. Put the object to be measured on the bottom hook. If the object will not stay on the hook, place it in a net bag. Then hang the bag from the hook.

3. Let go of the object slowly. It will pull down on a spring inside the scale. The spring is connected to a pointer. The pointer on the spring scale shown here is a small arrow.

4. Wait for the pointer to stop moving. Read the number of newtons next to the pointer. This is the object's weight. The mug in the picture weighs 3 N.

More About Spring Scales

You probably weigh yourself by standing on a bathroom scale. This is a spring scale. The force of your body stretches a spring inside the scale. The dial on the scale is probably marked in pounds—the English unit of weight. One pound is equal to about 4.5 newtons.

Here are some spring scales you may have seen.

Measure Temperature

Temperature is how hot or cold something is. You use a thermometer to measure temperature. A thermometer is made of a thin tube with colored liquid inside. When the liquid gets warmer, it expands and moves up the tube. When the liquid gets cooler, it contracts and moves down the tube. You may have seen most temperatures measured in degrees Fahrenheit (°F). Scientists measure temperature in degrees Celsius (°C).

Read a Thermometer

1. Look at the thermometer shown here. It has two scales—a Fahrenheit scale and a Celsius scale. Every 20 degrees on each scale has a number.

2. What is the temperature shown on the thermometer? At what temperature does water freeze? Give your answers in °F and in °C.

How Is Temperature Measured?

1. Fill a large beaker about one-half full of cool water. Hold the thermometer in the water by using a clamp. Do not let the thermometer bulb touch the beaker.

2. Wait until the liquid in the tube stops moving—about a minute. Read and record the temperature. Record the temperature scale you used.

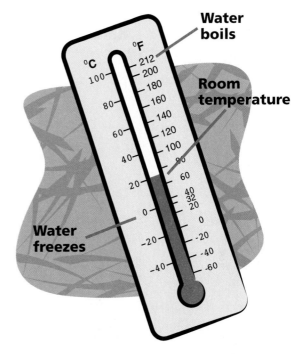

Water boils

Room temperature

Water freezes

3. Place the beaker with the thermometer on a hot plate and warm the beaker for two minutes. Be careful of the hot plate and warm water.

4. Record the temperature of the water. Use the same temperature scale you chose in Step 2.

Use Calculators: Add and Subtract

Sometimes after you make measurements, you have to add or subtract your numbers. A calculator helps you do this.

Add and Subtract Rainfall Amounts

The table shows the amount of rain that fell in a town each week during the summer.

Week	Rain (cm)
1	3
2	5
3	2
4	0
5	1
6	6
7	4
8	0
9	2
10	2
11	6
12	5

1. Make sure the calculator is on. Press the **ON** key.

2. To add the numbers, enter a number and press **+**. Repeat until you enter the last number. Then press **=**. You do not have to enter the zeros. Your total should be 36.

3. What if you found out that you made a mistake in your measurement? Week 1 should be 2 cm less, week 6 should be 3 cm less, week 11 should be 1 cm less, and week 12 should be 2 cm less. Subtract these numbers from your total. You should have 36 displayed on the calculator. Press **−**, and enter the first number you want to subtract. Repeat until you enter the last number. Then press **=**.

Use Calculators: Multiply and Divide

Sometimes after you make measurements, you have to multiply or divide your measurements to get other information. A calculator helps you multiply and divide, especially if the numbers have decimal points.

Multiply Decimals

What if you are measuring the width of your classroom? You discover that the floor is covered with tiles and the room is exactly 32 tiles wide. You measure a tile, and it is 22.7 centimeters wide. To find the width of the room, you can multiply 32 by 22.7.

1. Make sure the calculator is on. Press the **ON** key.
2. Press **3** and **2**.
3. Press **×**.
4. Press **2**, **2**, **·**, and **7**.
5. Press **=**. Your total should be 726.4. That is how wide the room is in centimeters.

Divide Decimals

Now what if you wanted to find out how many desks placed side by side would be needed to reach across the room? You measure one desk, and it is 60 centimeters wide. To find the number of desks needed, divide 726.4 by 60.

Remember that numbers have different values depending on what position they are in. A six in the ones place means six. In the tens place it means 60.

1. Turn the calculator on.
2. Press **7**, **2**, **6**, **·**, and **4**.
3. Press **÷**.
4. Press **6** and **0**.
5. Press **=**. Your total should be about 12.1. This means you can fit 12 desks across the room with a little space left over.

Suppose the room was 35 tiles wide. How wide would the room be? How many desks would fit across it?

Use Computers

A computer has many uses. The Internet connects your computer to many other computers around the world, so you can collect all kinds of information. You can use a computer to show this information and write reports. Best of all, you can use a computer to explore, discover, and learn.

You can also get information from CD-ROMs. They are computer disks that can hold large amounts of information. You can fit a whole encyclopedia on one CD-ROM.

Use Computers for a Project

Here's a project that uses computers. You can do the project in a group.

1. Use a collecting net to gather a soil sample from a brook or stream. Collect pebbles, sand, and small rocks. Keep any small plants also. Return any fish or other animals to the stream right away.

2. After the sample has dried, separate the items in the sample. Use a camera to photograph the soil, pebbles, small rocks, and plants.

3. Each group can use one of the photos to help them start their research. Try to find out what type of rocks or soil you collected.

4. Use the Internet for your research. Find a map and mark your area on it. Identify the type of soil. What types of plants grow well in that type of soil?

5. Find Web sites from an agency such as the Department of Environmental Protection. Contact the group. Ask questions about samples you collected.

6. Use CD-ROMS or other sources from the library to find out how the rocks and soil in your sample formed.

Use Technology

email: Dear Ms. Simpson, Thank you for helping with our project. How does the water in the stream help erode the rocks faster?

7. Keep the information you have gathered in a folder. Review it with your group and use it to write a group report about your soil sample.

8. Each group will present and read a different part of the report. Have an adult help you to record your reports on a video recorder. Show your photographs in the video and explain what each represents. If you'd like, use music or other sounds to accompany the voices on the video recorder.

9. Make a list of computer resources you used to make your report. List Web sites, CD-ROM titles, or other computer resources. Show or read the list at the end of your presentation.

10. Discuss how the computer helped each group to do their report. What problems did each group encounter using the computer? How were the problems solved?

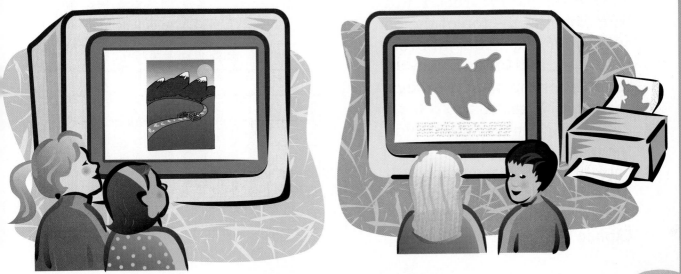

Represent Data

Make Graphs to Organize Data

Graphs can help organize data. Graphs make it easy to spot trends and patterns. There are many kinds of graphs.

Bar Graphs

A bar graph uses bars to show information. For example, what if you are growing a plant? Every week you measure how high the plant has grown. Here is what you find.

Week	Height (cm)
1	1
2	3
3	6
4	10
5	17
6	20
7	22
8	23

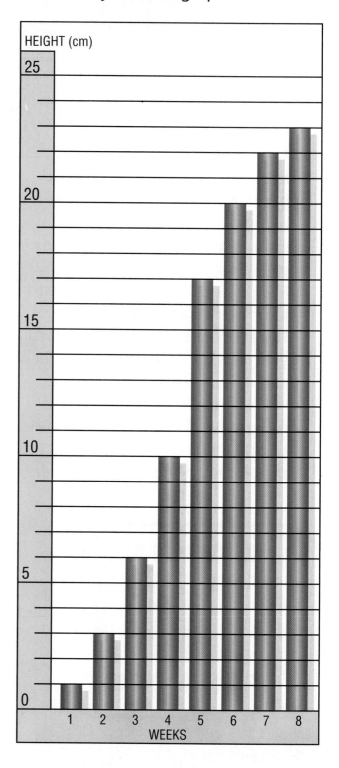

The bar graph at the right organizes the measurements so you can easily compare them.

1. Look at the bar for Week 2. Put your finger at the top of the bar. Move your finger straight over to the left to find how many centimeters the plant grew by the end of Week 2.

2. Between which two weeks did the plant grow most?

3. Look at the 0 on the graph. Is it just a label on a scale or does it have a meaning in the graph? Explain.

Represent Data

Pictographs

A pictograph uses symbols, or pictures, to show information. What if you collect information about how much water your family uses each day? Here is what you find.

Activity	Water Used Each Day (L)
Drinking	10
Showering	100
Bathing	120
Brushing teeth	40
Washing dishes	80
Washing hands	30
Washing clothes	160
Flushing toilet	50

You can organize this information into the pictograph shown here. In this pictograph each bottle means 20 liters of water. A half bottle means half of 20, or 10 liters of water.

1. Which activity uses the most water?
2. Which activity uses the least water?

A Family's Daily Use of Water

Drinking	
Showering	
Bathing	
Brushing teeth	
Washing dishes	
Washing hands	
Washing clothes	
Flushing toilet	

= 20 liters of water

Line Graphs

A line graph shows how information changes over time. What if you measure the temperature outdoors every hour starting at 6 A.M.? Here is what you find.

Time	Temperature (°C)
6 A.M.	10
7 A.M.	12
8 A.M.	14
9 A.M.	16
10 A.M.	18
11 A.M.	20

Now collect outside temperatures on your own each hour. Follow these steps to make a line graph.

1. Make a scale along the bottom and side of the graph as shown. Label the scales.
2. Plot points on the graph.
3. Connect the points with a line.
4. How do the temperatures and times relate to each other? Compare your graph to the one shown.

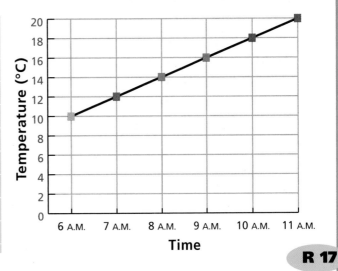

Represent Data

Make Maps, Tables, Charts

Locate Places

A map is a drawing that shows an area from above. Most maps have numbers and letters along the top and side. What if you wanted to find the library on the map below? It is located at D7. Place a finger on the letter D along the side of the map and another finger on the number 7 at the top. Then move your fingers straight across and down the map until they meet. The library is located where D and 7 meet.

1. What building is located at G3?
2. The hospital is located three blocks south and three blocks east of the library. What is its number and letter?
3. Make a map of an area in your community. It might be a park or the area between your home and school. Include numbers and letters along the top and side. Use a compass to find north, and mark north on your map. Exchange maps with classmates.

Idea Maps

The map below left shows how places are connected to each other. Idea maps, on the other hand, show how ideas are connected to each other. Idea maps help you organize information about a topic.

Look at the idea map below. It connects ideas about water. This map shows that Earth's water is either fresh water or salt water. The map also shows four sources of fresh water. You can see that there is no connection between "rivers" and "salt water" on the map. This reminds you that salt water does not flow in rivers.

Make an idea map about a topic you are learning in science. Your map can include words, phrases, or even sentences. Arrange your map in a way that makes sense to you and helps you understand the ideas.

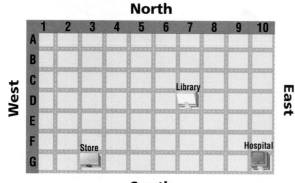

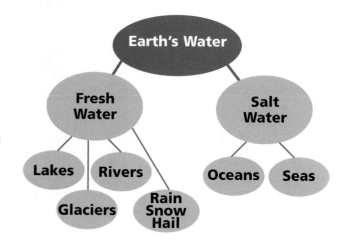

R 18

Make Tables and Charts to Organize Data

Tables help to organize data during experiments. Most tables have columns that run up and down, and rows that run across. The columns and rows have headings that tell you what kind of data goes in each part of the table.

A Sample Table

What if you are going to do an experiment to find out how long different kinds of seeds take to sprout? Before you begin the experiment, you should set up your table. Follow these steps.

1. In this experiment you will plant 20 radish seeds, 20 bean seeds, and 20 corn seeds. Your table must show how many of each kind of seed sprouted on days 1, 2, 3, 4, and 5.

2. Make your table with columns, rows, and headings. You might use a computer. Some computer programs let you build a table with just the click of a mouse. You can delete or add columns and rows if you need to.

3. Give your table a title. Your table could look like the one here.

Make a Table

Plant 20 bean seeds in each of two trays. Keep each tray at a different temperature and observe the trays for seven days. Make a table to record, examine, and evaluate the information of this experiment. How do the columns, rows, and headings of your table relate to one another?

Make a Chart

A chart is simply a table with pictures, as well as words to label the rows or columns. Make a chart that shows the information of the above experiment.

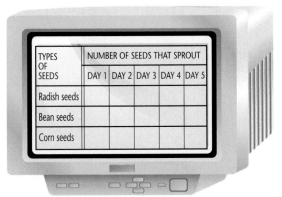

TYPES OF SEEDS	NUMBER OF SEEDS THAT SPROUT				
	DAY 1	DAY 2	DAY 3	DAY 4	DAY 5
Radish seeds					
Bean seeds					
Corn seeds					

The Skeletal System

The Skeleton

The skeleton is a system of the human body. It is the frame that supports the body. The skeleton is made up of bones and has several jobs.

- It gives the body its shape.
- It protects organs in the body.
- It works with muscles to move the body.

Each of the 206 bones of the skeleton is the size and shape best fitted to do its job. For example, long and strong leg bones support the body's weight. The skull protects the brain. The hip bone helps you move.

1. What is the skeleton?
2. Describe several jobs of bones.

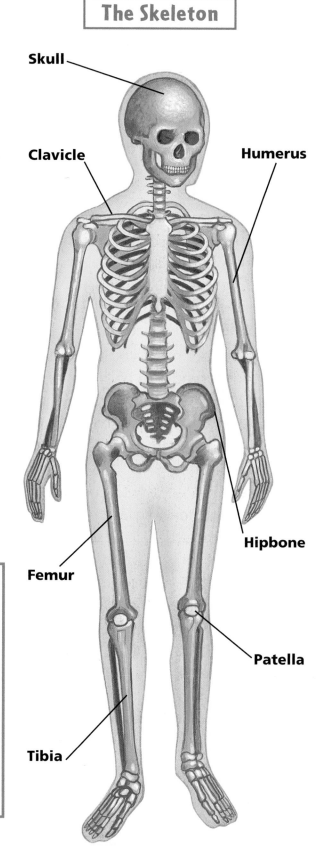

Skull
Clavicle
Humerus
Hipbone
Femur
Patella
Tibia

CARE!

- Exercise to keep your skeletal system in good shape.
- Don't overextend your joints.
- Eat foods rich in vitamins and minerals. Your bones need the minerals calcium and phosphorus to grow strong.

Bones

1 A bone is covered with a tough but thin membrane that has many small blood vessels. The blood vessels bring nutrients and oxygen to the living parts of the bone and remove wastes.

2 Inside some bones is a soft tissue known as marrow. Yellow marrow is made mostly of fat cells and is one of the body's energy reserves. It is usually found in the long, hollow spaces of long bones.

3 Part of the bone is compact, or solid. It is made up of living bone cells and non-living materials. The nonliving part is made up of layers of hardened minerals such as calcium and phosphorus. In between the mineral layers are living bone cells.

4 Red marrow fills the spaces in spongy bone. Red marrow makes new red blood cells, germ-fighting white blood cells, and cell fragments that stop a cut from bleeding.

5 Part of the bone is made of bone tissue that looks like a dry sponge. It is made of strong, hard tubes. It is also found in the middle of short, flat bones.

CARE!

- **Eat foods rich in vitamins and minerals. Your bones need the minerals calcium and phosphorus to grow strong.**
- **Be careful! Avoid sprains and fractures.**
- **Get help in case of injury.**

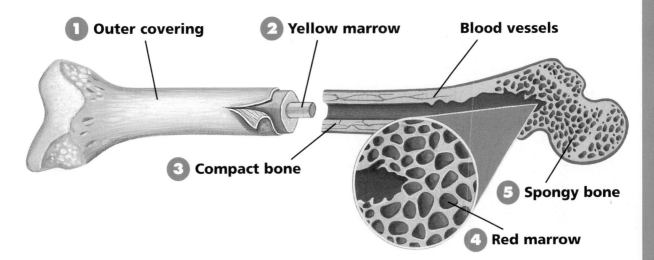

1 Outer covering   **2 Yellow marrow**   **Blood vessels**

3 Compact bone

5 Spongy bone

4 Red marrow

R 21

Joints

The skeleton has different types of joints. A joint is a place where two or more bones meet. Joints can be classified into three major groups—immovable joints, partly movable joints, and movable joints.

Types of Joints

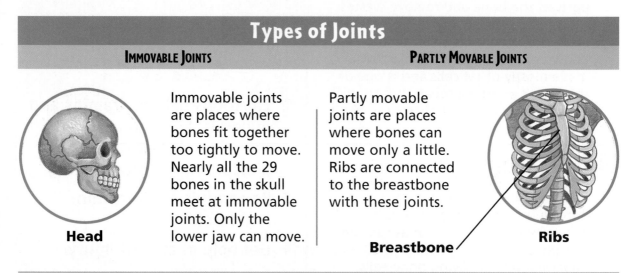

IMMOVABLE JOINTS

Immovable joints are places where bones fit together too tightly to move. Nearly all the 29 bones in the skull meet at immovable joints. Only the lower jaw can move.

Head

PARTLY MOVABLE JOINTS

Partly movable joints are places where bones can move only a little. Ribs are connected to the breastbone with these joints.

Breastbone

Ribs

MOVABLE JOINTS

Movable joints are places where bones can move easily. Use the information below to describe each type of movable joint. Explain how each type of joint allows movement.

Gliding joint

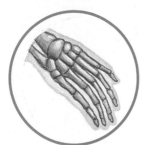

Hand and wrist

Small bones in the wrists and ankles meet at gliding joints. The bones can slide against one another. A gliding joint is similar to a sliding door. These joints allow some movement in all directions.

The hips are examples of ball-and-socket joints. The ball of one bone fits into the socket, or cup, of another bone. These joints allow bones to move back and forth, in a circle, and side to side.

Ball-and-socket joint

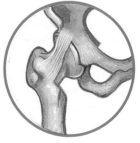

Hip

Hinge joint

The knees are hinge joints. A hinge joint is similar to a door hinge. It allows bones to move back and forth in one direction.

The joint between the skull and neck is a pivot joint. It allows the head to move up and down, and side to side. A pivot joint is similar to a compass.

Pivot joint

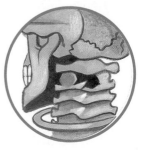

Knee

Neck

The Muscular System

1 A message from your brain causes this muscle, called the biceps, to contract. When a muscle contracts, it becomes shorter and thicker. As the biceps contracts, it pulls on the arm bone it is attached to.

2 Most muscles work in pairs to move bones. This muscle, called the triceps, relaxes when the biceps contracts. When a muscle relaxes, it becomes longer and thinner.

3 To straighten your arm, a message from your brain causes the triceps to contract. When the triceps contracts, it pulls on the bone it is attached to.

4 As the triceps contracts, the biceps relaxes. Your arm straightens.

Three types of muscles make up the body—skeletal muscle, cardiac muscle, and smooth muscle.

The muscles that are attached to and move bones are called skeletal muscles. These muscles are attached to bones by a tough cord called a tendon. Skeletal muscles pull bones to move them. Muscles do not push bones.

Cardiac muscles are found in only one place in the body—the heart. The walls of the heart are made of strong cardiac muscles. When cardiac muscles contract, they squeeze blood out of the heart. When cardiac muscles relax, the heart fills with more blood.

Smooth muscles make up internal organs and blood vessels. Smooth muscles in the lungs help a person breathe. Those in the blood vessels help control blood flow around the body.

1. Name the three types of muscles.
2. Describe how muscles cause the body to move.

CARE!

● **Exercise to strengthen your muscles.**

● **Eat the right foods, and get plenty of rest.**

The Circulatory System

The circulatory system consists of the heart, blood vessels, and blood. Circulation is the flow of blood through the body. Blood is a liquid that contains red blood cells, white blood cells, and platelets. Red blood cells carry oxygen and nutrients to cells. White blood cells work to fight germs that enter the body. Platelets are cell fragments that make the blood clot.

The heart is a muscular organ about the size of a fist. It beats about 70 to 90 times a minute, pumping blood through the blood vessels. Arteries carry blood away from the heart. Some arteries carry blood to the lungs, where the cells pick up oxygen. Other arteries carry oxygen-rich blood from the lungs to all other parts of the body. Veins carry blood from other parts of the body back to the heart. Blood in most veins carries the wastes released by cells and has little oxygen. Blood flows from arteries to veins through narrow vessels called capillaries.

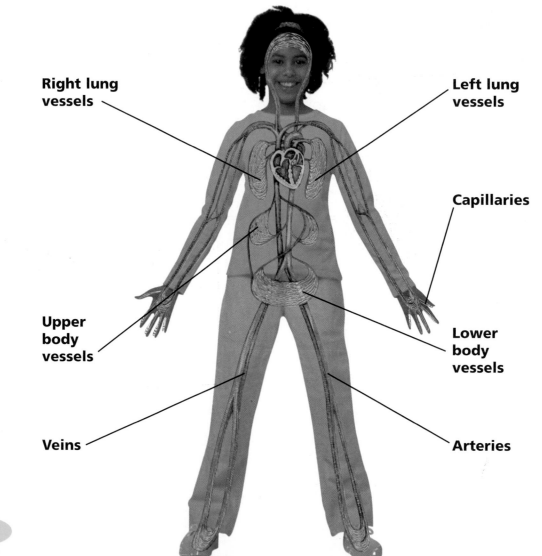

Right lung vessels

Left lung vessels

Capillaries

Upper body vessels

Lower body vessels

Veins

Arteries

The Heart

The heart has two sides, right and left, separated by a thick muscular wall. Each side has two chambers for blood. The upper chamber is the atrium. The lower chamber is the ventricle. Blood enters the heart through the vena cava. It leaves the heart through the aorta.

The pulmonary artery carries blood from the body into the lungs. Here carbon dioxide leaves the blood to be exhaled by the lungs. Fresh oxygen enters the blood to be carried to every cell in the body. Blood returns from the lungs to the heart through the pulmonary veins.

CARE!

- Don't smoke. The nicotine in tobacco makes the heart beat faster and work harder to pump blood.

- Never take illegal drugs, such as cocaine or heroin. They can damage the heart and cause heart failure.

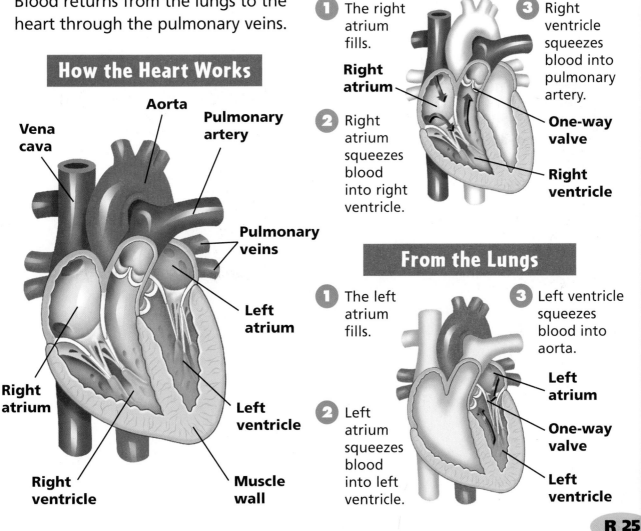

How the Heart Works

Vena cava

Aorta

Pulmonary artery

Pulmonary veins

Left atrium

Right atrium

Left ventricle

Right ventricle

Muscle wall

To the Lungs

1. The right atrium fills.

Right atrium

2. Right atrium squeezes blood into right ventricle.

3. Right ventricle squeezes blood into pulmonary artery.

One-way valve

Right ventricle

From the Lungs

1. The left atrium fills.

3. Left ventricle squeezes blood into aorta.

Left atrium

2. Left atrium squeezes blood into left ventricle.

One-way valve

Left ventricle

The Respiratory System

The process of getting and using oxygen in the body is called respiration. When a person inhales, air is pulled into the nose or mouth. The air travels down into the trachea. In the chest the trachea divides into two bronchial tubes. One bronchial tube enters each lung. Each bronchial tube branches into smaller tubes called bronchioles.

At the end of each bronchiole are tiny air sacs called alveoli. The alveoli exchange carbon dioxide for oxygen.

Oxygen comes from the air we breathe. The main muscle that controls breathing is a dome-shaped sheet of muscle called the diaphragm.

To inhale, the diaphragm contracts and pulls down. To exhale, the diaphragm relaxes and returns to its dome shape.

CARE!

- **Don't smoke. Smoking damages your respiratory system.**

- **Exercise to strengthen your breathing muscles.**

- **If you ever have trouble breathing, tell an adult at once.**

Air Flow

Carbon dioxide   **Oxygen**

Carbon dioxide diffuses into the alveoli. From there it is exhaled.

Capillary net

Throat

Trachea

Alveoli

Fresh oxygen diffuses from the alveoli to the blood.

Oxygen →   Carbon dioxide ←

Diaphragm

The air you breathe is about 21 percent oxygen.

The blood in the capillaries of your lungs has very little oxygen.

The blood has a higher concentration of carbon dioxide than air.

Lungs

Activity Pyramid

Physical fitness is the condition in which the body is healthy and works the best it can. The activity pyramid shows you the kinds of activities you should be doing to make your body more physically fit.

3–5 times a week Aerobic activities such as swimming, biking, climbing; sports activities such as basketball, handball

Occasionally
Inactive pastimes such as watching TV, playing board games, talking on the phone

2–3 times a week
Leisure activities such as gardening, golf, softball

Eating a variety of healthful foods and getting enough exercise and rest help people to stay healthy.

As people grow, the amounts and kinds of food and exercise the body needs may change.

Food Guide Pyramid

To make sure the body stays fit and healthy, a person needs to eat a balanced diet. The Food Guide Pyramid shows how many servings of each group a person should eat every day. Food provides energy and material for growth and repair of body parts. Vitamins and minerals keep the body healthy.

CARE!
- Stay active every day.
- Eat a balanced diet.
- Drink plenty of water— 6 to 8 large glasses a day.

Fats, oils, and sweets
Use sparingly

Milk, yogurt, and cheese group
2–3 servings

Meat, dry beans, eggs, and nuts group
2–3 servings

Vegetable group
3–5 servings

Fruit group
2–4 servings

Bread, cereal, rice, and pasta group
6–11 servings

The Digestive System

Digestion is the process of breaking down food into simple substances the body can use. Digestion begins when a person chews food. Chewing breaks the food down into smaller pieces and moistens it with saliva.

Digested food is absorbed in the small intestine. The walls of the small intestine are lined with villi. Villi are tiny fingerlike projections that absorb digested food. From the villi the blood transports nutrients to every part of the body.

It is important to eat healthful foods. Avoid eating foods with caffeine, sugar, and fat as these foods often lack the nutrients the body needs. Stay away from alcohol and drugs as these substances damage the body.

CARE!

- Chew your food well.
- Drink plenty of water to help move food through your digestive system.

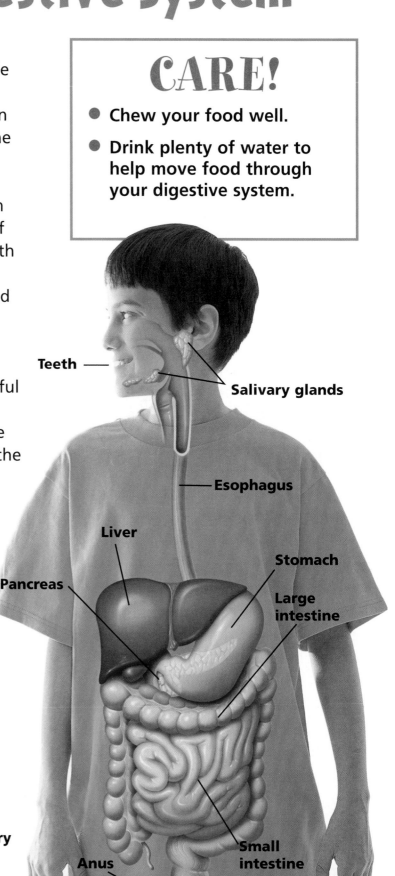

Capillary

Villi

Vein

Artery

Lymph vessel

Teeth

Salivary glands

Esophagus

Liver

Pancreas

Stomach

Large intestine

Small intestine

Anus

The Excretory System

Excretion is the process of removing waste products from the body. The liver filters wastes from the blood and converts them into urea. Urea is then carried to the kidneys for excretion.

The skin takes part in excretion when a person sweats. Glands in the inner layer of the skin produce sweat. Sweat is mostly water. Sweat tastes salty because it contains mineral salts the body doesn't need. There is also a tiny amount of urea in sweat.

Sweat is excreted onto the outer layer of the skin. Evaporation into the air takes place in part because of body heat. When sweat evaporates, a person feels cooler.

How You Sweat

Glands under your skin push sweat up to the surface, where it collects.

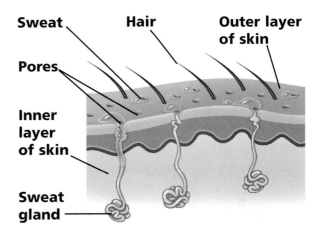

Sweat · Hair · Outer layer of skin · Pores · Inner layer of skin · Sweat gland

CARE!

- **Wash regularly to avoid body odor, clogged pores, and skin irritation.**

How Your Kidneys Work

1. Blood enters the kidney through an artery and flows into capillaries.

2. Sugars, salts, water, urea, and other wastes move from the capillaries to tiny nephrons.

3. Nutrients return to the blood and flow back out through veins.

4. Urea and other wastes become urine, which flows down the ureters.

5. Urine is stored in the bladder and excreted through the urethra.

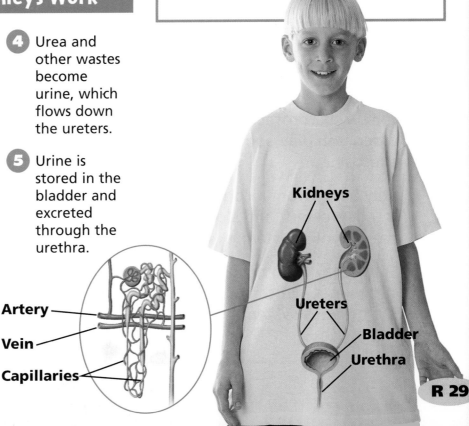

Artery · Vein · Capillaries · Kidneys · Ureters · Bladder · Urethra

The Nervous System

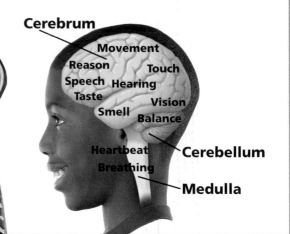

Cerebrum
Movement
Reason
Touch
Speech Hearing
Taste
Vision
Smell Balance

Heartbeat
Breathing Cerebellum

Medulla

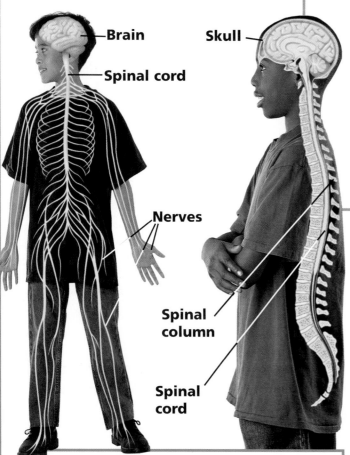

Brain

Skull

Spinal cord

Nerves

Spinal column

Spinal cord

The nervous system has two parts. The brain and the spinal cord are the central nervous system. All other nerves are the outer nervous system.

The largest part of the brain is the cerebrum. A deep groove separates the right half, or hemisphere, of the cerebrum from the left half. Both sides of the cerebrum contain control centers for the senses.

The cerebellum lies below the cerebrum. It coordinates the skeletal muscles. It also helps in keeping balance.

The brain stem connects to the spinal cord. The lowest part of the brain stem is the medulla. It controls heartbeat, breathing, blood pressure, and the muscles in the digestive system.

CARE!

- To protect the brain and spinal cord, wear protective headgear when you play sports or exercise.

- Stay away from alcohol, which is a depressant and slows down the nervous system.

- Stay away from drugs, such as stimulants, which can speed up the nervous system.

The Endocrine System

Hormones are chemicals that control body functions. A gland that produces hormones is called an endocrine gland. Sweat from sweat glands flows out of tubes called ducts. Endocrine glands have no ducts.

The endocrine glands are scattered around the body. Each gland makes one or more hormones. Every hormone seeks out a target organ. This is the place in the body where the hormone acts.

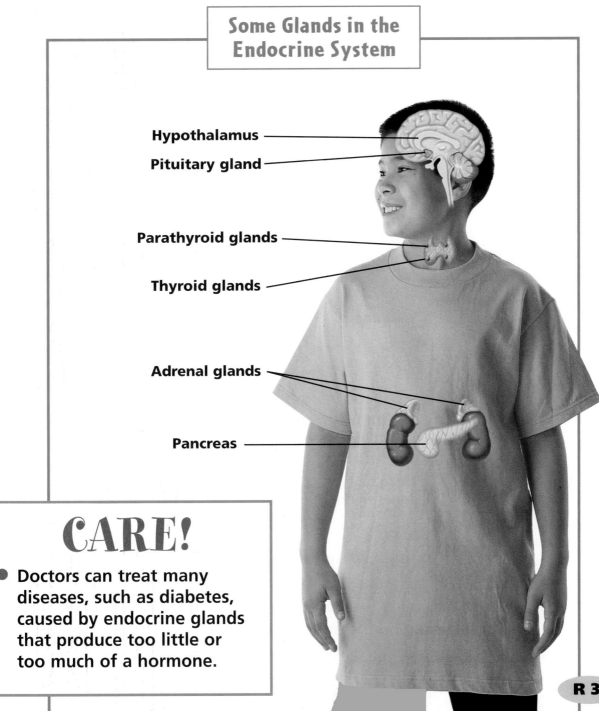

Some Glands in the Endocrine System

Hypothalamus

Pituitary gland

Parathyroid glands

Thyroid glands

Adrenal glands

Pancreas

CARE!

- Doctors can treat many diseases, such as diabetes, caused by endocrine glands that produce too little or too much of a hormone.

The Senses

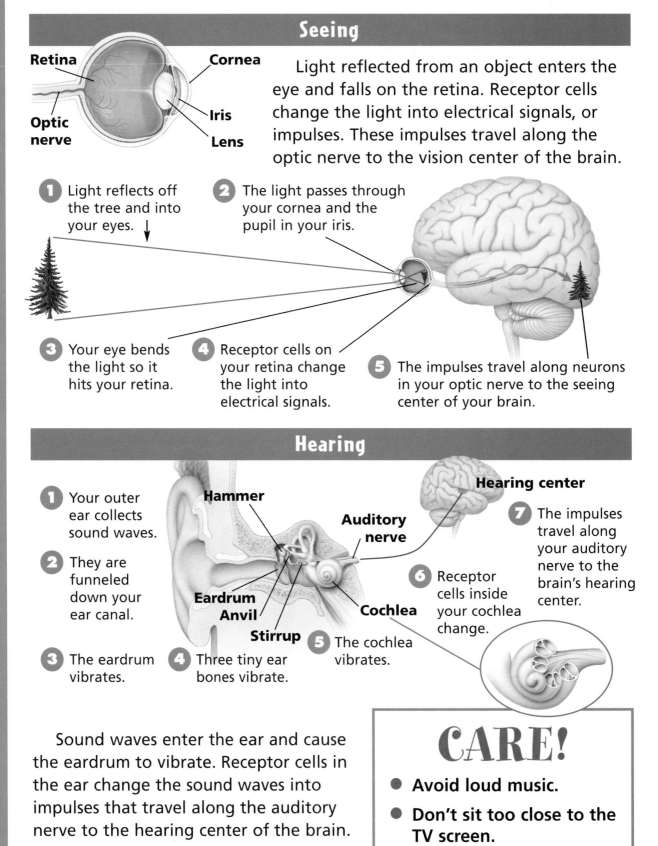

Seeing

Retina **Cornea** **Optic nerve** **Iris** **Lens**

Light reflected from an object enters the eye and falls on the retina. Receptor cells change the light into electrical signals, or impulses. These impulses travel along the optic nerve to the vision center of the brain.

1. Light reflects off the tree and into your eyes.

2. The light passes through your cornea and the pupil in your iris.

3. Your eye bends the light so it hits your retina.

4. Receptor cells on your retina change the light into electrical signals.

5. The impulses travel along neurons in your optic nerve to the seeing center of your brain.

Hearing

1. Your outer ear collects sound waves.

2. They are funneled down your ear canal.

3. The eardrum vibrates.

4. Three tiny ear bones vibrate.

5. The cochlea vibrates.

6. Receptor cells inside your cochlea change.

7. The impulses travel along your auditory nerve to the brain's hearing center.

Hammer **Auditory nerve** **Hearing center** **Eardrum** **Anvil** **Stirrup** **Cochlea**

Sound waves enter the ear and cause the eardrum to vibrate. Receptor cells in the ear change the sound waves into impulses that travel along the auditory nerve to the hearing center of the brain.

CARE!

- Avoid loud music.
- Don't sit too close to the TV screen.

The Senses

Smelling

The sense of smell is really the ability to detect chemicals in the air. When a person breathes, chemicals dissolve in mucus in the upper part of the nose. When the chemicals come in contact with receptor cells, the cells send impulses along the olfactory nerve to the smelling center of the brain.

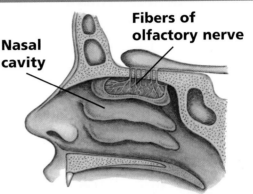

Nasal cavity

Fibers of olfactory nerve

Tasting

When a person eats, chemicals in food dissolve in saliva. Inside each taste bud are receptors that can sense the four main tastes—sweet, sour, salty, and bitter. The receptors send impulses along a nerve to the taste center of the brain. The brain identifies the taste of the food.

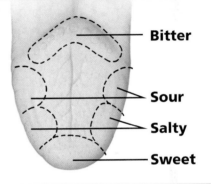

Bitter

Sour

Salty

Sweet

Touching

Receptor cells in the skin help a person tell hot from cold, wet from dry, and the light touch of a feather from the pressure of stepping on a stone. Each receptor cell sends impulses along sensory nerves to the spinal cord. The spinal cord then sends the impulses to the touch center of the brain.

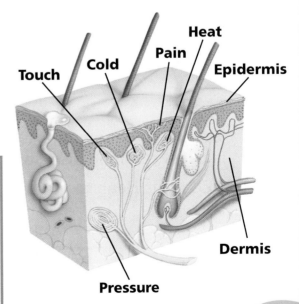

Touch Cold Pain Heat Epidermis

Dermis

Pressure

CARE!

- **To prevent the spread of germs, always cover your mouth and nose when you cough or sneeze.**

The Immune System

The immune system helps the body fight germs. Germs are tiny living things. The body is able to keep out harmful germs most of the time. Tears, saliva, and skin all help the body keep germs out. Sometimes germs get into the body. Usually white blood cells kill the germs before they can do any harm.

There are white blood cells in the blood vessels and in the lymph vessels. Lymph vessels are similar to blood vessels. Instead of blood, they carry lymph. Lymph nodes filter out harmful materials in the body. They also produce white blood cells to fight germs.

The white blood cells don't always get rid of the germs. Sometimes germs stay in the body and make it sick. When germs make the body sick, it is important to rest, eat healthful foods, and drink lots of water.

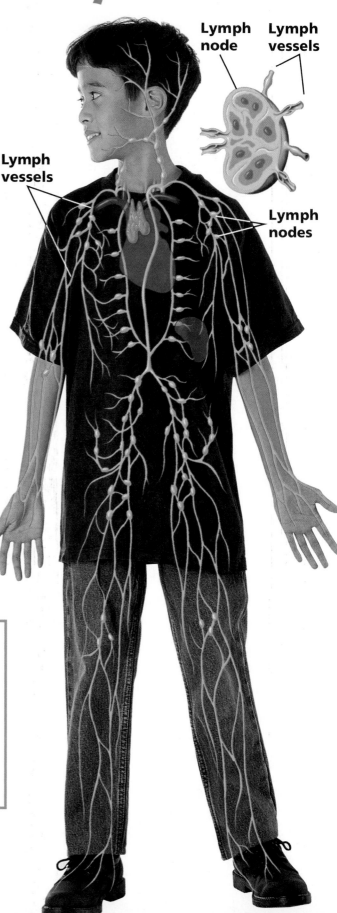

Lymph node

Lymph vessels

Lymph vessels

Lymph nodes

Lymph vessels run through your body to collect fluid and return it to the bloodstream.

CARE!

- Be sure to get immunized against common diseases.
- Keep cuts clean to prevent infection.

Nutrients

Nutrients are materials in foods that your body uses to grow and stay healthy. Without nutrients you could not grow, move, think, or even live. Most foods that provide you with nutrients come from plants and animals.

There are six kinds of nutrients and each helps your body in a different way. Some help you grow. Others help repair damaged tissues in your body. Some help your body function properly. Still others give you energy. The six kinds of nutrients found in foods are carbohydrates, vitamins, minerals, proteins, fats, and water. A balance of different foods will give your body the nutrients that it needs.

Carbohydrates

Your body needs a constant supply of energy to keep working. **Carbohydrates** are a main source of energy for your body. There are two kinds of carbohydrates. One is *starch* and the other is *sugar*.

Starches provide long-lasting energy. Your body is able to store energy from starches longer than many other nutrients. Foods with starches are rice, potatoes, bread, cereal, and pasta.

It is easy to see what starch looks like.

1. Cut a raw potato into several pieces on a chopping board. Be careful with the knife.
2. Look for a whitish, milky liquid on the potato and on the knife. That liquid contains starch.
3. Check other foods for starch, such as cooked pasta or cooked rice.

Energy from sugars doesn't last as long as energy from starches. Fruits such as apples and oranges are made of sugars.

How can you test a food to tell if it is made of sugars? One way is to test them for a chemical reaction.

Finding Sugar

1. Label each of five small paper cups *apple juice*, *orange juice*, *olive oil*, *milk*, and *water*. Pour a small amount of each liquid into its labeled cup.
2. Your teacher will give you one glucose strip for each cup. Do not touch the strips with your fingers. Use a tweezer to hold a glucose strip in each liquid for two seconds.
3. What happened to each of the test strips? Record your observations in a chart.

If the food you tested contains sugar, the yellow test strip will turn green. Which foods tested contained sugar?

Vitamins and Minerals

Vitamins keep your body tissues healthy and protect you from illness. They are found in foods that come from plants and animals.

Very small amounts of vitamins are present in many foods. But this is all our bodies need to grow and stay healthy. These are some common vitamins you can find in foods.

Vitamin	Sources	Benefits
A	Milk, fruit, carrots, green vegetables	Keeps eyes, teeth, gums, skin and hair healthy
C	Citrus fruits, strawberries, tomatoes	Helps heart, cells, and muscle function
D	Milk, fish, eggs	Helps keep teeth and bones strong

Minerals come from Earth. They are found in small amounts in foods that come from plants and animals. Minerals help your blood, muscles, and nervous system. They help your bones to grow and function.

Calcium is a mineral that builds strong teeth and bones. It's found in foods such as yogurt, milk, cheese, and green vegetables. *Iron* helps red blood cells. It can be found in meat, beans, fish, and whole grains. Your body uses *zinc* to grow and to heal wounds. It is found in meat, fish, and eggs.

Protein and Water

Two of the most important nutrients for any living thing are **protein** and water. Proteins are part of every living cell. They are needed by all organisms. They help your body grow and help repair body cells. Foods such as milk, dairy products, meats, fish, and nuts are good sources of protein.

You can see the protein in some foods. Have you ever cooked an egg in a frying pan? An egg is rich in protein. Even the colorless part of the egg is made of protein. As the egg cooks, you can see the protein in this part of the egg become white.

Water helps your body remove wastes. It also protects joints and other body parts. Water helps keep your body temperature normal. Your body is made of about 62% water. You could not live for even a week without water. Many fruits and vegetables are a source of water because they have water inside them.

Fats and Oils

Fats help your body to use other nutrients and to store vitamins. Fats keep your body warm and help brain cells and other body tissues work. Fats are found in meats, eggs, milk, butter, and nuts. Oils, such as those used in cooking, also contain fat.

While fat is needed for your body to work properly, it is needed only in small amounts. Some foods contain more fat than others.

Fat Check

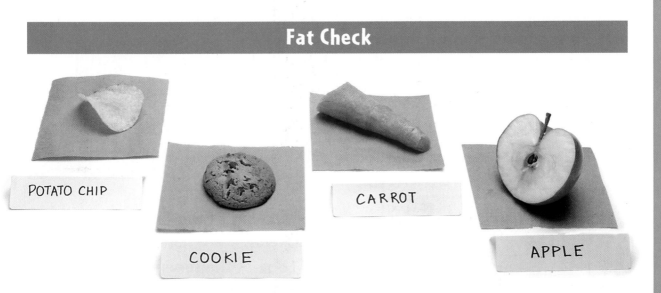

POTATO CHIP

COOKIE

CARROT

APPLE

Here's a way to find out which foods contain a lot of fats.

1. Gather various foods, such as a potato chip, cookie, carrot, and apple.
2. Cut a brown paper bag into 3-inch (7-cm) squares. Label each square with the name of one of the foods.
3. Rub some of each food on the square. Let the square dry.
4. Hold each square up to the light. What effect do the different foods have on the paper?

Foods that leave a greasy mark or stain on the paper contain a lot of fat, or oils. Too much fat in our bodies can cause health problems.

Calories

The chemical energy in foods is measured in a unit called a **calorie**. You take calories of food energy into your body by eating. Then you use, or burn, calories with everything you do. Breathing, eating, digesting food, walking, even doing your homework uses calories.

You can compare the chemical energy from different foods. Most food packages contain a label that gives information about the food's nutrients.

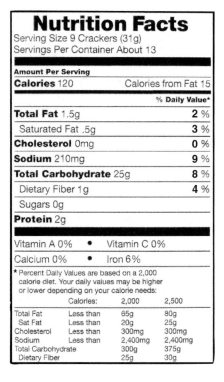

Nutrition Facts
Serving Size 9 Crackers (31g)
Servings Per Container About 13

Amount Per Serving	
Calories 120	Calories from Fat 15

	% Daily Value*
Total Fat 1.5g	2 %
Saturated Fat .5g	3 %
Cholesterol 0mg	0 %
Sodium 210mg	9 %
Total Carbohydrate 25g	8 %
Dietary Fiber 1g	4 %
Sugars 0g	
Protein 2g	

Vitamin A 0%	•	Vitamin C 0%
Calcium 0%	•	Iron 6%

*Percent Daily Values are based on a 2,000 calorie diet. Your daily values may be higher or lower depending on your calorie needs:

		Calories:	2,000	2,500
Total Fat	Less than		65g	80g
Sat Fat	Less than		20g	25g
Cholesterol	Less than		300mg	300mg
Sodium	Less than		2,400mg	2,400mg
Total Carbohydrate			300g	375g
Dietary Fiber			25g	30g

Nutrition Facts
Serving Size 7 Crackers (31g)
Servings Per Container About 9

Amount Per Serving	
Calories 140	Calories from Fat 45

	% Daily Value*
Total Fat 5g	8%
Saturated Fat 1g	5%
Polyunsaturated Fat 0g	
Monounsaturated Fat 1.5g	
Cholesterol 0mg	0%
Sodium 200mg	8%
Total Carbohydrate 21g	7%
Dietary Fiber 4g	14%
Sugars 0g	
Protein 3g	

Vitamin A 0%	•	Vitamin C 0%
Calcium 0%	•	Iron 8%

*Percent Daily Values are based on a 2,000 calorie diet. Your daily values may be higher or lower depending on your calorie needs:

		Calories:	2,000	2,500
Total Fat	Less than		65g	80g
Sat Fat	Less than		20g	25g
Cholesterol	Less than		300mg	300mg
Sodium	Less than		2,400mg	2,400mg
Total Carbohydrate			300g	375g
Dietary Fiber			25g	30g

Calorie Comparison

Compare the calories on the food labels of these two boxes of crackers.

1. Look at the serving size on both labels. How many grams (g) of crackers are in a serving of each? Are they equal?
2. Compare the calories listed on the labels.
3. Which cracker provides more chemical energy per serving? Which cracker contains more sugar?
4. Now compare labels on two different types of foods, such as cheese and butter. Be sure the serving sizes are equal before comparing calories.

FOLDABLES™

by Dinah Zike

Folding Instructions

So how do you make a Foldables data organizer? The following pages offer step-by-step instructions—where and when to fold, where to cut—for making 11 basic Foldables data organizers. The instructions begin with the basic shapes, such as the hot dog fold, that were introduced on page xv.

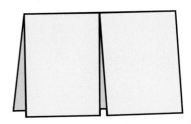

Half-Book

Fold a sheet of paper ($8\frac{1}{2}$" x 11") in half.

1. This book can be folded vertically like a hot dog or …

2. … it can be folded horizontally like a hamburger.

Folded Book

1. Make a Half-Book.

2. Fold in half again like a hamburger.

This makes a ready-made cover and two small pages inside for recording information.

Two-Tab Book

Take a Folded Book and cut up the valley of the inside fold toward the mountain top.

This cut forms two large tabs that can be used front and back for writing and illustrations.

Pocket Book

1. Fold a sheet of paper ($8\frac{1}{2}$" x 11") in half like a hamburger.

2. Open the folded paper and fold one of the long sides up two inches to form a pocket. Refold along the hamburger fold so that the newly formed pockets are on the inside.

3. Glue the outer edges of the two-inch fold with a small amount of glue.

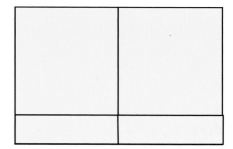

Shutter Fold

1. Begin as if you were going to make a hamburger, but instead of creasing the paper, pinch it to show the midpoint.

2. Fold the outer edges of the paper to meet at the pinch, or midpoint, forming a Shutter Fold.

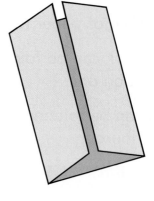

Trifold Book

1. Fold a sheet of paper ($8\frac{1}{2}$" x 11") into thirds.

2. Use this book as is, or cut into shapes.

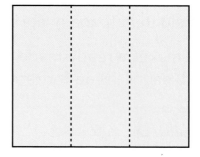

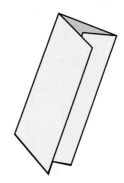

Three-Tab Book

1. Fold a sheet of paper like a hot dog.

2. With the paper horizontal and the fold of the hot dog up, fold the right side toward the center, trying to cover one half of the paper.

3. Fold the left side over the right side to make a book with three folds.

4. Open the folded book. Place one hand between the two thicknesses of paper and cut up the two valleys on one side only. This will create three tabs.

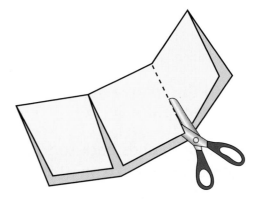

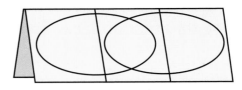

Layered-Look Book

1. Stack two sheets of paper ($8\frac{1}{2}$" x 11") so that the back sheet is one inch higher than the front sheet.

2. Bring the bottoms of both sheets upward and align the edges so that all of the layers or tabs are the same distance apart.

3. When all the tabs are an equal distance apart, fold the papers and crease well.

4. Open the papers and glue them together along the valley, or inner center fold, or staple them along the mountain.

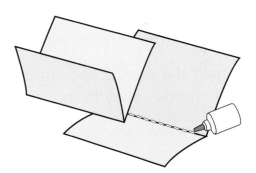

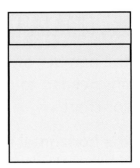

Four-Tab Book

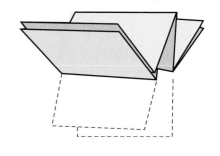

1. Fold a sheet of paper (8$\frac{1}{2}$" x 11") in half like a hot dog.

2. Fold this long rectangle in half like a hamburger.

3. Fold both ends back to touch the mountain top or fold it like an accordion.

4. On the side with two valleys and one mountain top, make vertical cuts through one thickness of paper, forming four tabs.

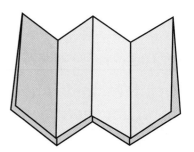

Four-Door Book

1. Make a Shutter Fold using 11" x 17" or 12" x 18" paper.

2. Fold the Shutter Fold in half like a hamburger. Crease well.

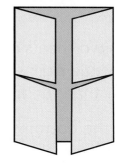

3. Open the project and cut along the two inside valley folds.

These cuts will form four doors on the inside of the project.

Folded Table or Chart

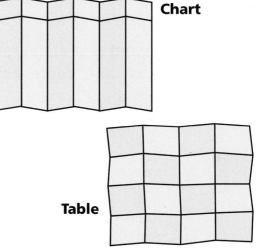

Chart

1. Fold the number of vertical columns needed to make the table or chart.

2. Fold the horizontal rows needed to make the table or chart.

3. Label the rows and columns.

Table

Glossary

This Glossary will help you to pronounce and understand the meanings of the Science Words introduced in this book. The page number at the end of the definition tells where the word appears.

A

adaptation (ad′əp tā′shən) A special characteristic that helps an organism survive. (p. B50)

air (âr) A mixture of gases and dust. (p. D6)

air pressure (âr presh′ər) The force of air pushing down on Earth. (p. D9)

algae (al′jē) *pl. n., sing.* (-gə) Tiny one-celled organisms. (pp. B9, B27)

amber (am′bər) Hardened tree sap, often a source of insect fossils. (p. C22)

amphibian (am fib′ē ən) An animal that spends part of its life in water and part of its life on land. (p. A72)

anemometer (an′ə mom′i tər) A device that measures wind speed. (p. D25)

aqueduct (ak′wə dukt′) A pipe or channel for carrying water over long distances. (p. C32)

atmosphere (at′məs fîr′) Gases that surround Earth. (p. D6)

atom (at′əm) The smallest particle of matter. (p. F28)

axis (ak′sis) A real or imaginary line through the center of a spinning object. (p. D37)

PRONUNCIATION KEY

The following symbols are used throughout the Macmillan McGraw-Hill Science Glossaries.

a	at	e	end	o	hot	u	up	hw	white	ə about
ā	ape	ē	me	ō	old	ū	use	ng	song	taken
ä	far	i	it	ôr	fork	ü	rule	th	thin	pencil
âr	care	ī	ice	oi	oil	ů	pull	th	this	lemon
ô	law	îr	pierce	ou	out	ûr	turn	zh	measure	circus

′ = primary accent; shows which syllable takes the main stress, such as **kil** in **kilogram** (kil′ə gram′).
′ = secondary accent; shows which syllables take lighter stresses, such as **gram** in **kilogram**.

B

bacteria, (bak tîr′ē ə) One-celled living things. (p. B18)

barometer (bə rom′i tər) A device for measuring air pressure. (p. D24)

bird (bûrd) An animal that has a beak, feathers, two wings, and two legs. (p. A73)

bulb (bulb) The underground stem of such plants as onions and irises. (p. A30)

C

camouflage (kam′ə fläzh) An adaptation that allows animals to blend into their surroundings. (p. B52)

carbon dioxide and oxygen cycles (kär′bən dī ok′sīd and ok′sə jən sī′kəlz) The process of passing oxygen and carbon dioxide from one population to another in both water and land habitats. (p. B27)

carnivore (kär′nə vôr′) An animal that eats only other animals. (p. B20)

cast (kast) A fossil formed or shaped inside a mold. (p. C23)

cell (sel) **1.** The basic building block of life. (p. A10) **2.** A source of electricity. (p. F72)

cell membrane (sel mem′brān′) The thin outer covering of a cell. (p. A10)

cell wall (sel wôl) A stiff layer outside the cell membrane of plant cells. (p. A11)

chemical change (kəm′i kəl chānj) A change that forms a different kind of matter. (p. F30)

chloroplast (klôr′ə plast′) One of the small green bodies inside a plant cell that makes foods for the plant. (p. A11)

circuit (sûr′kit) The path electricity flows through. (p. F72)

classify (klas′ə fī) To place materials that share properties together in groups. (pp. S3, A66)

communicate (kə mü′ni kāt′) To share information. (pp. S11, F20)

community (kə mü′ni tē) All the living things in an ecosystem. (p. B6)

competition (kom′pi tish′ən) The struggle among organisms for water, food, or other needs. (p. B42)

compound (kom′pound) Two or more elements put together. (p. F30)

compound machine (kom′pound mə shēn′) Two or more simple machines put together. (p. E57)

condense (kən dens′) *v.* To change from a gas to a liquid. (pp. C31, F17) —**condensation** (kon′den sā′shən) *n.* (p. D17)

conductor (kən duk′tər) A material that heat travels through easily. (p. F46)

conifer (kon′ə fər) A tree that produces seeds inside of cones. (p. A28)

conserve (kən sûrv′) To save, protect, or use something wisely without wasting it. (p. C34)

consumer (kən sü′mər) An organism that eats producers or other consumers. (pp. A40, B17)

crater (krā′tər) A hollow area in the ground. (p. D49)

cutting (kut′ing) A plant part from which a new plant can grow. (p. A30)

cytoplasm (sī′tə pla′zəm) A clear, jellylike material that fills both plant and animal cells. (p. A10)

D

decibel (dB) (des′ə bel′) A unit that measures loudness. (p. F69)

decomposer (dē′kəm pō′zər) An organism that breaks down dead plant and animal material. *Decomposers* recycle chemicals so they can be used again. (p. B18)

define based on observations (di fīn′ bāst ôn ob′zər vā′shənz) To put together a description that relies on examination and experience. (p. S5)

degree (di grē′) The unit of measurement for temperature. (p. F43)

PRONUNCIATION KEY

a at; ā ape; ä far; âr care; ô law; e end; ē me; i it; ī ice; îr pierce; o hot; ō old; ôr fork; oi oil; ou out; u up; ū use; ü rule; ù pull; ûr turn; hw white; ng song; th thin; <u>th</u> this; zh measure; ə about, taken, pencil, lemon, circus

desert (dez'ərt) A hot, dry place with very little rain. (p. B55)

development (di vel'əp mənt) The way a living thing changes during its life. (p. A6)

distance (dis'təns) The length between two places. (p. E7)

E

earthquake (ûrth'kwāk) A sudden movement in the rocks that make up Earth's crust. (p. C72)

ecosystem (ek'ō sis'təm) All the living and nonliving things in an environment and all their interactions. (p. B6)

electric current (i lek'trik kûr'ənt) Electricity that flows through a circuit. (p. F72)

element (el'ə mənt) A building block of matter. (p. F28)

embryo (em'brē ō) A young organism that is just beginning to grow. (p. A26)

endangered (en dān'jərd) Close to becoming extinct; having very few of its kind left. (p. B64)

energy (en'ər jē) The ability to do work. (pp. A18, E39)

energy pyramid (en'ər jē pir'ə mid') A diagram that shows how energy is used in an ecosystem. (p. B22)

environment (en vī'rən mənt) The things that make up an area, such as land, water, and air. (p. A8)

erosion (i rō'zhən) The carrying away of weathered materials. (p. C62)

evaporate (i vap'ə rāt') *v.* To change from a liquid to a gas. (pp. C31, F17) —**evaporation** (i vap'ə rā'shən') *n.* (p. D17)

experiment (ek sper'ə ment') To perform a test to support or disprove a hypothesis. (pp. S7, A12)

extinct (ek stingkt) Died out, leaving no more of that type of organism alive. (p. B66)

F

fertilizer (fûr'tə līz') A substance added to the soil that is used to make plants grow. (p. C42)

first quarter (fûrst kwôr'tər) A phase of the Moon in which the right half is visible and growing larger. (p. D47)

fish (fish) An animal that lives its whole life in water. (p. A71)

flood (flud) A great rush of water over usually dry land. (p. C71)

flowering plant (flou'ər ing plant) A plant that produces seeds inside of flowers. (p. A28)

fog (fôg) A cloud that forms near the ground. (p. D14)

food chain (füd chān) A series of organisms that depend on one another for food. (p. B17)

food web (füd web) Several food chains that are connected. (p. B20)

force (fôrs) A push or pull, such as the one that moves a lever. (pp. E14, E44)

form a hypothesis (fôrm ə hī poth'ə sis) To make a statement that can be tested in answer to a question. (pp. S5, C64)

fossil (fos'əl) The imprint or remains of something that lived long ago. (p. C22)

freeze (frēz) To turn from water to ice. (p. F17)

friction (frik'shən) A force that occurs when one object rubs against another. (p. E26)

fuel (fū'əl) A substance burned for its energy. (p. C26)

fulcrum (ful'krəm) The point where a lever turns or pivots. (p. E44)

full Moon (ful mün) or **second quarter** (sek'ənd kwôr'tər) The phase of the Moon in which all of its sunlit half is visible from Earth. (p. D47)

fungi, (fun'jī) *pl. n., sing.* **fungus** (fung'gəs) One- or many-celled organisms that absorb food from dead organisms. (p. B18)

G

gas (gas) Matter that has no definite shape or volume. (p. F14)

PRONUNCIATION KEY

a at; ā ape; ä far; âr care; ô law; e end; ē me; i it; ī ice; îr pierce; o hot; ō old; ôr fork; oi oil; ou out; u up; ū use;
ü rule; u̇ pull; ûr turn; hw white; ng song; th thin; <u>th</u> this; zh measure; ə about, taken, pencil, lemon, circus

germinate (jûr'mə nāt) To begin to grow, as when the right conditions allow a seed to develop. (p. A26)

glacier (glā'shər) A large mass of ice in motion. (p. C62)

gram (gram) A metric unit used to measure mass; 1,000 *grams* equals 1 kilogram. (p. F9)

gravity (grav'i tē) A pulling force between two objects, such as Earth and you. (p. E16)

groundwater (ground wô'tər) Water stored in the cracks of underground rocks and soil. (p. C33)

H

habitat (hab'i tat) The home of a living thing. (p. B7)

heat (hēt) A form of energy that makes things warmer. (p. F42)

herbivore (hûr'bə vôr') An animal that eats only plants. (p. B20)

heredity (hə red'i tē) The passing of traits from parents to offspring. (p. A27)

hibernate (hī'bər nāt') To rest or sleep through the cold winter. (p. A46)

host (hōst) An organism that a parasite lives with. (p. B31)

humus (hü'məs) Leftover decomposed plant and animal matter. (p. C14)

hurricane (hûr'i kān') A violent storm with strong winds and heavy rains. (p. C70)

I

igneous rock (ig'nē əs rok) A "fire-made" rock formed from melted rock material. (p. C8)

imprint (im'print') A shallow mark or print in a rock. (p. C23)

inclined plane (in klīnd' plān) A flat surface that is raised at one end. (p. E54)

infer (in fûr') To form an idea from facts or observations. (pp. S5, D20)

inherited trait (in her'i təd trāt) A characteristic that comes from parents. (p. A56)

inner planet (in′ər plan′it) Any of the four planets in the solar system that are closest to the Sun: Mercury, Venus, Earth, and Mars. (p. D56)

insulator (in′sə lā′tər) A material that heat doesn't travel through easily. (p. F46)

interpret data (in tûr′prit dā′tə) To use the information that has been gathered to answer questions or solve a problem. (p. S9)

K

key (kē) A table that shows what different symbols on a map stand for. (p. E10)

kilogram (kil′ə gram′) A metric unit used to measure mass; 1 *kilogram* equals 1,000 grams. (p. F9)

L

landform (land′fôrm′) A feature on Earth's surface. (p. C54)

last quarter (last kwôr′tər) or **third quarter** (thûrd kwôr′tər) The phase of the waning Moon in which the left half is visible but growing smaller. (p. D47)

leaf (lēf) A plant part that grows from the stem and helps the plant get air and make food. (p. A18)

learned trait (lûrnd trāt) Something that you are taught or learn from experience. (p. A56)

lens (lenz) A curved piece of glass. (p. D58)

lever (lev′ər) A straight bar that moves on a fixed point. (p. E44)

life cycle (līf sī′kəl) All the stages in an organism's life. (p. A26)

liquid (lik′wid) Matter that has a definite volume but not a definite shape. (p. F14)

liter (lē′tər) A metric unit used to measure volume. (p. F9)

load (lōd) The object that a lever lifts or moves. (p. E44)

PRONUNCIATION KEY

a at; ā ape; ä far; âr care; ô law; e end; ē me; i it; ī ice; îr pierce; o hot; ō old; ôr fork; oi oil; ou out; u up; ū use; ü rule; ů pull; ûr turn; hw white; ng song; th thin; th this; zh measure; ə about, taken, pencil, lemon, circus

loam (lōm) A kind of soil that contains clay, sand, silt, and humus. Plants grow well in loam. (p. C15)

luster (lus'tər) How an object reflects light. (p. F6)

M

machine (mə shēn') A tool that makes work easier to do. (p. E44)

magnetism (mag'ni tiz'əm) The property of an object that makes it attract iron. (p. F26)

make a model (māk ə mod'əl) To make something to represent an object or event. (p. S7)

mammal (mam'əl) An animal with fur that feeds its young with milk. (p. A74)

map (map) A flat drawing that shows the positions of things. (p. E10)

mass (mas) The amount of matter in an object. (p. F7)

matter (mat'ər) Anything that takes up space and has mass. (pp. D16, F6)

measure (mezh'ər) To find the size, volume, area, mass, weight, or temperature of an object, or how long an event occurs. (pp. S9, C16)

melt (melt) To change from a solid to a liquid. (p. F17)

metal (met'əl) A shiny material found in the ground. (p. F26)

metamorphic rock (met'ə môr'fik rok) A rock that has changed form through squeezing and heating. (p. C9)

metamorphosis (met'ə môr'fə sis) A change in the body form of an organism. (p. A52)

microscope (mī'krə skōp') A device that uses glass lenses to allow people to see very small things. (p. A10)

migrate (mī'grāt) To move to another place. (p. A46)

mimicry (mim'i krē) The imitation by one animal of the traits of another. (p. B53)

mineral (min'ə rəl) A naturally occurring substance, neither plant nor animal. (pp. A16, C6)

mixture (miks′chər) Different types of matter mixed together. The properties of each kind of matter in the mixture do not change. (p. F18)

mold (mold) An empty space in a rock that once contained an object such as a dead organism. (p. C23)

motion (mō′shən) A change in position. (p. E8)

mountain (moun′tən) The highest of Earth's landforms. *Mountains* often have steep sides and pointed tops. (p. C55)

N

natural resource (nach′ər əl rē′sôrs′) A material on Earth that is necessary or useful to people. (p. C38)

nectar (nek′tər) The sugary liquid in flowers that lures insects that aid in pollination. (p. A28)

new Moon (nü mün) A phase of the Moon in which none of its sunlit half is visible from Earth. (p. D47)

newton (nü′tən) The unit used to measure pushes and pulls. (pp. E17, F10)

niche (nich) The job or role an organism has in an ecosystem. (p. B44)

nonrenewable resource (non′ri nü′ə bəl rē′sôrs′) A resource that cannot be reused or replaced easily. (p. C41)

nucleus (nü′klē əs) The control center of a cell. (p. A11)

O

observe (əb sûrv′) To use one or more of the senses to identify or learn about an object or event. (pp. S3, B56)

omnivore (om′nə vôr′) An animal that eats both plants and animals. (p. B21)

PRONUNCIATION KEY

a at; ā ape; ä far; âr care; ô law; e end; ē me; i it; ī ice; îr pierce; o hot; ō old; ôr fork; oi oil; ou out; u up; ū use; ü rule; u̇ pull; ûr turn; hw white; ng song; th thin; <u>th</u> this; zh measure; ə about, taken, pencil, lemon, circus

opaque (ō pāk′) A material that doesn't allow light to pass through. (p. F54)

orbit (ôr′bit) The path an object follows as it revolves around another object. (p. D38)

organ (ôr′gən) A group of tissues that work together. (p. A62)

organism (ôr′gə niz′əm) Any living thing. (p. A6)

outer planet (out′ər plan′it) Any of the five planets in the solar system that are farthest from the Sun: Jupiter, Saturn, Uranus, Neptune, and Pluto. (p. D56)

oxygen (ok′sə jən) A gas that is in air and water. (p. A19)

P

parasite (par′ə sīt′) An organism that lives in or on a host. (p. B31)

perish (per′ish) To fail to survive. (p. B63)

phase (fāz) An apparent change in the Moon's shape. (p. D46)

physical change (fiz′i kəl chānj) A change in the way matter looks that leaves the matter itself unchanged. (p. F16)

pitch (pich) How high or low a sound is. (p. F66)

plain (plān) Wide, flat lands. (p. C55)

planet (plan′it) Any of the nine large bodies that orbit the Sun. In order from the Sun outward, they are Mercury, Venus, Earth, Mars, Jupiter, Saturn, Uranus, Neptune, and Pluto. (p. D54)

pollen (pol′ən) A powdery material needed by the eggs of flowers to make seeds. (p. A28)

pollution (pə lü′shən) The adding of harmful substances to the water, air, or land. (p. C42)

population (pop′yə lā′shən) All the members of a single type of organism in an ecosystem. (p. B6)

position (pə zish′ən) The location of an object. (p. E6)

precipitation (pri sip′i tā′shən) Water in the atmosphere that falls to Earth as rain, snow, hail, or sleet. (p. D19)

predator (pred′ə tər) An animal that hunts other animals for food. (p. B28)

predict (pri dikt′) To state possible results of an event or experiment. (pp. S7, D50)

prey (prā) The animals that predators eat. (p. B28)

prism (pri′zəm) A thick piece of glass that refracts light. (p. F57)

producer (prə dü′sər) An organism such as a plant that makes its own food. (p. B16)

property (prop′ər tē) Any characteristic of matter that you can observe. (p. F6)

pulley (pu̇l′ē) A simple machine that uses a wheel and a rope. (p. E48)

R

rain gauge (rān gāj) A device that measures how much precipitation has fallen. (p. D24)

ramp (ramp) Another name for an inclined plane. (p. E54)

recycle (rē sī′kəl) To treat something so it can be used again. (p. C44)

reduce (ri düs′) To use less of something. (p. C44)

reflect (ri flekt′) The bouncing of light off a surface. (p. F55)

refract (ri frakt′) The bending of light as it passes through matter. (p. F56)

relocate (rē lō′kāt) To find a new home. (p. B63)

renewable resource (ri nü′ə bəl rē′sôrs′) A resource that can be replaced or used over and over again. (p. C40)

reproduction (rē′prə duk′shən) The way organisms make more of their own kind. (p. A7)

reptile (rep′təl′) An animal that lives on land and has waterproof skin. (p. A72)

PRONUNCIATION KEY

a at; ā ape; ä far; âr care; ô law; e end; ē me; i it; ī ice; îr pierce; o hot; ō old; ôr fork; oi oil; ou out; u up; ū use; ü rule; u̇ pull; ûr turn; hw white; ng song; th thin; <u>th</u> this; zh measure; ə about, taken, pencil, lemon, circus

reservoir (rez'ər vwär') A storage area for fresh water supplies. (p. C32)

respond (ri spond') To react to changes in the environment. (p. A8)

reuse (rē ūz') To use something again. (p. C44)

revolve (ri volv') To move around another object. (p. D38)

river (riv'ər) A large stream of water that flows across the land. (p. C55)

root (rüt) A plant part that takes in water and grows under the ground. (p. A17)

rotate (rō'tāt) To turn around. (p. D36)

S

sand dune (sand dün) A mound of windblown sand. (p. C55)

sapling (sap'ling) A very young tree. (p. A6)

satellite (sat'ə līt') Any object that orbits another larger body in space. (p. D46)

scavenger (skav'ən jər) An animal that gets its food by eating dead organisms. (p. B29)

screw (skrü) An inclined plane wrapped into a spiral. (p. E56)

sedimentary rock (sed'ə men'tə rē rok) A kind of rock formed when sand, mud, or pebbles at the bottom of rivers, lakes, and oceans pile up. (p. C8)

seedling (sēd'ling) A young plant. (p. A27)

shelter (shel'tər) A place or object that protects an animal and keeps it safe. (p. A44)

simple machine (sim'pəl mə shēn') A machine with few or no moving parts. (p. E44)

soil (soil) A mixture of tiny rock particles, minerals, and decayed plant and animal materials. (p. C14)

solar system (sō'lər sis'təm) The Sun and all the objects that orbit the Sun. (p. D54)

solid (sol'id) Matter that has a definite shape and volume. (p. F14)

solution (sə lü′shən) A kind of mixture in which one or more types of matter are mixed evenly in another type of matter. (p. F19)

speed (spēd) How fast an object moves over a certain distance. (p. E9)

sphere (sfîr) A body that has the shape of a ball or globe. (p. D36)

spore (spôr) One of the tiny reproductive bodies of ferns and mosses, similar to the seeds of other plants. (p. A30)

star (stär) A huge, hot sphere of gases, like the Sun, that gives off its own light. (p. D55)

stem (stem) A plant part that supports the plant. (p. A17)

switch (swich) A lever that opens or closes an electric circuit. (p. F73)

system (sis′təm) A group of parts that work together. (p. A62)

T

telescope (tel′ə skōp′) A tool that gathers light to make faraway objects appear closer. (p. D58)

temperature (tem′pər ə cher) How hot or cold something is. (pp. D8, F43)

texture (teks′chər) How the surface of an object feels to the touch. (p. F6)

thermometer (thər mom′ə tər) An instrument used to measure temperature. (pp. D8, D24)

tissue (tish′ü) A group of cells that are alike. (p. A62)

tornado (tôr nā′dō) A violent, whirling wind that moves across the ground in a narrow path. (p. C70)

tuber (tü′bər) The underground stem of a plant such as the potato. (p. A30)

tundra (tun′drə) A cold, dry place. (p. B55)

PRONUNCIATION KEY

a at; ā ape; ä far; âr care; ô law; e end; ē me; i it; ī ice; îr pierce; o hot; ō old; ôr fork; oi oil; ou out; u up; ū use;
ü rule; ů pull; ûr turn; hw white; ng song; th thin; th this; zh measure; ə about, taken, pencil, lemon, circus

U

use numbers (ūz num'bərz) To order, count, add, subtract, multiply, or divide to explain data. (p. S9)

use variables (ūz vâr'ē ə bəlz) To identify and separate things in an experiment that can be changed or controlled. (pp. S7, F58)

V

valley (val'ē) An area of low land lying between hills or mountains. (p. C55)

vibrate (vī'brāt) To move back and forth quickly. (p. F64)

volcano (vol kā'nō) An opening in the surface of Earth. (p. C73)

volume (vol'ūm) **1.** A measure of how much space matter takes up. (p. F7) **2.** How loud or soft a sound is. (p. F67)

W

water cycle (wô'tər sī'kəl) The movement of Earth's water over and over from a liquid to a gas and from a gas to a liquid. (pp. C31, D19)

water vapor (wô'tər vā'pər) Water in the form of a gas in Earth's atmosphere. (p. D17)

weather (weth'ər) The condition of the atmosphere at a given time and place. (p. D6)

weather vane (weth'ər vān) A device that indicates the direction of the wind. (p. D25)

weathering (weth'ər ing) The process that causes rocks to crumble, crack, and break. (p. C60)

wedge (wej) Two inclined planes placed back-to-back. (p. E55)

weight (wāt) The measure of the pull of gravity between an object and Earth. (p. E17)

wheel and axle (hwēl and ak'səl) A wheel that turns on a post. (p. E47)

wind (wind) Moving air. (p. D10)

windlass (wind'ləs) A wheel and axle machine that is turned by a hand crank to lift a bucket in a well. (p. E47)

work (wûrk) The force that changes the motion of an object. (p. E38)

Index

* Indicates an activity related to this topic.

* Indicates an activity related to this topic.

* Indicates an activity related to this topic.

* Indicates an activity related to this topic.

* Indicates an activity related to this topic.

Credits

Cover Photos: c. Leeson Photography; bkgd. Roderick Chen/Superstock; spine Leeson Photography. Back Cover: bkgd. Roderick Chen/Superstock; t.l. Clive Druett/Papilio/CORBIS; t.r. Tim Flach/Stone/Getty Images; c.l. Donovan Reese/Stone/Getty Images; c.r. Earth Satellite Corporation/Science Photo Library/Photo Researchers, Inc.; b.l. James Marshall/The Stock Market/CORBIS; b.r. SuperStock. Endpaper: Roderick Chen/Superstock.

Photography Credits: All photos are by Macmillan/McGraw-Hill (MMH) and Ken Karp for MMH, Ray Boudreau for MMH, Dan Howell for MMH, David Waitz for MMH, Ron Tanaka for MMH, Dave Mager for MMH, Richard Hutchings for MMH and John Serafin for MMH except as noted below:

i: bkgd. Roderick Chen/Superstock; t.l, b.l. Leeson Photography. iii: Leeson Photography. iv: t. NASA/CORBIS; c., b. Courtesy Sally Ride; bkgd. Taxi/Getty Images. v: l. Mervyn Rees/Alamy; r. James L. Amos/CORBIS. vi: l. Victoria McCormick/Animals Animals; b. PhotoDisc/Getty Images. vii: l. inset Tim Davis/Stone/Getty Images; l. bkgd. Christer Fredriksson/Natural Selection Stock Photography; b. Runk/Schoenberger/Grant Heilman Photography, Inc.; ants PhotoDisc. viii: l. Donovan Reese/Stone/Getty Images; b.c. Francois Gohier/Photo Researchers, Inc.; b.r. American Museum of Natural History. ix: l. Earth Satellite Corporation/Science Photo Library/Photo Researchers, Inc.; c. NASA/Photo Researchers, Inc.; r. John Sanford/Photo Researchers, Inc. x: l. Ron Stroud/Masterfile; b. Peter Weimann/Animals Animals/Earth Scenes. xi: l. Superstock; r. D. Boone/CORBIS. xiv: l. Roderick Chen/Superstock. xvi: b.r.: PhotoDisc. SO: Danny Lehman/CORBIS. S0-S1: James L. Amos/CORBIS. S2-S3: Tom Bean/CORBIS. S4: Mervyn Rees/Alamy. S5: DK Images. S6-S7: Ira Block/National Geographic. S8-S9: Robert Campbell/CORBIS. S10-S11: Richard Cummins/CORBIS.

Unit A: AO: Clive Druett/Papilio/CORBIS. A0-A1: Victoria McCormick/Animals Animals. A2-A3: Alan Oddie/PhotoEdit. A4-A5: Douglas Peebles/CORBIS. A6: l. Tony Wharton/CORBIS; t., b. Terry Eggers/The Stock Market/CORBIS; r. The Stock Market/CORBIS. A6-A7: Frank Siteman/Stock Boston. A7: PhotoDisc/Getty Images. A8: t. Gerard Fuehrer/DRK Photo; b. SuperStock. A9: t. Norbert Wu/Peter Arnold, Inc.; c. Secret Sea Visions/Peter Arnold, Inc.; b. Joe McDonald/Visuals Unlimited, Inc. A10: t. Kent Wood/Photo Researchers, Inc.; b. Dwight R. Kuhn. A11: Moredun Animal Health LTD/Science Photo Library/Photo Researchers, Inc. A13: Carl Roessler/Animals Animals/Earth Scenes. A14: t.l. Doug Peebles/Panoramic Images; r. Mark Segal/Panoramic Images. bkgd. Ryan McVay/PhotoDisc/Getty Images; bkgd. PhotoDisc/Getty Images; c. Allen Prier/Panoramic Images. A16: bkgd. Runk/Schoenberger/Grant Heilman Photography; inset E. Webber/Visuals Unlimited. A17: b. Jim Zipp/Photo Researchers, Inc.; r. Jenny Hager/The Image Works. A18: l. Runk/Schoenberger/Grant Heilman Photography; r. C.G. Van Dyke/Visuals Unlimited. A19: t. Dave M. Phillips/Visuals Unlimited. A20: t. Bill Beatty/Visuals Unlimited; b. Pat O'Hara/DRK Photo. A22: l. Stan Osolinski/Dembinsky Photo Associates; r. Larry West/Taxi/Getty Images. A22-A23: Randy Green/Taxi/Getty Images. A23: t. John M. Roberts/The Stock Market/CORBIS; b. J. H. Robinson/Photo Researchers, Inc. A24-A25: Neil Gilchrist/Panoramic Images. A26: t. D. Gavagnaro/Visuals Unlimited; t.c.r. Kevin Collins/Visuals Unlimited; c.r. Tony Freeman/PhotoEdit; Inga Spence/Tom Stack & Associates. A26-A27: Inga Spence/Visuals Unlimited. A27: D. Gavagnaro/Visuals Unlimited. A29: Gerald and Buff Corsi/Visuals Unlimited. A30: t., c., David Young-Wolff/PhotoEdit; b.l. Ed Reschke/Peter Arnold, Inc.; b.r. Jeff J. Daly/Visuals Unlimited. A32: Ed Galindo. A32-A33: l., c., t. Ed Galindo; b.r. C Squared Studios/PhotoDisc/Getty Images. A36-A37: Stephen J. Krasemann/Photo Researchers, Inc. A38-A39: Jade Albert/FPG International/Getty Images. A40: t. Fritz Polikng/Bruce Coleman, Inc.; b.l. Joe McDonald/DRK Photo; b.r. Dale E. Boyer/Photo Researchers, Inc. A41: Kevin Schafer/Peter Arnold, Inc. A42: inset W. Gregory Brown/Animals Animals. A42-A43: Michael S. Nolan/Tom Stack & Associates. A44: t. Eric & David Hosking/CORBIS; c. John Cancalosi/DRK Photo; b. Ted Levine/Animals Animals. A45: t. Zoran Milich/Allsport USA/Getty Images; b. Mark Newman/Bruce Coleman, Inc. A 46: t. David Madison/Bruce Coleman, Inc.; c. Runk/Schoenberger/Grant Heilman Photography; b. John Cancalosi/DRK Photo. A48: t. Robert P. Carr/Bruce Coleman, Inc.; b. Skip Moody/Dembinsky Photo Associates. A48-A49: Ken Lucas/Visuals Unlimited. A49: t.l., t.r., b. Robert P. Carr/Bruce Coleman, Inc.; c. Jon Dicus. A50-A51: Tim Davis/Photo Researchers, Inc. A52: b. Dwight R. Kuhn; b. Arthur Morris/Visuals Unlimited. A53: t.l. Gelnn M. Oliver/Visuals Unlimited; t.c. Pat Lynch/Zipp/Photo Researchers, Inc.; t.r. Robert P. Carr/Bruce Coleman, Inc.; c.l. Nuridsany et Perennou/Zipp/Photo Researchers, Inc.; c.r. Robert L. Dunne/Bruce Coleman, Inc.; b.l. Sharon Cummings/Dembinsky Photo Associates; b.r. John Mielcarek/Dembinsky Photo Associates. A54: t. SuperStock; c. Lynn Rogers/Peter Arnold, Inc.; b.l. Erwin and Peggy Bauer/Bruce Coleman, Inc.; b.r. Pat

and Tom Leeson/Photo Researchers, Inc. A55: t.l. Cabisco/Visuals Unlimited; t.c.l. E.A. Janes/Bruce Coleman, Inc.; t.r. Lindholm/Visuals Unlimited; b.c.l. Fred Breummer/DRK Photo; b.r. Dave B. Fleetham/Visuals Unlimited; b.l. M H Sharp/Photo Researchers, Inc. A56: l. George Shelley/The Stock Market/CORBIS; r. Richard Hutchings/PhotoEdit. A58: Bill Banaszewski/Visuals Unlimited. A58-A59: J.C. Carton/Bruce Coleman, Inc. A60-A61: Robert Maier/Animals Animals. A62: l. M.I. Walker/Science Source/Photo Researchers, Inc. A63: t. R. Dowling/Animals Animals/Earth Scenes; b. Joe McDonald/Animals Animals/Earth Scenes. A64: Robert Winslow. A64-A65: Tom Brakefield/CORBIS. A65: t. James Watt/Animals Animals/Earth Scenes; b. Jeff Rotman/Jeff Rotman Photography. A66: PhotoDisc/Getty Images. A68-A69: VCG/FPG International/Getty Images. A69: t.r. Stephen Dalton/Animals Animals/Earth Scenes; t.c.r. Tony Wharton/CORBIS; b.c.r. Brian Parker/Tom Stack & Associates; b.r. Lisa and Mike Husar/DRK Photo; c.l. EyeWire; b.l. Kichen and Hurst/Tom Stack & Associates; c. G.W.Willis/Animals Animals/Earth Scenes. A70: l. Darryl Torckler/Stone/Getty Images; r. Rob Simpson/Visuals Unlimited. A71: t. Breck P. Kent/Animals Animals/Earth Scenes; inset George Bernard/Animals Animals/Earth Scenes. A72: t. Jane Borton/Bruce Coleman, Inc.; b. E.R. Degginger/Animals Animals/Earth Scenes. A73: l. S. Nielson/DRK Photo; r. Robert Winslow. A74: Jeff Rotman/Jeff Rotman Photography. A74-A75: Dave Watts/Tom Stack & Associates. A75: t. Erwin & Peggy Bauer/Bruce Coleman, Inc.; b. Lynn M. Stone/Bruce Coleman Inc. A77: SuperStock. A78: Photo courtesy of Dan Lausser/University of Wisconsin-Madison. A78-A79: c. Photo courtesy Jeff Miller/University of Wisconsin-Madison; bkgd. StockTrek/Photodisc Green/Getty Images, Inc. A80: l. Jeff J. Daly/Visuals Unlimited; r. David Young-Wolff/PhotoEdit.

Unit B: BO: Tim Flach/Stone/Getty Images. B0-B1: Christer Fredriksson/Natural Selection Stock Photography. B1: Tim Davis/Stone/Getty Images. B2-B3: Raymond Gehman/CORBIS. B4-B5: Johnny Johnson/Animals Animals/Earth Scenes. B5: PhotoDisc/Getty Images. B6: Nicholas DeVore/Stone/Getty Images. B6-B7: Joseph Van Os/The Image Bank/Getty Images. B12: inset Lance Nelson/The Stock Market/CORBIS; c. Jeff Greenberg/Visuals Unlimited; b. Jeff Greenberg/PhotoEdit. B13: t. Gerard Lacz/Peter Arnold, Inc.; b. PhotoDisc/Getty Images. B14-B15: L. Lenz/Natural Selection. B16: t. Kim Taylor/Dorling Kindersley Ltd. B18: t. SuperStock; b.l. Michael P. Gadomski/Photo Researchers, Inc. B18-B19: Dwight Kuhn Photography. B22: t. John Warden/Stone/Getty Images; c. Tom J. Ulrich/Visuals Unlimited; b.c. John Shaw/Bruce Coleman, Inc.; b. Runk/Schoenberger/Grant Heilman Photography, Inc. B24-B25: Michael Simpson/FPG International/Getty Images. B26: William H. Mullins/Photo Researchers, Inc. B26-B27: bkgd. Kent Foster/Photo Researchers, Inc. B28: t. Kim Taylor/Dorling Kindersley Ltd.; c. John Shaw/Bruce Coleman, Inc.; branch Kim Taylor/Dorling Kindersley Ltd.; b. Arthur Morris/The Stock Market/CORBIS. B28-B29: inset Kim Taylor/Dorling Kindersley Ltd.; bkgd. M. C. Chamberlain/DRK Photo. B29: t. Jeremy Woodhouse/PhotoDisc/Getty Images; b. Jerry Young/Dorling Kindersley Ltd. B30: t. Nawrocki Stock Photo; b. Carl Roessler/Bruce Coleman, Inc. B30-B31: S. Dimmitt/Photo Researchers, Inc. B31: t. James H. Robinson/Photo Researchers, Inc.; b.l. Stone/Getty Images; b.r. Runk/Schoenberger/Grant Heilman Photography, Inc. B32-B33: Kim Taylor/Dorling Kindersley Ltd. B34: l. Trevor Barrett/Animals Animals/Earth Scenes; b. George D. Lepp/Photo Researchers, Inc. B34-B35: John Elk III. B35: Kjell B. Sandved/Visuals Unlimited. B37: l., c. Runk/Schoenberger/Grant Heilman Photography, Inc.; r Arthur Morris/Visuals Unlimited. B38-B39: Robert Winslow. B40-B41: The Stock Market/CORBIS. B42: t. Stephen Dalton/Animals Animals/Earth Scenes; b. Richard Day/Panoramic Images. B43: t.l. Steve Maslowski/Visuals Unlimited; t.r. James P. Rowan/DRK Photo; b.l. George D. Dodge/Bruce Coleman, Inc.; b.r. Michael Dwyer/Stock Boston. B44: t. Gail Shumway/FPG International/Getty Images. B46: Paul McCormick/Getty Images. B47: Gil T Friedman. B48: Richard & Susan Day/Animals Animals/Earth Scenes. B48-B49: Johnny Johnson/DRK Photo; c. Tom and Pat Leeson/DRK Photo. B50: t. Gail Shumway/FPG International/Getty Images; c. Jack Jeffrey/Photo Resource Hawaii; b. John Cancalosi/DRK Photo. B50-B51: t. Francis/Donna Caldwell/Visuals Unlimited; b. Kim Taylor/Dorling Kindersley Ltd. B51: Heather Angel/Natural Visions. B52: t. Gregory Ochoki/Photo Researchers, Inc.; b. Breck P. Kent/Animals Animals/Earth Scenes. B53: t. Stephen J. Krasemann/DRK Photo; b.l. John Eastcott/Yva Momatiuk/DRK Photo; b.r. A. Cosmos Blank/Photo Researchers, Inc. B54: t. Zig Leszcynski/Animals Animals/Earth Scenes; b. Michael Fogden/DRK Photo. B54-B55: Michael Fogden/DRK Photo. B55: t.l. Pat O'Hara/DRK Photo; t.c. Don Enger/Animals Animals/Earth Scenes; t.r. Richard Kolar/Animals Animals/Earth Scenes; b.l. Jim Steinberg/Photo Researchers, Inc.; b.r. Stephen J. Krasemann/Photo Researchers, Inc. B57: Chris Johns/National Geographic . B58-B59: Gary Braasch/CORBIS. B60: t. Charles Palek/Earth Scenes; b. Pat and Tom Leeson/Photo Researchers, Inc.

B60-B61: Brett Baunton. B61: Wayne Hacker/Alamy. B62: l. Kent and Donna Dannen/Photo Researchers, Inc.; t.r. Diana L. Stratton/Tom Stack & Associates; t.c.r. Doug Sokell/Visuals Unlimited; b.c.r. Sharon Gerig/Tom Stack & Associates; b.r. Pat and Tom Leeson/DRK Photo. B63: t. Joe & Carol McDonald/Visuals Unlimited; b. Stephen J. Krasemann/DRK Photo. B64: t. M.C. Chamberlain/DRK Photo; b.l. Erwin and Peggy Bauer/Bruce Coleman Inc.; b.r. G. Prance/Visuals Unlimited. B65: M.C. Chamberlain/DRK Photo. B66: t. Stephen J. Krasemann/DRK Photo; b. Science VU/Visuals Unlimited. B69: l. Pat and Tom Leeson/Photo Researchers, Inc.; r. Robert Madden/National Geographic . B70: Smithsonian. B70-B71: b. PhotoDisc/Getty Images; bkgd. Cartesia/PhotoDisc. B71: t. Martin Harvey/CORBIS; b. Royalty-free/CORBIS.

Unit C: CO: Donovan Reese/Stone/Getty Images. C0-C1: David Muench/Stone/Getty Images. C2-C3: David Muench/CORBIS. C4-C5: Chip Porter/Stone/Getty Images. C6: t. Joyce Photographics/Photo Researchers, Inc.; b.l. Bill Bachmann/Index Stock Imagery; b.r. Runk/Schoenberger/Grant Heilman Photography. C7: t., c. Tom Pantages. C8: Adam G. Sylvester/Photo Researchers, Inc. C9: t.l. Joyce Photographics/Photo Researchers, Inc.; t.r. Runk/Schoenberger/Grant Heilman Photography; b.l. Charles R. Belinky/Photo Researchers, Inc. C10: t. Frederik D. Bodin/Stock Boston; c. Erich Lessing/Art Resource; b. Boleslaw Edelhajt/Gamma-Liaison/Getty Images. C12-C13: Bo Brannhage/Panoramic Images. C14-C15: Jeff Lepore/Panoramic Images. C15: l. Stephen Ogilvy for MMH. C17: Runk/Schoenberger/Grant Heilman Photography. C18: t. The National Archives/CORBIS; b. G. Buttner/Okapia/Photo Researchers, Inc.; inset, c.r. Roy Morsch/The Stock Market/CORBIS. C19: bkgd. Arthur C. Smith/Grant Heilman Photography; t. Roy Morsch/The Stock Market/CORBIS. C20-C21: bkgd. Jeff J. Daly/Visuals Unlimited. C22: Tom Bean/DRK Photo. C23: t. Runk/Schoenberger/Grant Heilman Photography. C24: t. Louis Psihoyos/MATRIX; inset Mehau Kulyk/Photo Researchers, Inc.; b. Francois Gohier/Photo Researchers, Inc. C24-C25: Biophoto Associates/Photo Researchers, Inc. C25: Stephen J. Krasemann/DRK Photo. C26: Ray Ellis/Photo Researchers, Inc. C28-C29: F. Stuart Westmorland/Photo Researchers, Inc. C30-C31: Tom Van Sant/Photo Researchers, Inc. C32: t. Davis Barber/PhotoEdit; b. C.C. Lockwood/DRK Photo. C36-C37: Grant Heilman/Grant Heilman Photography. C38: Emma Lee/Life File/PhotoDisc/Getty Images. C38-C39: t. David R. Frazier/Photo Researchers, Inc.; b. Charles Mauzy/Natural Selection. C39: John Elk III. C40: t. Don and Pat Valenti/DRK Photo; b. Gary Gray/DRK Photo. C41: t. American Museum of Natural History; inset Will and Deni McIntyre/Photo Researchers, Inc.; b. George Gerster/Photo Researchers, Inc. C42: t. Ruth Dixon/Stock Boston; b. David Ulmer/Stock Boston. C42-C43: Simon Fraser/Science Photo Library/Photo Researchers, Inc. C44: t.l. Larry Lefever/Grant Heilman Photography; t.c.l. EyeWire; b.c.l. RJ Erwin/DRK Photo; b.l., b.r. Tony Freeman/PhotoEdit. C46: t. David Young-Wolff/PhotoEdit; b. Chromosohm/Sohm/Stock Boston. C47: t. Spencer Grant/PhotoEdit; b. Bonnie Kaman/PhotoEdit. C50-C51: Addison Geary/Stock Boston. C52-C53: Allen Prier/Panoramic Images. C53: t. Peter Miller/Panoramic Images; t.c. Richard Sisk/Panoramic Images; c. Mark Heifner/Panoramic Images; b.c. Kim Heacox/Stone/Getty Images; b.r. Don Pitcher/Stock Boston; b.l. Jack Krawczyk/Panoramic Images. C56: t.l. Jim Wiebe/Panoramic Images; t.r. Peter Pearson/Stone/Getty Images; b.l. Richard Sisk/Panoramic Images; b.c. Mark Heifner/Panoramic Images; b.r. Tom Bean/Stone/Getty Images. C57: t. Jack Krawczyk/Panoramic Images. C58-C59: David L. Brown/Panoramic Images. C60: t. Michael P. Gadomski/Photo Researchers, Inc.; b. John Anderson/Animals Animals/Earth Scenes. C62: t. Thomas Fletcher/Stock Boston; inset PhotoDisc/Getty Images; b. Jeff Greenberg/PhotoEdit. C63: t. Kathy Ferguson/PhotoEdit; b. Runk/Schoenberger/Grant Heilman Photography. C65: PhotoEdit. C66: Adam Jones/Photo Researchers, Inc. C66-C67: The National Archives/CORBIS. C67: t. W. E. Ruth/Bruce Coleman, Inc.; inset Pat Armstrong/Visuals Unlimited; c. Sylvan H. Wittaver/Visuals Unlimited; b. John Sohlden/Visuals Unlimited. C68-C69: David Young-Wolff/PhotoEdit. C70-C71: t. Ana Laura Gonzalez/Animals Animals/Earth Scenes; b. Art Montes De Oca/FPG International/Getty Images. C72: t. David Bartruff/FPG International/Getty Images; b. Will & Deni McIntyre/Photo Researchers, Inc. C73: G. Brad Lewis/Stone/Getty Images. C74: t. David Weintraub/Stock Boston; b. Archive Photos/Library of Congress. C78: M. Olsen/College of William and Mary. C78-C79: inset Woods Hole Oceanographic Institute; bkgd. Ralph White/CORBIS.

Unit D: DO: bkgd. Earth Satellite Corporation/Science Photo Library/Photo Researchers, Inc. D0: t. John Sanford/Science Photo Library/Photo Researchers, Inc. D0-D1: bkgd. Science Photo Library/Photo Researchers, Inc; inset Photo Library International/Photo Researchers, Inc. D2-D3: Jack Krawczyk/Panoramic Images. D4-D5: Ariel Skelley/The Stock Market/CORBIS. D8-D9: Didier Givois/Photo Researchers, Inc. D10: David Young-Wolff/PhotoEdit. D11: l. Barbara Stotzen/PhotoEdit; r. D. Boone/Corbis. D12: Jim Reed/CORBIS. D13: t.

Jim Reed/Photo Researchers, Inc.; b. StockTrek/Photodisc Green/Getty Images. D14-D15: Clifford Paine/CORBIS. D16: t. Myrleen Ferguson/PhotoEdit; c. Paul Silverman; b. Michael Newman/PhotoEdit. D17: t. Diane Hirsch/Fundamental Photographs; b. Jeff Greenberg/Peter Arnold, Inc. D21: P. Quittemelle/Stock Boston. D22-D23: Bob Krist/CORBIS. D24: t., b.l. Tom Pantages; b.r. Jeff J. Daly/Stock Boston. D25: t. Charles D. Winters/Photo Researchers, Inc.; b. Tony Freeman/PhotoEdit. D27: b. NOAA/Science Photo Library/Photo Researchers, Inc. D28: Michael P. Gadomski/Photo Researchers, Inc. D28-D29: F. Stuart Westmorland/Photo Researchers, Inc. D32-D33: Michael Hovell/Index Stock Imagery. D34-D35: Robert Mathena/Fundamental Photographs. D37: t. Ken Lucas/Visuals Unlimited; b. Thomas Barbudo/Panoramic Images. D41: Bob Daemmrich/Stock Boston. D42: Roger Ressmeyer/CORBIS. D43: Photo Network/Alamy. D44-D45: Peter Menzel/Stock Boston. D46: Frank Cara/Bruce Coleman, Inc. D47: John Sanford/Photo Researchers, Inc. D48: NASA/Science Source/Photo Researchers, Inc. D49: l. Mark E. Gibson/Visuals Unlimited; r. NASA/Science Photo Library/Photo Researchers, Inc. D52-D53: Frank Zullo/Photo Researchers, Inc. D56: t. U.S .Geological Survey/Photo Researchers, Inc.; c. NASA/Mark Marten/Photo Researchers, Inc.; b.l. Stock Boston; b.r. NASA/Tom Pantages. D56-D57: Ross Ressmeyer/NASA/CORBIS. D57: t.r. NASA/Photo Researchers, Inc.; c.l. Space Telescope Space Institute/Photo Researchers, Inc.; c.r. NASA/Tom Pantages; b. Space Telescope Space Institute/Photo Researchers, Inc. D58: t. Tony Freeman/PhotoEdit. D62: t. National Weather Service; c., b. NOAA/AFP/Getty Images. D62-D63: bkgd. Don Farrall/PhotoDisc/Getty Images. D64: b. bkgd. Bruce Heinemann/PhotoDisc/Getty Images.

Unit E: EO: James Marshall/The Stock Market/CORBIS. E0-E1: Ron Stroud/Masterfile. E2-E3: Bernard Asset/Photo Researchers, Inc. E4-E5: S. Dalton/Photo Researchers, Inc. E5: t. Will Hart/PhotoEdit. E6: leaves Foodpix; snails Gregory K. Scott/Photo Researchers, Inc.; b.l., b.r. Zoran Milich/Allsport USA/Getty Images. E8: t. Robert Winslow; b. Fritz Polking/Peter Arnold, Inc. E8-E9: bkgd. The Stock Market/CORBIS. E9: t. Joseph Van Os/The Image Bank/Getty Images; b. Peter Weimann/Animals Animals/Earth Scenes. E12-E13: Craig J. Brown/Flashfocus. E16: l. NASA. E17: NASA/Earth Scenes. E18: PhotoDisc/Getty Images. E19: t. Art Resource. E26: t. Tony Freeman/PhotoEdit; b. John Coletti/Stock Boston. E27: c. Michael Groen for MMH. E30-E31: Dale Sanders/Masterfile. E31: B&C Gill Gillingham/Index Stock Imagery. E34-E35: Addison Geary/Stock Boston. E36-E37: Tom Salyer/Silver Image for MMH. E38: t.l. David Young-Wolff/PhotoEdit; b.r. John Eastcott/Yva Momatiuk/DRK Photo. E39: David Matherly/Visuals Unlimited. E40: Dan Howell for MMH. E42-E43: Bob Daemmrich/Stock Boston. E46: t.r. Michael Newman/PhotoEdit; c.r. Tony Freeman/PhotoEdit; b.r. Siede Preis/PhotoDisc/Getty Images. E46-E47: b. Eric Roth/Flashfocus. E47: t. Roger Wilmshurst/Frank Lane Picture Agency/CORBIS; c. CORBIS; b. Eric Roth/Flashfocus . E51: Washington Metropolitan Area Transit Authority. E52-E53: McCutchean/Visuals Unlimited. E54: Richard Hutchings/Photo Researchers, Inc. E55: Donald Specker/Animals Animals/Earth Scenes. E56: Mark Burnett/Stock Boston. E57: t., c. PhotoDisc/Getty Images; b. David Young-Wolff/PhotoEdit. E59: Jodi Jacobson. E62-E63: NASA. E64: b. John Neubauer/PhotoEdit.

Unit F: FO: SuperStock. F0-F1: Kunio Owaki/The Stock Market/CORBIS. F2-F3: Myrleen Ferguson/PhotoEdit. F6: c. RDF/Visuals Unlimited; b. PhotoDisc/Getty Images. F7: t.l. Spencer Grant/PhotoEdit; t.c. PhotoDisc/Getty Images; t.r. Diane Padys/FPG International/Getty Images; b. Index Stock Imagery. F8: l. Spencer Grant/PhotoEdit; r. Diane Padys/FPG International/Getty Images. F10: l. VCG/PhotoDisc/Getty Images; r. Stock Boston. F12-F13: Alan Kearney/FPG International/Getty Images. F14: PhotoDisc/Getty Images. F15: c., r. PhotoDisc/Getty Images. F16: b. David Young-Wolff/PhotoEdit; r., inset Lawrence Migdale . F17: t.l., b.r. SuperStock; t.r. Hutchings Photography; b.l. Amanda Merullo/Stock Boston. F18: t. PhotoDisc/Getty Images. F20: Peter Scoones/TCL/Masterfile. F21: l. Tony Freeman/PhotoEdit. F22: t.c.l. Steve Kline/Bruce Coleman, Inc.; dice Norman Owen Tomalin/Bruce Coleman, Inc. F22-F23: Bruce Byers/FPG International/Getty Images. F23: t. Norman Owen Tomalin/Bruce Coleman, Inc. F24-F25: Spencer Grant/PhotoEdit. F26-F27: t. Bo Brannhage/Panoramic Images; b. PhotoDisc/Getty Images. F27: t. Burke/Triolo Productions/Foodpix; b. PhotoDisc/Getty Images. F28: t. D. Boone/CORBIS. F29: The Stock Market/CORBIS. F30: l. PhotoDisc/Getty Images; c. EyeWire; r. PhotoDisc/Getty Images. F31: c.l. PhotoDisc/Getty Images. F32: t. Ernie Friedlander/Flashfocus; c.l. Gabriel Covian/The Image Bank/Getty Images; c. Fred J. Maroon/Photo Researchers, Inc.; c.r. David Sieren/Visuals Unlimited; b.l. Stephen Shepherd/Alamy Images . F34-F35: t. Joel Sartore/Grant Heilman Photography; c. Leonard Lessin/Peter Arnold, Inc.; b. James L. Amos/Peter Arnold, Inc. F35: Gabe Palmer/The Stock Market/CORBIS. F37: l. Tom Pantages; r. Richard Megna/Fundamental Photographs. F38-F39: Glenn Vanstrum/Animals Animals/Earth Scenes. F40: Kim Fennema/Visuals Unlimited. F40-F41: Tom Bean/DRK Photo. F43: b. Bill Bachmann/